Nature's Yellowstone

Nature's Yellowstone

Richard A. Bartlett

UNIVERSITY OF NEW MEXICO PRESS

Albuquerque

*To my family
all of whom love Yellowstone.*

Acknowledgments

The most peaceful daylight hour in Yellowstone is the one just before sunset. The tourists are settled at the campgrounds, inns, and cottages, park personnel have gone home, and only the vehicle of an occasional latecomer breaks the wilderness silence. During the long summer days of my research in the park I used to drive out from Mammoth toward Tower Falls, or from Mammoth toward Norris, at this silent time. I would park the car and walk through a meadow, stand still and hear the rustle of the grass in the gentle breeze, catch glimpses of rabbits, mice, deer, elk, and — once — a moose. Often I would visit Mammoth Hot Springs, vacant now, and in the stillness I could hear the sound of the hot waters, just as they had bubbled up for thousands upon thousands of years. What came through at this quiet hour was the sense, the feel, of timelessness, of the steady, inexorable ways of nature. The blacktopped road became a scar to be healed, and the absence of humanity placed me, with the long shadow I cast from the westering sun, as a god overlooking ten million years of Yellowstone's history. It is to present for the reader something of this feeling that I have written this book.

In conducting research I was helped with grants or financial aid from the Florida State University Research Council, the Huntington Library, the American Philosophical Society, and the Yellowstone Library and Museum Association.

I have crossed paths with dozens of historians, park authorities, librarians, archivists, and just plain people possessing some knowledge of the park. It is impossible to list all of these people, though I have appreciated the help of every one of them. I owe a special debt to Aubrey L. Haines, formerly the Yellowstone Park historian, whose aid to me far exceeded any requirements of his position. Miss Nellie Carico of the U.S. Geological Survey aided with photographs and as a liaison with professional U.S.G.S. personnel. Mrs. Marion Drew and Mrs. Jean Newhouse of the Yellowstone Library, the late

Miss Catherine Dempsey and Mrs. Harriett Meloy at the Montana Historical Society, Mr. Ed Carpenter at the Huntington Library, Mrs. Alys Fries at the Western History Room of the Denver Public Library, and N. Orwin Rush, Joe Evans, and the late Reno Bupp of the Robert Manning Strozier Library at Florida State University all contributed of their time and experience.

Edmund B. Rogers, Horace Albright, Gene Gressley, Ray Allen Billington, W. Turrentine Jackson, Fred Nicholson, the late Willard Fraser, Don Russell, Harry Kelsey, and Richard Dillon have aided me by way of conversations and occasional correspondence germane to Yellowstone. Mr. Irvin Alhadeff, a graduate student at Florida State, helped with proofreading and in other ways. My wife, Marie Cosgrove Bartlett, and Rich, Margy, Mary, and Tom benefited by way of trips to Yellowstone and, perhaps, suffered from my long hours at research and writing. Yet for all the wonderful aid of the above people and institutions, errors will probably appear; for them I accept full responsibility.

Contents

Preface xi

PART I   Nature's Age 1

    Map 2

    Chapter 1   The Mountain Bastions 3

    Chapter 2   The Plateau Inside 23

    Chapter 3   Flora and Fauna 51

PART II   Wanderers and Explorers 73

    Chapter 4   The Wanderers 75

    Chapter 5   The First White Men 93

    Chapter 6   The Prospectors 117

    Chapter 7   Two Yankee Quakers and a Dane 143

    Chapter 8   The Washburn–Langford–Doane Expedition
                 and the First Hayden Expedition 164

    Chapter 9   The Creation of Yellowstone National Park 194

Notes 211

A Brief Essay on Sources 238

Index 247

ILLUSTRATIONS

Following page 114

1. Soda Butte Creek
2. Black Sand Basin
3. Crater of Giant Geyser
4. Monad in Hayden Valley
5. Seismic geyser
6. Madison Canyon slide
7. Mammoth Hot Springs
8. Beaver
9. Grizzly bear
10. Bighorn sheep
11. Pronghorn antelope
12. Wapiti
13. Bison
14. Cormorants

15. Swans
16. Clark's map
17. Doane expedition map
18. Thomas Moran
19. The *Anna*
20. Hayden Survey camp
21. Hayden Survey, 1871
22. Barlow and Heap expedition map
23. Hayden Survey map
24. Hayden Survey, 1872
25. Hayden Survey, 1872
26. Crater of Lone Star Geyser

Preface

Today man's urge for adventure has led him beyond the earth to the barren, mysterious satellite of his own planet — the moon. Man can be justly proud of this achievement — and yet, something is missing. There is no vegetation on the moon — no grass and colorful flowers, no shady trees. There are no singing birds, no raccoons or rabbits, coyotes or antelope, deer or elk, bear or mountain lions. Nor are there any insects or serpents, nor any "Moondians" to challenge the primitive nature of man the hunter, man the killer. Let's admit it: for anyone but a scientist, the moon is a dull place. Poor, tired old mother earth looks awfully good by comparison.

But what if the moon were full of green growing things? — of forests and lush meadows, with delicate flowers waving in mountain breezes? What if it contained rippling streams and sparkling lakes, their waters full of edible fish, myriads of aquatic birds skimming over their surfaces? And what if the land gave sustenance to all manner of beasts, and over it walked a few primitive peoples who remained in the Stone Age because food was so abundant that there was no challenge for them to change or improve themselves?

Indeed, were the moon another earth, the clamor to get there would be deafening. Every youth would dream of going there to explore and develop it and make his fortune by growing up with the country.

Hard to believe, but less than a century and a half ago a new world on earth lay open to man. It was the vast land extending west from the Appalachians to the Pacific. The white man — "western man," as historians call him — advanced into this new country. There he explored and panned for gold, trapped the beaver and shot the buffalo in a disgraceful display of cruelty and avarice, and nearly destroyed the natives, the American Indians.

Occasionally one of the more sensitive white men discovered a place so lovely that words could hardly describe it. One preacher thought Heaven was a "Kentucky of a place." And Old Gabe — the trappers' name for Jim Bridger — and John Colter, Osborne Russell, and William Ferris, saw the Yellowstone country and waxed ecstatic, as much as their limited vocabularies would allow, over the beauty of the place. Russell camped in Yellowstone's Lamar Valley and wished a world so beautiful, so peaceful, so rich in all good things, could be preserved unchanged. At a later date, Cook and Folsom, two young Quakers, gazed upon the Grand Canyon of the Yellowstone and thanked God for the privilege.

For these men and others mentioned in the following pages, the Yellowstone region (by which we mean the park and its surrounding areas) was as new as the Garden of Eden. The tiny clusters of Tuka-rikas — Sheep Eater Indians — who occupied the mountains were so scarce as to qualify, were they alive today, as an endangered species. Save for a shooting incident or occasional attacks by angry grizzly bears or by Indian marauders, who sometimes made forays into the mountains from their hunting grounds on the buffalo plains, a man was totally safe there.

Then more white men came, and still more. They took over the Yellowstone region, constructing roads, hotels, campgrounds, and boat-launching ramps. Man still finds Nature there, but it is hardly the Yellowstone visited by Colter, Bridger, Russell, Ferris, Cook, Folsom, and a few others.

What *was* Yellowstone like — back then? What is the secret story of its birth and early millennia? What of the lichen and the grasses and the woods, what of the petrified burial grounds of successive generations of flora? What of its insects, animals, fish, and birds? And what of the early two-legged creatures who explored it, bathed in its warm waters, shivered with fear when the earth trembled, huddled in wickiups or caves as the cold winds blew down off the frigid glaciers?

This is the story of the Yellowstone region as Nature created it, of her agony as she blew millions of tons of lava and ash sky high, as a giant caldera was created, and as oozing volcanoes discharged more millions of tons of molten rock across Yellowstone's surface. It is the narrative of the cold eras when glaciers moved across the land with imperceptible sureness, and of other times when hot, dry winds blew across the uplands. It is a story of flora and fauna also, from lichen to lodgepole pines, from white-footed mice to moose. And finally, it is the story of the white man's entrance into the region. What man has done with Yellowstone is another story.

And if, after reading this book, you wish you could have been a primitive man, a Sheep Eater Indian, a Colter, Bridger, Russell, Ferris, Cook, or Folsom, and could, like them, have seen Yellowstone before the people came, then the mission of this book will have been successful.

PART I
Nature's Age

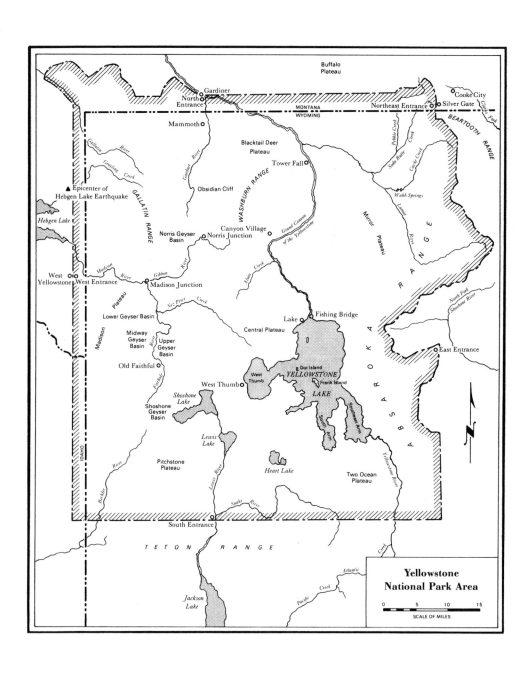

Yellowstone National Park Area

0   5   10   15
SCALE OF MILES

1

The Mountain Bastions

Up in the northwest part of our country, where a man casts a shadow even at high noon on the longest day and winter is never far off, where the altitude is high, the mountains are rugged, and the sky is a deep blue, there is a place of intense interest to man. Whether he knows it intellectually or merely senses it in his heart, the impact of this land is profound and of lifelong duration. For here man meets infinity. The human mind cannot comprehend timelessness, and in the void man feels as though he were lost in a vacuum. He does not soon forget the experience.

Here man also meets nature's power, and the comprehension comes hard. His standard of values is based upon horsepower or British Thermal Units or even megatons. But what are these compared with the powers of nature? Lava flows to leave a plateau thousands of feet thick, waters boil for fifty millennia, the perpetual energy of water erosion cuts a 1000-foot-deep canyon not once but three times. The force that can uplift a great block of land several thousands of feet, the patience that allows it to erode to a low plain, and the power that raises it up again; the grinding movement of glaciers that drop billions of tons of drift hundreds of feet deep — these are nature's doings and they must be measured on her scale or not at all.

Fortunately nature has been relatively quiescent for the past ten thousand years. The naked, rocky gashes have softened with weathering and taken on colors pleasant to the eye; the once reddish, molten, steaming lava beds have hardened and a lush cover of grass, wild flowers, and lodgepole pines has grown over the terrible burn; the waters have carved out streams and lakes or have soaked into the ground, there to unite with subterranean heat to rise again as hot springs or geysers. The uplifted land masses are etched with glacial cirques and cold, clear moraine lakes teaming with rainbow, cutthroat, and native trout; snow covers the highlands in patterns that fire the imagination, and on the tundra grow forget-me-nots, harebells, Indian paintbrush, buttercups, and many other wild flowers that bloom for only a few days. Birds — woodpeckers, warblers, jays, thrushes, ospreys, swans, eagles, ducks, pelicans, terns, sparrows, hummingbirds, flycatchers, and ravens — add their songs to the streams and forests. Animals — bear, moose, elk, deer, antelope, sheep, goats, coyotes, bobcats, and rodents of many kinds — populate the land. The terrible is beautiful, and life abounds.

This is what civilized man saw, and he liked it so much that in a moment of rare intelligence he drew some arbitrary boundaries and created a park for all people. He left much beautiful nearby country outside his reservation, but even so, his pleasuring ground was as large as Rhode Island and Delaware combined, or a thousand square miles larger than the largest Swiss canton, or half the size of Wales. "The Americans," remarked an Englishman, "do their pleasuring as gigantically as they do anything else."[1] The reservation was named Yellowstone National Park.

This book describes Nature's Yellowstone. It is primarily about the park region prior to the most recent one thousandth of one percent of its history. Even then, as the reader will see, there were occasions when modern man came into contact with nature. We mention such incidents, but always from the point of view of nature, not man.

Nature: the seismograph at the park headquarters at Mammoth registers the instability of the land; hot springs break out in the middle of blacktopped park roads, nascent geysers come to life, and active ones go dormant. Two million affluent human beings visit nature's wonders and drive on. Overhead, B-52s from Malmstrom Air Force Base at Great Falls, Montana, leave their vapor trails like white scars in the blue sky as their crews return from practice missions. But nature ignores the vapor trails and the two million human beings. Activities that have been going on ten thousand times ten thousand years continue according to a grand plan only nature understands. Two million visitors a year? Half a million internal combustion engines? Planes overhead bearing nuclear bombs? All of this is nothing to her. Let Man care for himself; Nature will continue according to her Plan.

Before there were grass and flowers and trees, insects and animals, fishes and birds, there was the cold planet Earth. In the vast span of geologic time the earth grew more spherical and more compact. Heavier elements concentrated at its core; lighter elements moved outward into concentric spheres, and at the surface was the emulsion, the matter remaining after the concentration had taken place. Radioactivity probably heated the core elements, gases arose, volcanic activity erupted, and the earth, at least somewhat as we know it today, came into being. The story of nature's Yellowstone begins, then, with geologic history, a history still being made today.

To maintain clarity in our story of the geology of Yellowstone, we are going to imagine the park as the face of a clock. We will pivot the hands at the center of the park, and our descriptions will work around the clock from noon to noon. We will go twice around the clock, first describing the lands just outside or on the fringe of the park boundaries, and then, on the second sweep, examining the country inside the reservation. According to this pattern, we will look first at the great Beartooth Plateau to the northeast of the park.

We must travel back through eons of time to reach the beginnings of Yellowstone. The story begins 2.5–4.5 billion years ago, with the earth whirling around its orbit in space. The rays of a gradually brightening sun brought warmth to the earth's surface, water began to flow, erosion set in, sedimentary rocks began to be created, and the land began to take shape. Some of the oldest rocks known to man have been found in the Beartooth Mountains of Wyoming and Montana.[2]

The Beartooth Plateau is the northeastern bastion of the Yellowstone. Viewed from the air the snow-covered plateau looks something like the top of a gigantic loaf cake, with the snow its white icing. Comprehension of the geological phenomenon that formed it is somewhat easier for a passenger in a plane than for a tourist on the ground. Indeed, for those who cross the Beartooth on U.S. Route 212 from Roosevelt Lodge in the park east through the Lamar Valley, through the Northeast Entrance out through Silver Gate and Cooke City, then up onto the plateau, across it, and abruptly down the other side to Red Lodge, Montana, it is simply spectacular mountain scenery. Little does the airline passenger or the automobiling summer tourist realize that in the Beartooth Range rocks have been found with an estimated age of 2.6–3.5 billion years.[3]

It is one of the ruggedest mountain ranges in the United States, and its geologic history is as spectacular as its summits, lakes, and high plateaus. The southern boundary, the canyon of the Clarks Fork River, is about 30 miles northwest of Cody, Wyoming. The northern ramparts of the Beartooth end 70–80 miles northwestward at the Yellowstone Valley above Livingston, Montana. It is a broad range, 30 miles wide just south of its central portion. A small section crosses the extreme northeast boundary of the park, and Archean rocks (the oldest known rocks) linked with the Beartooth are found down the Lamar Valley and at Specimen Ridge. Druid, Bison, and Barronette* peaks in the eastern part of the park are parts of the Beartooth.[4]

In two areas there has been some confusion as to its limits. In the southwest the Beartooth tends to blend with the Absarokas, which rise to the south and west; in the northwest a trough beween the mountains, called by some geologists the "Cooke City sag zone," separates the range from another one extending from Livingston southeast to Cooke City, and this branch of the mountains has often been designated separately as the Snowy Mountains. Modern terminology, however, includes all these mountains under the name Beartooth, and where, as in the southwest, it is difficult to determine where the one range ends and the other begins, the water divides have provided an answer. Waters flowing south and west to the Yellowstone River identify their mountains as the Absarokas, while waters flowing north and east — which also flow into the Yellowstone, but far out on the northern or northeastern plains of Montana — are considered as draining the Beartooth.[5]

Thus from the northeast — from high noon to about a quarter after the hour on our improvised clock — Yellowstone is protected by a formidable mountain barrier. From the east, the mountain wall rises very abruptly from the 6,000-foot level of the Bighorn Basin, to which the Beartooth is closely related geologically. After the ascent to altitudes of 9–11,000 feet, the range flattens into a series of plateaus or "upland flats," 10–20 miles in width, of remarkably similar elevations. These constitute a "sub-summit plateau . . . the remnants of a once continuous plain."[6] Northeasterly flowing streams

---

*Named for "Yellowstone Jack" Baronett. Just why the name is spelled Barronette on U.S. topography maps is an unsolved mystery.

have cut the plain with valleys and canyons 3–4,000 feet deep, adding to the beauty of the highland area. Another 2,000 feet higher is the actual Beartooth Plateau, the principal remainder of an earlier plain that was some 2,000 feet above the subsummit plateau. There are twenty-five peaks over 12,000 feet in the Beartooth, but the highest, Granite Peak (12,799 feet and the highest point in Montana) is so little higher than the rest that the similarity in top elevations suggests that all the peaks represent the surface of an ancient eroded plateau.

The geology of these mountains is complex and enigmatic, but scientists have untangled most of it. Their findings appear in recent professional publications; more reports are to come.[7] Just a few miles east, in the Bighorn Basin, the surface of the so-called crystalline basement is 10,000 feet or more *below* sea level, whereas in the Beartooth, rocks of that same crystalline basement stand 10–12,000 or more feet *above* it. The core of the mountains consists for the most part of pre-Cambrian granite and granite-gneiss — "pre-Cambrian" on the geologic time chart indicating an age of at least 550 million years. There is evidence of one great uplift in pre-Cambrian Proterozoic times (1,250 million years ago), and strata have been identified of nearly all the geologic periods in the Paleozoic era (550 million down to 215 million years ago). At Beartooth Butte, just 18 miles east of the park boundary and 3 miles south of the Montana line in Wyoming, there are sediments containing fossilized crustacea and armored fish that existed at one time or another from middle Cambrian to middle Devonian times — roughly from 500 million down to 200 million years ago.[8]

Yet while the Beartooth Mountains are composed of ancient rocks and numerous stratifications, it should be kept in mind that the range itself is relatively young. The Beartooth is a part of the great Laramide revolution of 60–75 million years ago, when the original Rocky Mountains were formed. Prior to this incredible uplifting, the land had been covered for millions of years in the Mesozoic era by a great sea that spanned the entire Mississippi Valley from the Appalachians to beyond the Rockies, which had yet to appear. Vast amounts of sediment were laid down, and then, near the beginning of the Cenozoic (or most recent) era, about 75 million years ago, the great orogeny took place.[9]

This mountain making, which proceded the volcanism, was even more spectacular in the region now occupied by the Beartooth than elsewhere (not that there was anyone around to appreciate it). It created the range which, in technical language, is described as a "huge, overturned anticline and the great overthrust fault along its northeastern flank."[10] Visualize it this way: if you lay a sheet of paper on the floor and push both sides against the middle, an upward thrust and a ridge are created. If the paper were a carpet of billions of tons of earth and rock, this could — and in this case did — happen. But then, unlike the paper, one side snapped, and, in an overthrust, slid up over the other side, completely overturning it and burying it below that mass of overthrust rock. This is why a younger stratum may today, after millions of years of erosion, be covered by hundreds or thousands of feet of geologically older strata, defying the logic that the older deposits should be on the bottom and the youngest on top. Certainly they should — if the earth would not buckle and rise and snap.

In the case of the Beartooth, erosion carried off much of the lighter sediment; at least a fifth of the Beartooth Plateau is hard, gneissic rock.[11] And in the time from 70 million years ago to the present, there was erosion, and there were uplifts, faults, thrusts, and some tilting of the entire mountain range toward the southwest.

Then, about a million years ago, the climate cooled and the first of four glacial periods struck the region. Streams that had been carving out canyons and valleys in the form of a V froze over and filled with hard, glacial ice, which slowly extended down those valleys in long, frigid fingers, and, after melting, left the valleys in the shape of a U. When the four glacial periods were over, the scars of the cold period could be seen etched into the rocks. Millions of tons of glacial detritus lay where it was dropped, and cirques and moraines remained, cutting the great Beartooth Plateau into the beautiful jagged contours that the range preserves for us today. Such, very briefly, is the geology of the mountains seen by the tourist who travels U.S. Route 212 between the Northeast Entrance and Red Lodge, Montana.

When compared with the Beartooth, the Absarokas — from a quarter after the hour to about the half hour on our map-clock— seem to lack something. Perhaps it is the absence of hard rock; possibly it is their barren appearance from a distance. Their best known landmarks, Pilot and Index peaks, seen from the Beartooth, do have a rugged beauty that is nevertheless marred by their coarse, dirty, unstable aspect. Their geologic pedigree, one suspects, is not impressive; and yet, the range is still striking.

And indeed their lineage goes back only to Eocene times, about 50 million years ago. While the Beartooth is an uplifted lowland, the Absarokas are almost entirely the products of volcanism, of terrible times in the earth's past when incredible amounts of ejectamenta — breccias, tufas, and massive quantities of basalt — were thrown from or flowed out of volcanoes so long extinct that their exact locations are uncertain. It is believed, however, that on Hurricane Mesa in the Crandall Basin, less than ten miles east of the park, there is an excellent example of an extinct volcano of the type that accomplished the work. It is identified by the gabbros and diorites, hard rocks which constituted the core of the volcano that brought the molten lava to the surface. Dikes radiate from this center; they exuded molten materials along many miles of fissures. Although this volcano — if it was a volcano — may once have had an elevation in excess of 13,000 feet, only its hard core remains, but a geologist's vision can piece together the story of subterranean activity.[12]

There has been considerable squabbling over the name as well as over the geographical limits of the Absarokas. At various times and by different explorers the range has been called the Snowy, the Yellowstone, and the Shoshone, but earth scientists, as well as the local inhabitants, now call the range Absaroka.[13]

The geographical limits of the Absarokas are fairly well defined except in the south. The northern boundary is the southern side of Clarks Fork, whose northern side begins the Beartooth. The western boundary is in many places identical with park boundaries, although many westerly spurs or ridges crest into peaks inside the park all the way to the eastern slope of Yellowstone Lake (The Needle, Hoodoo Peak, Mount Chittenden, Mount Humphrey, Mount Schurz, and others); the eastern boundaries are the western foot of the Bighorn Basin or the Great Plains, with the range being at the most 50 miles wide. Southward the Absarokas extend 30–40 miles past Cody, Wyoming, making their north-south length 70–80 miles. Their loftiest summits are in the southern parts, and with their steep, narrow canyons and rugged peaks (Washakie Needles, Needle Mountain, Yount's Peak, Fortress Mountain, and others) all looming 12–13,000 feet above sea level, the range is one of the most spectacular in America. South of Cody this barrier has often been called the Shoshone Range, but regardless of its nomenclature, the end of the range comes with the end of the volcanic cover at a vague geographic area where the so-called Owl Creek Range and the Wind River Range begin. It is "so closely connected with the Wind River Plateau," wrote the great geologist of the park, Arnold Hague, "that any line of separation between them must be drawn arbitrarily."[14]

The Absarokas were the primary barrier to exploration of the Yellowstone country. With their summits and canyons covered much of the year with deep snow and their narrow, rocky gorges, once packed with extensive glaciers, now filled with raging snow waters during the warmer season, they constituted a formidable barrier whose rifts took time to discover. And in fact only a few passes do exist through the range, among them Jones Pass, never heavily used; Isha-wooa Pass, 10 miles east of the park boundary, and Sylvan Pass, through which U.S. Route 14 comes into the park at the East Entrance. Drained by Clarks Fork and two branches of the Shoshone (formerly known as the Stinkingwater, a name adopted from the Indians and derived from some ill-smelling sulphur springs close to the river), this area, nearly 80 percent covered with pine, spruce, and fir, to this day constitutes one of the finest wilderness regions in the United States. Camping, hunting, fishing, and of course, hiking, are popular pastimes there.

If Colter's Hell (see Part II, Chap. 2) was the hot springs above Cody, Wyoming, in the area now inundated by the Shoshone Reservoir, it was in the Absarokas, as were some caves of ancient man that have been found southwest of Cody. The old Dead Indian Trail, used by the red man before the coming of the whites, ran up in the Sunlight Basin, northwest of Cody, and then crossed over to the Lamar River drainage in the park. John Colter could easily have used this path, but whether he was going to Yellowstone or coming from there we will probably never know. Today the road through the Sunlight Basin is blacktop, and several dude ranches attract visitors to the area.

By now we are at the half hour on our imaginary geographical clock. In a sweep from about 25 minutes after the hour to 25 of, we have a brief respite from the exhausting mountain wastelands. The country is rough, somewhat undulating, and high, but it is a plateau rather than a mountain barrier. On the west it blends into the declining northerly spurs of the spectacular Tetons; eastward it includes the drainage area of the upper Snake River and the dwindling spurs first of the Gros Ventre Mountains and then of the long, broad Wind River Range, which extends 120 miles southward into central Wyoming. The Wind River Range constituted a barrier to explorers until the 1870s, when Togwotee Pass and Union Pass, both south of the park, began to be used.[15]

This area, just above and below the southeastern boundary of the park, though cut only by trails except for the highway up from Jackson Hole, is not without interest and beauty. Big Game Ridge, and Chicken Ridge, Pinyon Peak, Bobcat Ridge, Huckleberry Mountain, and Bobcat Peak are all examples of the dominant sedimentary rock in this area. From Mount Hancock, 9,328 feet high, the mountain climber gains a magnificent view of the Tetons, the Wind Rivers, the entire west face of the Absarokas and the Beartooth, the Park Plateau and the lake, and the Gallatin Mountains far to the northwest. From Chicken Ridge to the northeast, one can look down into Outlet Canyon, so named because it once drained the waters of the Yellowstone Lake into the Snake–Columbia River system. Eastward is the moisture-soaked Two Ocean Plateau, related in its volcanic materials to the Absarokas, with the Continental Divide snaking its way across it from southeast to northwest, and unused Two Ocean Pass at its southern limits below the park boundary. Early explorers were profoundly and philosophically impressed by discovering streams a few feet apart flowing toward different oceans, so Pacific Creek and Atlantic Creek are prominent streams in the area.[16] Flowing northward from the base of Yount's Peak, southeast of the park, where the Absarokas and Wind Rivers join, is the Upper Yellowstone River. It is joined by Thorofare Creek west of the Absarokas; thus enlarged, it flows through swampy land due east of Two Ocean Plateau and after 30 miles empties into the Yellowstone Lake.

On the other (west) side of the Snake River are the final northerly outcroppings of the Tetons, not at all spectacular up this far, but of geologic interest because they contain the Archean base on which the Tetons are formed. They also constitute the water divide between the Snake River and the Falls River Basin in the southwest corner of the park. Owl and Berry creeks on the east side flow into the Snake, and Conant and Boone creeks on the west are tributaries of Falls River.[17]

Although it is not filled with thermal phenomena (though there are a few active hot springs and many signs of considerable activity in ages past), this southern section of the park and the great block of land extending on down into Wyoming is still not a section of country where man can tread without caution. The mighty Tetons, a separate national park, take their annual toll of mountain climbers, and the dangerous canyons of the rampaging Snake are an invitation to the adventurous. In June 1925, Sheep Mountain, on the Gros Ventre, a tributary of the Snake, toppled 50 million cubic yards, 1,700–2,000 feet into the river and created a lake 5 miles long; two years later this slide dam gave way just as residents had warned it would do, inundated the hamlets of Kelly and Wilson, and drowned seven or eight people.[18] Great mud slides which substantially change the terrain have occured in recent years in the Tetons.[19]

Between the half and the three-quarter hour on our clock, we come to a high plateau extending far westward into Idaho and Montana, and carrying us to about twelve minutes to the hour. This Cascade Corner, as it is often designated, is a conifer-covered, generously watered, liberally drained wilderness area, famous for its excellent fishing in streams with many cascades and waterfalls. This same terrain extends west beyond the boundaries of the park.

Up toward the hour, however, the forested Madison Plateau is broken by canyons and cleft at right angles by three short mountain ranges running north and south between their drainage systems. The three rivers were named by Lewis and Clark the Gallatin, the Madison, and, far out of the park, the Jefferson. South and southwest are Targhee Pass, used by the Nez Perces, and Raynolds Pass, separating the Madison from the Snake River drainage, both crossing the Continental Divide. Both passes are significant in the history of Yellowstone exploration, along with Henry's Lake, a wooded haven known to the Indians and mountain men who figure in the early history of Yellowstone exploration.

But the area west of the northwest corner of the park, no matter how beautiful its terrain, should be no more casually trodden upon by man than the Teton and Gros Ventre country to the south. Earthquakes always characterize volcanic areas, and they are common in the Yellowstone country.[20] On the moonlit night of August 17,

1959, at 11:37, the time came as it had at least fifty-three other times since 1770 in southwestern Montana.[21] Earthquake!

The greatest devastation was in the Madison Canyon, through which runs the principal highway to the West Entrance of the park. Both the highway and the river turn northward just outside West Yellowstone. The river enters the upper, eastern reaches of Hebgen Lake, and the road turns west and follows the lake sinuously along the north shore, with the steep sides of the southern Madison Range on the other (north) side of the road. The canyon, which runs west-north-west now for about 25 miles, is at times narrow and up to 3,000 feet deep, and again it pushes aside the mountains and makes room for lush hay meadows, dude ranches, and motels. At a point where it is barely 700 feet wide the Montana Electric Power Company built a high, concrete-core dam, thus creating Hebgen Lake, which extends 15 miles east and has a maximum breadth of 6 miles. By 1959, in the forty-four years since the dam was activated in 1915, the canyon had become one of the busiest arteries to Yellowstone, and was itself a vacation spot. The fishing in the Madison River was excellent, and sleeping beneath the stars to the music of roaring water and whispering pines was soul-satisfying to a tired city-dweller. One in-gredient of contentment is safety, and what could be safer than bedding down in a Montana river canyon? No one had informed the 300–500 people camping there that night that every other year an earthquake occurred within a radius of 75 miles of Hebgen Dam.[22]

Was the family dog particularly nervous that night? Or was he just baying at the moon? Were the coyotes howling more than usual? Did the animals sense insecurity welling up from the earth into their nerve centers by way of their paws? No one knows for sure.

But at 11:37:15:0 P.M., Mountain Standard Time, Monday, August 17, 1959, man was once more reminded of the unstable, uncontrollable forces of nature. The fifteenth strongest earthquake ever recorded in the United States, and the strongest one ever in Montana,[23] triggered an almost simultaneous series of devastating events. The epicenter of the quake was a few miles northwest of Hebgen Dam — actually the point, 10–12 miles below the surface, is fixed at 44° 50′ N, 111°05′ W. This spot is on Grayling Creek, which flows into Hebgen Lake from near the west side of the Gallatin Mountains. The site is just within the northwest boundary of the park. The initial shock lasted from five seconds to a minute (opinions differ), and was followed by aftershocks up to the middle of October 1959. Several shocks did minor damage in the next twenty-four hours, about two hundred were perceptible to man, and the remainder were only recorded on instruments. The initial shocks were felt over a 600,000 mile area extending from the Pacific coast east to western North Dakota, and water levels fluctuated in wells as far away as Hawaii and Puerto Rico.[24]

The reasons for the instability of this land mass are complex and not entirely understood. In the area just north of Hebgen Lake geologists have long known of the existence of several normal faults — places where the earth has fractured and one side has moved in relation to the other. One of these, the Red Canyon Fault, "'follows a curved line along Kirkwood Ridge and Red Canyon Creek and then tapers off in a line parallel to the lake." The shorter Hebgen Fault parallels the lake shore. Two smaller ones, the Kirkwood and the West faults, are also north of the lake; westward is the Madison Range Fault. The Henry's Lake Basin and the Continental Mountains to the south owe their existence to the phenomenon of faulting. In a larger sense, of course, the entire Yellowstone area is heavily faulted and, as would be expected, changes took place all over the park as a result of this earthquake.[25]

New or reactivated fault movements are commonly marked by what geologists call scarps, and after 11:37 that night, there were enough scarps in the neighborhood of Hebgen Lake to delight a regiment of geologists. One of the first to be aware of this heavy scarping was Irving Witkind of the United States Geological Survey. He was asleep in his trailer about a mile north of the lake when the time came. "My first reaction to the shaking," he recalls, "was that my trailer had broken loose from its moorings and was carrying me downhill." When he stumbled outside and saw trees swaying without the wind, he realized, after clearing his mind a bit, that it was an earthquake. A few minutes later he climbed into his car to make a survey of the countryside. "I discovered my access road displaced by a fault scarp fifteen feet high," he reported. The car remained in camp.[26]

In the days that followed he discovered an enormous amount of scarping. The Red Canyon Fault scarp, whose eastern end was near the epicenter of the quake, blossomed out with fissures and scarps extending 14 miles. The Red Canyon Fault scarp maintains an average height of about 10 feet, although at places it is 20 feet and near its west end only about 2 feet. Near the junction of State Road 499 (since changed to U.S. Route 287) and U.S. 191 (the Duck Creek Wye), there are two scarps displacing the roads, and one of the scarps increases in height until at the Blarneystone Ranch it is 14 feet high. The Hebgen Fault scarp runs parallel to the northeast shore of the lake at an average height of about 10 feet, although it did reach 20 feet in a few places, dwindled to 2 feet at the ends, and at its southeast terminus became a mile and a half of deep parallel fissures in a zone about 100 feet wide. Both of these, the principal scarps, represent reactivations of old faults. They are described as "vertical normal faults." When passing through bedrock each followed a single trace, but in alluvium or colluvium, they tended to divide into several smaller scarps.[27]

After the quake, men walked along these scarps with awe. Here would be a gap where the simple scarp had pulled away from the higher side; a man could stand easily in the gap and his head would still be lower than the surface of the upper side. At the Blarneystone Ranch, buildings unfortunately stood athwart the Red Canyon Fault scarp, and when the earth fell 10 feet, the buildings were wrecked. Culligan's haystack entered geological history because it lay above the track of "a minor scarp of about two feet displacement. . . . On both sides of the fault scarp undamaged bales were broken and sheared off — the only known example of gouge in a haystack."[28] There was compaction of the earth, too: at the Narrows Motel a flower bed that had been 18 inches wide on the night of August 17 was squeezed to 8 inches the next morning.[29]

As the scarps indicate, the earth slumped. The entire lake basin and the obsidian sand plain to the south of it settled with a downward tilt toward the northeast so pronounced that, just as it obliterated roads and buildings to the northeast, it exposed the shoreline on the southwest side. Scientists estimate that "an area 43 miles long and 14 miles wide subsided measurably. . . . The maximum subsidence, 22 feet, was in part of Hebgen Lake basin where a tract of about 60 square miles dropped more than 10 feet. The lower Madison Canyon dropped 7 to 8 feet, dwindling out to a few tenths of a foot at its mouth, while the area above the dam subsided 6 to 14 feet. Cliff

Lake, west of the upper Madison valley, likewise tilted, while north
of the slumped canyon there was a slight elevation of 0.1 to 1.7
feet."[30]

Such an abrupt change in the lake floor, accompanied by water
spilling over the shorelines, naturally made the water in Hebgen Lake
turbulent. Geologists now know that the main body of the lake bed
subsided more than either the Madison Arm (the southeast extremity)
or the dam. This warped the body of water so that at one time the
Madison Arm "stood 5 feet higher than the dam and 10 to 15 feet
higher than water in the main part of the lake." Nature could never
tolerate such a condition, and with a great surge the water rushed
northward and then on down the lake to the dam, which it over-
topped by perhaps four feet; it then receded, only to go over the dam
at least three more times. The water meanwhile sloshed about, raised
itself into vertically bouncing waves, and acted in a most unorthodox
fashion for hours afterward. It was the first surge that hit the Hilgard
Lodge, one mile from the dam, with a 9-foot-high wave that carried
off some buildings and wrecked the rest.[31]

Fortunately the forty-six-year-old dam held, though it cracked
in three places, one of the cracks being 4 inches wide. When the
initial quake was over, the northeast end was a foot lower than the
southwest end, and some water appeared to be seeping through the
bottom. But it held.[32]

Although we can only describe one event at a time, everything
happened at once. The highways split asunder, or slipped into the
lake, or were broken at right angles by scarps, or were covered by
landslides or by the rapidly rising water of Earthquake Lake below
the dam. A camper fortunate enough to be above the road and
above the dam, rather than below it, was still not out of danger, for
looming above him from the canyon floor were limestone or sandstone
ledges, and these were so shaken that great boulders came rolling
down the mountainsides, cutting a swath through the trees as if they
were matchsticks, bouncing with a Paul Bunyanesque thud which
left pits in the earth big enough for a man to sit in. In one case, at
a campsite 15 miles west of the dam, 8-ton boulders leapfrogged over
a picnic table and landed on an unfortunate couple camped there,
killing them instantly.[33]

Up from the northeast side of the lake the very earth began to
move slowly forward. This was named the "Kirkwood earth flow,"

and it consisted of a half-mile tongue of earth, 400–800 feet wide, which spent a month moving forward about 100 feet, cutting a trail in two and carrying a wedge of the path 100 feet downhill.[34]

But the greater damage and loss of life was caused not by the falling boulders, nor by the scarps, nor by the earth or mudflows, but by the terrible rockslides the quake unleashed. Along the northeast side of Hebgen Lake the slides carried 3,000 feet of the highway into the water, and the largest one moved 350,000 cubic yards of earth below the surface of the lake.[35]

The most horrifying event was the so-called Madison Slide, occurring 6 miles down the canyon from Hebgen Dam, 17 miles southwest of the epicenter of the quake. Until 11:37 P.M., August 17, 1959, a campground built and maintained by the United States Forest Service was located slightly northeast of this point. Here and farther down the canyon a number of people had bedded down for sleep on this moonlit summer night.

Probably the twenty-six unfortunate people who were killed suffered a few moments of stark terror before the landslide engulfed them. (Two others were killed by a falling boulder elsewhere in the canyon.) Tales told by the survivors indicate that about twenty seconds elapsed after the first quake awakened them and before the mountain fell. And then it happened: 37 million cubic yards of the upper parts of the mountain on the south side of the canyon broke loose from the harder, dolomite pilings and slid into the narrow canyon (500-1000 feet across) and up the other side, burying the river and the highway for a mile to depths up to 220 feet. Nine people are known to have been killed, and nineteen more are presumed dead and buried beneath the slide.[36]

Such a massive wrenching of the earth's surface caused a blast of air stronger than a hurricane; it turned cars on end and whisked people into the air like so many straws before dashing them to their deaths. It sent the waters of the Madison River speeding back upstream in a tidal wave full of rocks, mud, and timber which engulfed the Rock Creek campground and created a new lake by blocking the river's progress downstream. On the downstream side it created a wave that flooded a terrace 15 feet above the stream. It raised an enormous dust cloud that obliterated the moon. And then there was silence, punctuated by occasional falling rocks or the screams of survivors.

When morning came the immensity of the slide area and the reason for the survivors' terror became apparent. A raw, light-colored wound extended from the top of the mountain (in some places, even 200–300 feet down the back side), downward to where the new slide mass began. The green conifers, the grasses, the black topsoil that belonged there were gone. Geologists measured the break: 2,200 feet wide and 1,300 feet high, with the depth of the scar 100–300 feet below the former crest of the mountain, creating a concave surface where the ridge had previously been convex. Where the canyon wall was steepest, at the west end, scientists estimated that the mass traveled 100 miles an hour for twenty seconds, catching air beneath it which broke out as an air blast, and carrying rocks as much as 430 feet above the river, which was the highest point the slide touched, as it plowed up the other side of the canyon. On the east side the slide moved down more slowly.[37]

What, other than earth tremors, caused the slide? The geologists list a number of factors: hard spurs of brittle dolomite stuck at a steep angle into a thick, badly weathered covering of gneiss and schist which anchored the sloping mass, but not securely: friction was necessary to keep it all in place. The earthquake unleashed the mass, and it became 37 million cubic yards of fluid rock, rushing downward into the narrow canyon.[38]

Morning also revealed that the Madison River was building a lake upriver on the east side of the slide. At first it rose rapidly with the quantities of the four sloshovers from Hebgen Lake, plus the regular flow of the river, so that by 6:30 that first morning 20 feet of water covered the Rock Creek campground. For the next three weeks water rose at a decreasing rate, and was finally down to about a foot a day so that it was once more safe to control the outflow from Hebgen Dam.

But how strong was this "instant" dam — the slide, with a new lake backing behind it? When a 240-foot wall of water built up behind, might it not give way as had the Gros Ventre dam, which had killed several people in 1925? And what if the waters of Earthquake Lake, backed up to the Hebgen Dam, undermined it so that it gave way and released seven times as much water as in Earthquake Lake? All the towns down the Madison Valley would be imperiled. Confronted with these problems, the Army Corps of Engineers bulldozed a spillway across the slide area and drained nearly half the water behind the slide, thus ending the danger.[39]

Today the Madison flows freely north, meeting the Gallatin and the Jefferson to form the Missouri. Every summer thousands travel to see the slide and Earthquake Lake; to read the plaque on the highest boulder thrown up on the north side of the canyon, commemorating the deaths of the nineteen presumed buried by the slide and the others killed by the quake; to trace the deteriorating blacktop highway that runs right into the lake; and to scan the ridge for the Red Canyon Fault scarp (14 miles long and 14 feet high at midpoint) or the Hebgen Fault scarp (7½ miles long and 20 feet high near its midpoint).[40] They try to comprehend the immense power of nature, then climb back into their automobiles and hustle out of the canyon. "How far is Old Faithful? How far is Virginia City?"[41]

Up in the park all manner of earthquake-activated phenomena occurred. A mudflow in Secret Valley upturned trees. There were rockslides at Tuff Cliff, Mount Jackson, Mount Everts, and along the Gibbon and Fire Hole canyons, where only the fortunate absence of tourists on the highway prevented the loss of human life. The water table being jarred, most of the streams and ponds were muddied up, and waterflow increased with the release of groundwater. According to William A. Fischer, park geologist, more geysers and hot springs were in action immediately following the quake than at any other time since the opening of the park in 1872. Well over 150 geysers erupted that had no previous record of eruption, the temperature of the water increased 6 degrees Fahrenheit, and the discharge of water increased by 10 percent. Most changes were recorded in the Lower, Midway, and Upper Geyser basins. Old Faithful behaved normally except for a slight lengthening of the interval between eruptions, but this leveled off by 1960.[42] Guests at Old Faithful Inn were doused when the sprinkler system was activated; cracks in the chimneys prompted authorities to close the inn, but one wing was later reopened for 350 guests. The "savages" (student waiters) who poured coffee all night for the interrupted sleepers commented that "there was more steam and water in the rooms than at the geysers." The Union Pacific line to West Yellowstone was cut, thus setting ahead by fifteen or twenty days the date the company had chosen to terminate that part of its service permanently. That no one was hurt within the park is due partly to luck, and also to the fact that park campgrounds are situated away from cliffs and mountain slopes.[43]

Although probably two-thirds of the 18,000 people in the park that night slept through the quake, the visitors were sufficiently impressed by nature's power that 7,000 of them left the following day and only 50 percent of the usual tourist load filled the park for the remainder of the season.

Our imaginary clock, superimposed upon the Yellowstone country, is now at about twelve minutes to the hour, the hands stretching from their center in the park out through Hebgen Dam. Let us find out what is left outside the park up to high noon, the point from which we started, which is just east of Gardiner. What of the terrain bordering the northwestern corner of the park?

It is primarily the country of the Gallatin, Madison, and Jefferson rivers, the first two of which originate in the park. They all flow north, more or less parallel to each other, separated by similarly named mountain ranges on their eastern flanks. At Three Forks, Montana, they merge and create the Missouri. It was at Three Forks that Lewis and Clark had three choices and chose the one river— the Jefferson — which would lead them eventually to the Snake– Columbia system and thence to the Pacific Ocean.

The Jefferson Range is beyond our interests, but the Madison was the scene of the earthquake, and farther down the canyon lies Virginia City, near Alder Gulch, from which more than $60 million in gold was extracted in the early days of Montana Territory. A very small eastern segment of the range extends into the northwest corner of the park.[44]

Most of the Gallatin Range, which, like the Beartooth, contains some of the most ancient igneous rocks known to man[45] lies within the reservation. The visitor views it west of Swan Lake Flats, running parallel with the road. Its more prominent crests include Mount Holmes on the south (10,336 feet high, with a fire tower that can be seen faintly from the highway); Electric Peak, so prominent none can miss it (11,196 feet and the highest point of the range, second highest point in the park); and, north of the boundary, Mount Blackmore (10,196 feet), named for the wife of British entrepreneur William Blackmore. She died at Bozeman in the summer of 1872 while her husband was preparing their visit to the park with Dr. Ferdinand V. Hayden of the United States Geological Survey of the Territories.[46]

The Gallatin River rises in the mountains of the same name and flows on the west side some 120 miles north to its junction with the Madison and the Jefferson. Along the parallel highway, U.S. 191, one arrives at the Gallatin Gateway, a hamlet built by the Chicago, Milwaukee and St. Paul Railroad as a point of embarkation for its passengers bound for Yellowstone. Ten miles farther north one comes to Bozeman, which, until the coming of the Northern Pacific and the founding of Livingston in 1882, was the chief outfitting point, besides Virginia City, for trips to the park. It was also the site of old Fort Ellis, of which nothing remains today but a marker at the site on the eastern fringes of the town.

Rounding the northwest corner of the park, the valley and mountain country north of Electric Peak and west of the town of Gardiner (and of the Yellowstone River) is beautiful ranch country. The great depressions or mountain parks are Cinnabar Basin and Tom Minor Basin. Coal of good coking quality has been mined in these areas in the past, especially on the slopes of Electric Peak.[47]

Descending to the west bank of the Yellowstone, the tourist will notice the Devil's Slide on Cinnabar Mountain. Old-timers say that a mountain man once lived at the foot of the slide, and whenever he got hungry, he just stepped outside his cabin door, drew a bead on a curious elk peering down from the top of the slide, shot it, and waited. In due time the elk slid to the bottom, the meat nicely roasted from the friction heat, and the hide beautifully tanned. This story may lack credibility, but there is no question that, to geologists, Cinnabar is a most fascinating mountain. Hayden first noticed it in 1871: "On the west side of the Yellowstone River," he said, "there is an exhibition of uplifted strata. It is sometimes called Cinnabar Mountain, from a brick-red band of clay which extends from the summit down the slide, and was supposed to be cinnabar. . . ." In his report of the following year, Hayden went into greater detail: "Cinnabar Mountain comprises a group of nearly vertical beds," he wrote; " . . . it . . . is about one mile in length, and in this distance are exposed probably 10,000 feet of strata. . . . "[48] Indeed, the strata are lined up like so many books, and the trained geologist can read their designations as easily as one can read the titles of books on a shelf.

Still working east toward high noon on our geographical clock, we follow the Yellowstone River, which flows out of the park just east of the hamlet of Gardiner, is joined near there by the river of the same name (but spelled without the i), and then flows in a northwest-by-north direction. This takes it placidly through Cinnabar Valley, angrily down through Yankee Jim Canyon (also known as the Second Canyon), dreamily through a 30-mile stretch appropriately named Paradise Valley, then through the First (or Lower) Canyon, or Gate of the Mountains, into the great terraced valley that it will follow all the way to its junction with the Missouri.

This section from the northern park boundary to Livingston, Montana, 56 miles away, is especially beautiful, as several million visitors will attest; it is also geologically linked with the park, because the course of the river was also the scene of massive glaciation in prehistoric times. Here one can see blocks of granite the size of small cottages, weighing as much as 150 tons. In Yankee Jim Canyon there are granite spurs as "smooth, polished and striated as those at the margin of any Swiss or Norwegian glacier." The striae point upward over the ridge, mute testimony of "how the ice had been pressed out of the gorge over this opposing barrier of rock."[49] This glacier was a slow-flowing river of ice extending far up the Yellowstone into the park.

As the hands of our clock approach noon, we find ourselves once more in the high, rugged Beartooth, locally called the Snowy Mountains. They loom spectacularly from the east side of Paradise Valley, with Emigrant Peak a landmark, and with Emigrant Gulch, leading into the mountains, reminding the historically minded visitor of mining camps established there as early as July 1864.[50]

And so we have completed the circle. "Wonderland," as the park was called by early visitors, is indeed surrounded by mountains — Snowy or Beartooth, Absaroka, Owl Creek, Wind River, Gros Ventre, Teton, the Madison Plateau, the Madison Valley and Mountains, the Gallatins, and the Jeffersons on the far west, then the Yellowstone Valley and back to high noon and the Snowy Mountains again. Man has cut roads into these barriers, he has robbed them of some of their precious metals, but he cannot remove the mountains. There they are, protective walls to the basin within, beautiful, formidable, forboding, by their very presence prompting the curious to ask, What lies inside?

2

The Plateau Inside

Nearly surrounded by mountains is the greater portion of a plateau or basin, relatively flat, 75 miles across east to west and 65 miles north to south, averaging 7,500 feet above sea level. The geology of this plateau (as we shall call it hereafter, though "basin" would be equally acceptable) is of great interest. Volcanism, ice, water, and wind, together with cataclysmic changes in the earth's crust, have all played their parts in creating its contours.

The most important event of all, though not even theorized by geologists until the late 1950s, was the formation of the Yellowstone caldera. (A caldera is the craterlike basin of a volcano.) Such a basin is formed when volcanic gases cause an eruption; the remaining surface of the earth collapses into the void below. Krakatoa is the best known caldera of modern times, but the explosion causing it was small compared with the two that Yellowstone experienced: the first was 2 million years ago, the second one — and the one geologists can most easily study — about 600,000 years ago. These must have been earth-shattering explosions. The caldera they created was about 45 miles long and 30 miles across; it included much of Yellowstone Lake, plus the heart of the Yellowstone plateau. In subsequent millennia lava oozed over the caldera floor and built up the surface several thousand feet to the present level. Fractures caused by the pressure of the gases became channels by which lava and heat moved upward; those channels give Yellowstone the heat which, meeting with water seeping from above, provides the ingredients for hot springs and geysers. The airborne ash from the explosions settled across most of the central and western states.[1]

The discovery of the two massive explosions and the resultant calderas also blew sky-high ninety years of painstaking geologic research; conversely, new problems arose which have yet to be solved. Yet the basic fact that lava poured out over the basin, or caldera, remains established, though not all the orifices from which it oozed have been identified. We know that it almost completely covered the central and southwestern parts of Yellowstone, leaving the Washburn Range and the Red Mountains as islands. It lapped at the foothills of the hardening ranges and headed southwest where there were no mountains to stop it; it continued on out of the park to a point where a scarp of unknown origin stopped it as the terrain dropped abruptly to the Snake River plain.[2]

The lava was not thrown or exploded out of volcanoes; it poured out — perhaps just oozed out — from fissures and spread over the area according to the laws of gravity, like fudge being poured onto a dish. One massive intrusion after another flowed over its predecessor, creating the Yellowstone plateau. Eventually the rhyolite would be thousands of feet thick, and although the extent of this plateau is not as great nor the thickness as impressive as was believed by Arnold Hague a half-century ago, Hague's statement that "the mass can not be considered otherwise than as a geographical unit" remains essentially correct.[3]

So the plateau is the basic geographic feature of Yellowstone. Yet it is a broken plateau, partly because of faults and blocking, no doubt, but mostly because of water and ice erosion. The former we can witness at work today, but the glaciation has ended, and only its results can be seen. Still, glaciation is perhaps the most easily understood geologic phenomenon, and an awareness of the Ice Age and a knowledge of what it left behind can increase our appreciation of nature's work in the park.

It has long been known that there were several ice ages during Pleistocene and Quaternary times, from about a million years ago until as recently as 8,000 years ago. It was also obvious to geologists that the Yellowstone area, one of the largest highlands in North America, should have been affected by it. But it took a stormy day in December for the full importance of the glacial era to impress one of Hayden's geologists, William Henry Holmes. He was going about his task of sketching geologic phenomena between "'the Grand Canyon from the falls to the base of Mount Washburn," he wrote, "and during a storm of rain and sleet took shelter under the overhanging edge of a great rock in the dense timber. Considerably to my surprise I found it to be a very compact, coarsely crystalline feldspathic granite. . . . It is within a stone's throw of the brink of the Canyon and rests upon a sheet or series of rhyolite, not less than one thousand feet in thickness. . . . "

Like the apple falling on Newton's head, the shelter given Holmes by this rock set him to thinking. For the boulder did not belong there. The Yellowstone plateau, the Absarokas on the east, the upper reaches of the Yellowstone River Valley above the lake — they were all of purely volcanic origin. But that huge boulder was granite. Where did it come from? How did it get there?

Holmes reasoned that the rock could have come from one of two areas: from the Gallatins, 20 miles to the northwest, or from the Beartooth Plateau, 20 miles to the northeast. Because the Gallatins appeared too small to have produced glaciers large enough to carry the boulder to its present location, he rejected that possibility and concentrated on the other one. The massive granite highland to the northeast could have been the source of the boulder, and it could have spawned a river of ice sufficiently large to have carried it there and spilled it over to one side of the Yellowstone Canyon.[4]

More recent study bears out many of Holmes's preliminary conclusions. Two glaciers had cut and disfigured the once-solid plateau. One of these was the Lamar Glacier, which flowed down the valley of the same name from the Beartooth and Absaroka ranges. It was 35 miles long from its head to its junction with the north-running Yellowstone Glacier.

From its junction with the Lamar, the Yellowstone Glacier extended south 30 miles to its head. In its course it included the basin that constituted the Yellowstone Lake and the Upper Yellowstone Valley above it (known as the "Thorofare" today). There it received the ice from the southern Absarokas much as the Yellowstone River receives most of its waters from them today. However, these two glaciers did not inevitably meet at the Lamar–Yellowstone junction: at one time Beartooth ice appears to have spread southward over the plateau, submerging the Grand Canyon of the Yellowstone, engulfing Hayden Valley, and even extending westward into the geyser regions. The ice dropped granite when it receded. Thus there is a rational explanation for the presence of the lonely boulder that protected

William Henry Holmes from the elements.[5]

Since the retreat of the glaciers 8,000–10,000 years ago, no major changes are known to have occurred in Yellowstone's geologic history. We know that thermal activity was present during and probably before the glaciation, and earthquakes and landslides, faulting and blocking, are continuing phenomena of the area. But the geologic drama essentially ends with the retreat of the last great glacial covering. The latest chapter in the continuing story is concerned with the inexorable, incredibly slow action of erosion.

Let us circle our imaginary clock once again but this time with big quarter-hour leaps, and staying at all times within the park boundaries. High noon will still be a few miles east of Gardiner, whose main street is the park boundary, and 12:15 is just north of Mount Chittenden. This quarter of the park is dominated by the Yellowstone and Lamar (once called the East Fork) rivers and their tributaries.

The Yellowstone River was called *Roche Jaune* by early French trappers who probably adapted a name given it by Indians of the upper Missouri and Yellowstone country. Lewis and Clark simply anglicized the name in 1805. Apparently the river derives its name from the yellowish bluffs along its lower reaches. It could have received its name from the cream and citrine tints of the Grand Canyon of the Yellowstone, but there is no evidence that white men had seen that spectacle prior to John Colter's adventurous, lonesome exploration, and we cannot be sure that he saw it.[6] In fact, the grandeur of the Upper Yellowstone was not known to the civilized world until nearly three-quarters of a century after his journey.

After beginning at the foot of Yount's Peak southeast of the park and flowing into Yellowstone Lake, the Yellowstone River runs out of the northernmost point of the lake and for about 10 miles winds langorously north by northwest, protected on the west by a plateau-like ridge known as the Elephant Back Mountains, and on the east by the Sulphur Hills. Then, on the west side, the stream enters the open country known as the Hayden Valley. In this grassy, ancient lake bed, moose, elk, deer, and an occasional bison may be seen, for both Trout Creek and Alum Creek furnish water as they run through the valley toward their union with the Yellowstone. There is some thermal activity here, notably from the Mud Volcano and Black Dragon's Caldron. Fishermen are attracted to this stretch of the river, as are large flocks of aquatic birds.

Then the flow of the water increases, a roar is heard, and the river spills 109 feet over a precipice called the Upper Falls. It then travels rapidly another third of a mile (1,600 feet), spills 308 feet over a second precipice, the Lower Falls, and continues through a deepening canyon 800–1200 feet below the surface of the plateau. Not until it has reached the junction with the Lamar River, 24 miles to the northeast, is this fourth canyon, the Grand Canyon of the Yellowstone, at an end. It is an awe-inspiring sight.

But to the geologists of a Princeton University expedition to the park in 1926, the "prominent dark reddish brown pinnacle known as Red Rock," had more than beauty to offer. They saw the rock on the west side of the canyon just below the Lower Falls, sheer on the river side but attached to the canyon rim by an earthen hinge which surrounded it three-quarters of the way up. In the depression between the pinnacle and the canyon wall they were able to detect, and later to prove, the existence of an earlier river channel.[7] Theirs was not so much a new find as a rediscovery of something Holmes had mentioned in 1883, when he had found indisputable evidence of a stream "600 feet below the top of the present valley, and about 400 feet above the present river." But, he added, "I had not time to go on with this interesting investigation."[8]

Both Holmes and the Princeton group were correct about previous channels, but because of the simplicity of geology at that time, some of their conjectures were wrong. In recent decades Yellowstone geology has been complicated by the identification of more and more stages in its history, but clear and surprisingly convincing answers are now forthcoming.

At present, all evidence indicates that the older channel of the Yellowstone was filled to the brim as a result of damming by Pleistocene glaciers which, in the course of tens of thousands of years, dropped quantities of rocky drift. These deposits were followed, as the glaciers receded, by the lacustrine deposits of a glacier-made lake much larger than the present Yellowstone Lake. Before the end of the Ice Age, erosion had set in once more and the old channel was cut again — "resurrected," as the Princetonians put it. The original channel had been cut through the rhyolite, and one of the questions recently answered is whether basaltic lavas had filled the channel prior to Pleistocene (Ice Age) times. The answer is negative,

save for the Tower Creek span of the Yellowstone Canyon, where
three valleys — the present one, a Pleistocene, and a pre-Pleistocene
one — can be traced. Furthermore, evidence indicates that the
Yellowstone's course has not changed significantly for many thousands
of years; and if the lake ever did drain into the Snake River–Columbia–Pacific Ocean system, it was for a very short period, or periods,
of time.[9]

As it rushes downward in response to the law of gravity, the
river passes the marshy Solfatara Plateau. Then, veering abruptly
northeast, the Yellowstone flows by a range of mountains to the
northwest whose actual contours in the park are misunderstood (if
they are considered at all) by most casual visitors. This is the Washburn Range, which is "horseshoe-shaped, with the open end to the
northeast"; the great interior amphitheater thus created is drained by
Tower Creek, whose striking falls are one of the most photographed
sights in the park. Washburn itself is an old volcano, standing high
because of the collapse of the Yellowstone terrain into the great caldera directly to the south.[10]

The views from Mount Washburn (10,243 feet and highest point
in the range) are truly worth the bus fare up. Fine vistas may also
be enjoyed by those who choose to climb Dunraven Peak, just west
of the pass of the same name, over which runs the road between
Tower and Canyon; or from Cook, Folsom, and Prospect peaks,
among the twenty or more crests in the range.

The river flows out of the Fourth Canyon at the Lamar Junction, where the Lamar River flows in, at a low, grassy, peaceful
stretch of land. For years the only bridge below the falls was here,
just above the junction of the two rivers. It was called Baronett's
Bridge, after its owner, Jack Baronett (see note, p. 6) and it had
a long and adventurous history.[11]

To the west of Lamar Junction and the Yellowstone lies Pleasant
Valley, another of those lovely, quiet meadowlands in which Yellowstone abounds. The modern traveler pays no attention, but a quick
glance at the map will attest to its strategic location in the days when
there was considerable horse and wagon traffic between Gardiner
and Cooke City, up the Lamar River and out of the park. An un-
reconstructed old rebel named "Uncle John" Yancey established a
tavern and stables there, catering to the draymen and visitors who
were men enough to stay and stomach the swill he served for food.

Uncle John was especially proud of his own special brand of "Kentucky tea," which he served from two incredibly dirty glasses, neither of which, he boasted, had ever been tainted by a drop of water.[12]

And the Yellowstone, swollen with the waters of the Lamar, enters the steep, narrow Third Canyon. It cuts through rugged, broken country, some of it of Beartooth granite, some of it of volcanic origin. Now it cuts through a narrow pass 2,500 feet high (as in the Black Canyon), now it flows through relatively open country. At places the Third Canyon is indeed rugged and spectacular, but it is more conventional than the Grand Canyon of the Yellowstone and is therefore largely ignored.

The Yellowstone's flow is increased by the flow of Lost Creek, Blacktail Deer Creek, and Lava Creek flowing out of the southwest; all three streams drain the rolling, grassy Blacktail Deer Plateau. To the northeast, where the Beartooths loom, Little Buffalo Creek, Slough Creek, and Hellroaring Creek add to its swelling size. The Gardner River, which rises on Sepulcher Mountain southwest of Mammoth Hot Springs, joins the mother stream just north of the boundary and east of the town of Gardiner.

As our imaginary clock works toward the quarter-hour it passes the Buffalo Plateau, then those spectacular outcroppings of the Beartooth, Druid Peak, Barronette Peak, Abiathar Peak, Mount Norris, and others, all of them between 10,000 and 11,000 feet high. The hands of our clock also touch briefly on part of the Lamar River, whose grassy turf was for hundreds of years a feeding ground for deer, elk, moose, mountain sheep, and the American bison (which we shall call *buffalo* from now on).

In this area, south of Soda Butte, is Death Gulch and Wahb Springs. Death Gulch, which holds deadly gases so concentrated that birds and rodents that happen into it are asphyxiated, was the scene of the death of Wahb, the bear in Ernest Thompson Seton's *The Biography of a Grizzly.*

About midway between Lamar Junction and the Northeast Entrance (which leads on to Cooke City, the Beartooth Highway, and then to Deer Lodge, Montana), is Soda Butte, the lone indication of thermal activity in this alpine valley. Its waters are cold now, and the flow is very slight, but at one time there was substantial hot flow. All the signs of former hot-spring activity are present there. Soda Butte also gave its name to the southwest running creek which flows into the Lamar about two miles below the Butte; when the Lamar veers southeast, Soda Butte Creek creates the canyon up which Cooke City-bound people make their way. At one point by the road is Icebox Canyon, where the sun's rays are so rare that ice remains all year round.

Returning to the junction of the Lamar with the Yellowstone, as we work southward toward our quarter hour, embracing the northeast quarter of the park, we shall note on the south side of the Lamar, and east of the Yellowstone, a long, elliptical elevation known as Specimen Ridge. Here is one of nature's own museums, in which a petrified forest of prehistoric trees still stands. Although few of the park's visitors see it (one must wade the Lamar to reach it), this sight can impress us with the longevity of the earth and the precariousness of the present more, perhaps, than can any other phenomenon in a park full of nature's surprises.

This forest was first described in detail by William Henry Holmes, who was impressed by what he saw on the south side of the Lamar Valley, near the junction with Soda Creek. "As we ride up the trail that meanders the smooth river bottom, we have but to turn our attention to the cliffs on the right hand to discover a multitude of the bleached trunks of the ancient forests," he wrote. "Prostrate trunks, 40 and 50 feet in length, are of frequent occurrence, and not a few of these are as much as 5 or 6 feet in diameter . . . . One upright trunk . . . rises . . . to the height of 12 feet. By careful measurements, it was found to be 10 feet in diameter . . . The bark . . . retains perfectly the original deeply-lined outer surface." Often he found the wood completely opalized or agatized, with "beautiful crystals of quartz and calcite" present in the cavities of decayed trunks.[13]

More recent studies, notably that of Professor Erling Dorf of Princeton University, have led to the identity of as many as twenty-seven separate fossil forests on Yellowstone's Specimen Ridge. They are piled one on another, with volcanic debris in between, to a height of 1,675 feet. Dr. Dorf believes that each forest was covered in days or weeks, that it takes at least 200 years for volcanic debris to change to a soil in which vegetation can thrive, and that most of the activity took place during the Eocene epoch, 40–60 million years ago.[14]

East of Specimen Ridge lie the well-watered Mirror Plateau, the northwest-flowing Lamar River, and the western heights of the Absaroka Range. Here are the weird volcanic formations in what is called the Hoodoo Region. This is another area reached only by trail, but the visitor coming into the park through the East Entrance, up from Cody, has an idea of what the Hoodoos are like, for similar formations of volcanic debris weathered into strange forms exist along the Shoshone River Canyon.

According to the peripatetic Philetus W. Norris, second superintendent of Yellowstone, the Hoodoo Region was named by the same unfortunate prospectors who discovered the Clarks Fork gold vein in 1870 and were later attacked by Indians, who killed several of them. Norris was determined to explore this country for himself, and in 1880 he got his opportunity. He pushed through the headwaters of the Lamar and the Stinkingwater (also known as Stinking River, and finally the North Fork of the Shoshone), and climbed Hoodoo Peak (whose height he figured at 10,700 feet: its height is now determined to be 10,546 feet). On the southern side of this mountain he found his Hoodoos. "Here," he wrote in his annual report, " . . . the frosts and storms of untold ages in an Alpine climate have worn about a dozen labyrinths of countless deep, narrow, tortuous channels amid the long, slender, tottering pillars, shafts, and spires of the conglomerate breccia and other remaining volcanic rocks."[15]

As the hands of our imaginary clock sweep down through the second quarter of the park, the southeast section, it is clear that the dominant landmark is the Yellowstone Lake. Situated 7,731 feet above sea level, 20 miles long by 14 miles wide, with a 100-mile shoreline and a total area of 139 square miles, in places at least 300 feet deep, the lake alone, surrounded by woods and mountains, would be sufficient justification for a national park. Its outline is so jagged that it can be compared with nothing that any ordinary imagination could conjure up, although the early explorers compared the lake, with its three "arms" and its "'thumb," to a hand — surely a badly mangled one.[16] Within the lake are several islands, of which Frank Island, Dot Island, and Stevenson Island are the best known.

This great body of water is partly in a Pleistocene depression and partly within the caldera proper. Geologists are convinced, and with good reason, that at one time the lake was as much as 600 feet higher than it is at present, and they know of at least four shallow grassy or swampy cols through which it could have drained out into the Snake River–Columbia System.[17]

On the east side of the lake are the Absarokas, of course, where Sylvan Pass provides access for automobile traffic from the east, and a superheated steam vent by the lake shore, on Steamboat Point, attracts attention. South of this area are a number of peaks bearing the names of important men in Yellowstone history: Mount Doane, for Lieutenant Gustavus C. Doane, who explored the park several times, first in 1870; Mount Langford, named for Nathaniel P. Langford, who was with the 1870 group and was the first superintendent of the park, and Mount Stevenson, named for Hayden's executive officer. A few are named after politicians, for the sake of public relations: among these are Mount Arthur and Mount Schurz. Mount Humphreys is named for General A. A. Humphreys, chief of the Army Corps of Engineers.

Advancing southward to about twenty-five minutes past the hour, we come to the valley of the Upper Yellowstone. Now called the Thorofare, it is 2–3 miles wide, grassy and well watered, even marshy, with "dark, somber rocks of volcanic origin" on either side. Ferdinand Hayden, exploring the valley in 1871, was deeply impressed by the beauty of this canyon, which is still inaccessible to automobiles. "Looking up the valley from some high point," he wrote, "one could almost imagine that he was in the presence of the ruins of some gigantic city, so much like old castles, cathedrals of every age and clime, do these rocks appear. . . . "[18] After about 15 miles the mountains close in, and the Yellowstone, a small stream here, heads to the southeast at the foot of Yount's Peak, while other streams, notably Atlantic Creek on the west and Thorofare Creek on the east, soon join it to add to its volume.

At just about the half-hour the hands of our clock, having passed across Two Ocean Plateau, Mount Hancock, and Big Game Ridge, cross Heart Lake and the Red Mountains. Heart Lake — really *Hart* Lake for a mountain man of that name — is a beautiful body of water just southwest of the South Arm of Yellowstone Lake. It is one of the sources of the Snake River. On Witch Creek, a warm stream flowing into the lake from the west, there is a geyser rarely observed by tourists, since, like the lake, it is accessible only by trail.

Looking down upon Heart Lake from 10,308 feet is Mount Sheridan, the highest peak in the Red Mountains. This impressive range on the south and west side of the lake is made up of sedimentary rocks overlaid by rhyolite.[19]

And now we enter the third quarter in our trip around the Yellowstone Clock. On the outer fringes of this southwest corner of the park is the well-watered, tree-covered Cascade Corner, drained by several streams, of which the Bechler River and Mountain Ash Creek are most important. Northeast lies the Pitchstone Plateau, northwest, the Madison Plateau: the rapid drop-offs from these rhyolite plains have given the Cascade Corner its name.

Northeast of the Cascade Corner, the hands of our clock will pass two other lakes of importance in the Yellowstone story. The first of these is Lewis Lake, 7,779 feet above sea level; in its waters, on a clear, still morning, the Tetons are perfectly reflected, though they rise up from the plain 40–50 miles to the south. The highway from the South Entrance follows the eastern shore of Lewis Lake for several miles.

About 5 miles northwest-by-north of the lake via the Lewis River Canyon is Shoshone Lake, 7,791 feet high, close to the Canyon–Old Faithful Highway but still a hike of several miles away. The Lewis River flows from Shoshone Lake into Lewis Lake, at the extreme south end of which it then flows out again, passes south through a narrow canyon, and joins the Snake River just north of the Yellowstone boundary. (The Snake heads far to the east. Its trickling beginnings are actually south of the park, but it receives most of its waters in the park, especially from the Heart and Lewis rivers as well as from dozens of smaller tributaries).

As the hands of our clock move on, touching the Madison Canyon, the Madison Valley, and finally the Gallatin Mountains, the absence of substantial lakes indicates a good system of rapid drainage. This system consists of three rivers whose shape on a map may be compared to an upside down Y whose branches are rivers, with the stem the single stream created by them. The southern branch is known as the Firehole River. It begins at little Madison Lake, about 20 miles south of Madison Junction, and wends its way north toward its junction with the other branch. The Firehole runs past many hot springs and geysers, and it is the principal drainage for the

Upper, the Midway, and the Lower geyser basins. There is also one spectacular drop in the Firehole Canyon: Keppler Cascades.

"Firehole" is simply a descriptive name, although its origin is probably not quite what the visitor would conclude. "Hole" was the word used by the mountan men to describe well-watered, protected, grassy openings in the mountains; such a description was fitting for some sections of this river, save for the prevalence of fires along it — thus the name Firehole.[20]

The north branch of the reversed Y is the Gibbon River, which originates about 15 miles northeast by east of the Norris Geyser Basin, on the Solfatara Plateau. It pushes westward, falling at beautiful Virginia Cascades, winds through the Norris Geyser Basin and flows southwest, swelled by the thermal waters, on through the less spectacular Gibbon Geyser Basin, through the narrow Gibbon Canyon and Gibbon Falls; then it turns due west, accepts the waters of the Firehole at Madison Junction, and finally becomes part of the Madison and continues on through the Madison Canyon out of the park. The river is called Gibbon in honor of General John Gibbon of the U.S. Army, who led several Indian campaigns in Montana.[21]

Although we have not emphasized them as we circled the park, we have passed many places where thermal action has been observed: there are hot springs on the Mirror Plateau, on the south side of Mount Washburn, up Pelican Creek southeast of the lake, and they become increasingly prevalent after we have passed the half-hour on our clock. At the west end of Heart Lake, at the West Thumb of Yellowstone Lake, on the western shores of Lewis Lake, and on the southwest shores of Shoshone Lake, there are places where the magmatic vault underlying the entire park has heated the waters and sent them bubbling, steaming, or spouting up through fissures in the earth to appear on the surface as springs or geysers. Yet this has been only a portent of what is to come in our journey toward noon at the center of the northern boundary.

For the greatest geyser area in the world lies between twenty and ten minutes to the hour on the clock. The Upper, Midway, Lower, Gibbon, and Norris basins await our geologic examinations. They constitute an elliptical area of about 1,800 square miles. Along with the clusters of hot springs that are found up to 10 miles east of the Yellowstone River, south along the Snake River to the boundaries of the park, and north nearly to the border, there are about 100 groupings of thermal activity, involving at least 3,000 individual springs.[22] Impressive as this area is, there are also significant thermal areas in New Zealand and Iceland.[23] But while a geyser is a hot spring, the reverse is not necessarily true, and there are more geysers — over 300 — in Yellowstone than at any other single place in the world. New Zealand boasts of having the world's greatest geyser, but it has been dormant since 1916. This was the spouter called Waimangu, which threw up muddy water to a height of 900–1,500 feet. This geyser area is similar to the Yellowstone in its shape (20 miles wide, 150 miles long) and also consists predominantly of rhyolite pumice dating from Miocene times. Steam vents, fumaroles, and mud pots — aptly called "porridge pots" by the New Zealanders — increase its similarity to Yellowstone.[24]

Iceland has several thousand hot springs but probably not over thirty geysers, or perhaps 1 percent of the total number of hot springs. Some are in remote places, and there may be a few that have never been seen. The known geysers are in five clusters, spread across the volcanic belt that crosses the island from southwest to northeast. It is in Iceland that western man probably gained his first acquaintance with this beautiful natural phenomenon, for the Reykir Geyser in Olfus (an Icelandic province) has been famous as long as historical records have been kept. In 1647 Bishop Sveinson applied the name *geysir* (gusher) to one of the spectacular spouters, and the name has been accepted. Icelandic geysers assume some additional historical significance because of the research on geyser activity that has been conducted there.[25]

In the United States there are geysers at Beowawe Hot Springs in Eureka County, Nevada, and well over 150 miles to the southwest, at Steamboat Springs near Reno; at Soda Springs, Idaho; and on Umnak Island in Alaska. In general these are small geysers, erupting 1–5 feet. Tibet, the Azores, Chile, and the Pacific islands of New Britain and New Ireland are said to possess a few.[26] But the sum total is small: geysers are among nature's rarest phenomena.

In Yellowstone Park the thermal activity is directly related to the rhyolite plateau — that enormous covering of lava thousands of feet thick that flowed over the area after the great explosions of 2 million and 600,000 years ago. This extrusion came in repeated horizontal flows, and its most striking characteristics are its chemistry and its physical appearance. Wherever it is found in the park its chemical-mineralogical composition is 70–75 percent silicon, although — strangely — its physical appearance is diverse. Its texture can differ almost from foot to foot, and its colors range from black to white, with yellows, reds, browns, splotches, speckles, and multicolored layers common. It can be dull or brilliant, rough or smooth, porous or compact, or it can be glassy, as at Obsidian Cliff south of Swan Lake Flats.[27] But regardless of its diverse physical aspects, the structure of the rhyolite makes it extremely receptive to the circulation of water throughout the myriad of cracks and seams that characterize masses of this kind of rock.[28]

It is assumed that there is an enormous magmatic source of heat one to four miles below the rhyolite plateau, and it is known that somehow heat is transferred to waters which rise to the surface as hot springs. But how long has this been going on? How is the heat applied to the waters, and where do the waters come from?

Geologists are in general agreement that the thermal activity began with the cessation of the rhyolite flows and has continued consistently ever since. Their "Exhibit A" is Terrace Mountain, west of Mammoth Hot Springs. In that area the rhyolite came up against Mississippi and Jurassic limestones (300 million and 150 million years old), and the percolating waters laid down horizontal beds of calcium carbonate (travertine) up to 250 feet thick. "And," emphasizes Arnold Hague, the travertine rests "directly on fresh, unaltered rhyolite." Then the Ice Age came, and glaciers from the Gallatins moved right over the top of Terrace Mountain; when they retreated, they dropped glacial fragments of crystalline. So Terrace Mountain consists of layers: fresh rhyolite beneath travertine beneath glacial drift.[29]

The other two problems — the origin and transmittal of the heat and the source of the water — have been tentatively solved, although together they constitute "the hot spring problem" and have troubled the minds of geologists for more than a century. Investigations by Geological Survey scientists in the early 1960s at Steamboat Springs, Nevada, and in the late 1960s at Yellowstone confirm with greater proof the conclusions reached more than a generation ago by two researchers from the Carnegie Institution.* "There are no convenient

*The conclusions of the Yellowstone researchers have not been published as this book goes to press, although many of the results of their investigations ap-

mine shafts in the hot-spring country," complained Professor Arthur L. Day, who, with E. T. Allen, conducted exhaustive investigations in the 1920s and 1930s. "Moreover," he wrote, "hot springs are evanescent mechanisms in geologic history which leave no permanent exposures from which the sources of energy and water supply may be confidently traced."[30]

Regardless of the obstacles, Professors Allen and Day set out to find some answers. The prevalence of innumerable boiling springs was already well known, but scientists did not understand the substantial number that were superheated, with surface temperatures above the boiling point of water. In 1929 Allen and Day discovered that nearly a hundred superheated springs existed, many of them in a constant state of ebullition only explicable in terms of a constant source of heat from below. If in addition to the boiling and superheated springs we consider the near-boiling springs, the mudpots, and the geysers — when we estimate several million years of continuous thermal activity — the source of energy and its transmission seem increasingly mysterious.[31]

Allen and Day got their tentative answer not from the hot springs and geysers but from steam vents or fumaroles. Most visitors ignore steam vents, but the geologists found eleven in the park that were peculiar in that they blew out superheated steam. The hottest vent, the Black Growler in Norris Basin, registered 138.2°C., and Beryl Spring, seen along the highway above Norris, shoots out a hot 97°C.[32]

Where did the steam originate? To help solve this question and others in the realm of physics and chemistry, these men of the Geophysical Laboratory of the Carnegie Institution of Washington hired an experienced steam-well driller to sink boreholes, one in the Upper Geyser Basin and one in the Norris Basin. The scientists planned to

---

pear in U.S.G.S. Bulletin No. 1487, pp. 79-82. Basically the scientists have used isotopes to confirm that at least 95 percent of the water is of surface origin, and is heated "largely by thermal conduction through solid rock." The ultimate source of heat is, of course, volcanic masses two to four miles beneath the surface. See Donald E. White, "Some Principles of Geyser Activity, Mainly from Steamboat Springs, Nevada," *American Journal of Science* 165, no. 8 (October 1967): 641–84.

In the absence of published information about the more recent investigations in Yellowstone, I have chosen to narrate the experiences and conclusions of Allen and Day.

measure temperatures and pressures and take core samplings with which to analyze the underground structures and determine the chemical composition of the rocks.

They chose for the first borehole a site several hundred yards west of Old Faithful. Here they drilled down through the sileceous sinter that covers the basin, through hardened gravels containing rhyolite pebbles, and then, at 62 feet, they struck steam. They drilled to 406 feet before they sealed the hole with concrete and journeyed down to Norris to drill the second hole. (Although the steam had not been superheated and only reached a pressure of 57 pounds per square inch, they were sure that the absence of superheated steam was due to the prevalence of groundwater in the area penetrated.)[33]

At the Norris Basin they chose a site on "hot ground" near Congress Pool and just west of the highway. Solid rock, not gravel, was very close to the surface, but as they drilled through it, the fissures and joints that were believed to characterize these deposits resulted in rapid and surprising changes in pressures and temperatures. Thus on September 11, 1930 (drilling having been halted in the fall of 1929 and resumed in August of the following year), the pressure was 89 pounds; later that day it shot up to 225 pounds, then, on September 13, to 250 pounds. At this stage the drill contractor feared that rock would be blown out, leaving a steaming crater where the drill rig was. So drilling was halted for several days while a covering of concrete and iron rods was placed around the drill hole, with the steam blowing off at full force all this time. Not that this did any good: when the pressure was measured a few days later, before drilling was resumed, it stood at 297.5 pounds above atmospheric pressure, with its temperature at 205°. Because of difficulties in taking the measurements the scientists were sure that the pressure actually exceeded 300 pounds per square inch. The greatest depth they reached was 264 feet, 10 inches. Again, groundwater prevented the steam from being superheated.

"According to calculations," writes the chronicler of this scientific adventure, "the pressure was more than sufficient to lift the weight of a column of rock extending from the bottom of the hole to the surface. Apparently it was only because of the interlocking of the jointed masses that there was not an upheaval." When drilling was resumed, it was found nearly impossible to force the feedwater to the bottom. Instead, some of it went out through the threaded joints of the pipes, and the rest was vaporized. Then the pressure dropped to 125 pounds as, 25 feet to the south, a blowout of steam occurred in an opening of the ground, followed in rapid order by other steaming fissures in the earth to the west and north, some of them small and some "several feet in diameter at the mouth."

Then the drill hole blocked up at 36 feet, apparently due to the collapse of the casing under great pressure. All attempts at reopening it failed, and the decision was made to abandon the experiment. Five tons of cement were rammed down the hole as fast as possible, the top was sealed off, and, after two more blowouts 75 and 50 feet away, the venture ended. When we note that most of the steam was allowed to escape unchecked, we can begin to appreciate the pressure, the heat, and the limitless source of the energy.[34]

The pressures and temperatures had increased as the drilling progressed, indicating beyond a doubt that the origin of the steam was very deep. The next problem was to analyze the constituents of the partially liquid rock magma whence the steam originated. "Its major volatile components," wrote Day, "are water vapor upwards of 95%, carbon dioxide in the neighborhood of 2%, and the remainder distributed between compounds of the more active elements chlorine, fluorine, and sulphur, of which the most important is probably hydrogen sulfide, and occasional traces of boron and arsenic." Such gases, it is speculated, are given off by magma in the process of slow crystallization. When superheated steam containing these ingredients pushes up through a rock cover, their chemicals should combine with those of the rock (the rhyolite) which would then "appear as chlorides, fluorides, and bicarbonates with smaller amounts of sulphates or sulfides, borates, and arsenates." "These," added Day, "are the magmatic components which must be sought in the hot spring water, and when their presence there is established they afford conclusive evidence of the participation of magmatic emanations in hot spring activity."[35]

The source of the energy, then, is understood in a general way, and so is the manner in which the heat is carried upward, which is much like the way steam heat works in an office building, except that the fissures and joints are substituted for iron pipes. But here the analogy must cease, for while Yellowstone has its steam vents and fumaroles, it has mostly hot springs. So the next question is: What is the source of the hot spring water? Does it, too, originate with the magma, and has it never before been exposed to the atmosphere? Or is it of meteoric origin — from rain and snowfall?

On this question A.C. Peale in 1883, Arnold Hague in 1910, Allen and Day in 1935, and the U.S.G.S. in the late 1960s are in general agreement, and the research conducted by each succeeding geologist only strengthened the same conclusion: the hot springs waters are meteoric.[36]

The facts that Yellowstone is a highland encircled by mountains on the other sides of which are lower, semiarid regions; that precipitation is consequently heavier in the Yellowstone area; and that the Yellowstone, Snake, Madison, and Gallatin rivers all originate in the Yellowstone area, led Arnold Hague to accept the meteoric theory for the water supply of the hot springs. He noted that the region is filled with lakes, ponds, meadows, bogs, and marshes, and that many of them (such as the Yellowstone and Shoshone lakes) are 500–700 feet above the Upper Geyser Basin. He was aware of the long winter, of the forests which cover more than 80 percent of Yellowstone, and of the slow melting process, with much of the snow and rain cover seeping into the ground. "I believe," he wrote, "the supply of water greatly exceeds the amount carried away by surface streams." If he was correct, then the water source of the hot springs was readily explained.[37]

During their seven years of research Allen and Day began with the same premise, but they proceeded to take systematic measurements of water discharge. This was not too difficult, for most hot springs either held their water in the orifice or else discharged it in ditches that existed solely from the hot springs' discharge. The scientists' conclusions, based upon resultant statistics, are convincing. They measured flow with weirs and meters.

Their assessment was that the "aggregate discharge of hot water in the park from the various groups of springs [was] about 109 second feet." (A second foot is a unit of flow of 1 cubic foot per second.) In view of the fact that the single valley of the Upper Geyser Basin has a total drainage of 132 second feet, it is readily seen that the extent of rainfall is more than sufficient: enough rain and snow fall in the small area of that one drainage basin to supply all the hot water in the park. Even so, the discharge is greater, so far as is known, than in any other thermal area on earth.[38]

With rain and snowfall established as the source of the hot spring waters, a question arises about seasonal changes. Yellowstone has freezing temperatures for more than six months of the year, the thermometer sometimes sinking to 40° below zero. For months the water source for the hot springs is latent in the forms of snow and ice. Does this affect the hot springs or the geysers? "Speaking broadly," wrote Professor Day, "there is no difference to be noted by experienced observers in the behavior of the geysers during the winter season or in the amount of water discharged. The hot springs likewise show no pertinent differences in temperature during the winter months." This seems to indicate, he adds, that "the amount of meteoric water circulating below ground is so large that the water partially withheld from circulation in the snow and ice of a six-months winter is inadequate to disturb it seriously. Neither does the freezing of several feet of ground surface produce any measurable effect. . . . "[39]

With the source of energy and its means of transmission determined, and the source of water supply verified, it remains for us to examine the "'hot ground" areas and describe the variations in hot-spring activity. This is a fairly simple matter, for there are only three types of hot ground areas.

The first, and most prevalent, type are "acid tracts," and they are usually small, often located on hillsides, as at Mary Mountain or Sulphur Mountain or, 4.5 miles north of Norris Junction, at Roaring Mountain. These areas are characterized by a paucity of water (even when pools exist, they are shallow) and by sulphur in all forms to the almost complete exclusion of other chemicals. The gases working up from the magma do not strike water until near the surface, perhaps 100 feet down, and it is the acid reaction (almost always sulfuric acid) upon the "subadjacent surface rocks," that produces odor and — where those multicolored pools called "paint pots" exist in these areas — the "porridge while the iron content provides the paint." Fumaroles and occasional superheated steam vents may also be found in these acid areas. And they are truly in hot ground. On a cold, clear winter's day, steam puffs of all sizes may be seen rising spectacularly from all over Roaring Mountain.[40]

The second type of hot ground area is that of which Mammoth Hot Springs is the prime and almost the only example. The Jurassic and Mississippian limestones in the vicinity are taken up in solution by carbon dioxide, one of the major ingredients of rhyolite, and

carried to the surface as bicarbonate in water. At the surface carbon
dioxide is released, leaving the carbonate solution. Some of it will be
deposited as travertine. The water is clear, heavily alkaline, and at
a temperature below 75°C. The absence of boiling waters and the
weakness of travertine as a container of water explain the lack of
geysers at Mammoth. Other similar travertine areas are at the nascent Soda Butte 17 miles east of Tower Junction, and along the
Snake River in the lower part of the park.[41]

The third type of hot ground region in Yellowstone is the
alkaline area or geyser basin. These are larger than the acid tracts
and more numerous than the travertine. They are found on valley
floors or in drainage basins. Here function the deep, clear, bluish
springs of neutral or alkaline reaction, containing bicarbonates and
chlorides but very little sulphur. Their only deposit worth noting is
sileceous sinter, the silica crust which is responsible for the white
linings and cones of hot springs and which covers substantial parts
of the basins, although it may have been reduced by time and the
elements to sands and gravels. There will be no algae in these hot
waters, for algae cannot exist in waters hotter than 85°C. Incidentally, the blue coloring in such pools as Gentian and Sapphire is
not due to sky reflection — the pools are blue even on cloudy days —
but to several factors including the depth of the water and the
scattering of molecules in the spring. Thermal activity is high in
these alkaline areas, with much boiling or even superheated water,
and many geysers.[42]

Regardless of the type of hot ground — acid tract, travertine,
or alkali geyser basin — the hot springs will be characterized by the
emission of gases. Steam and carbon dioxide are the most abundant,
followed by hydrogen sulphide, some hydrogen, methane, nitrogen,
and argon. Interestingly, the geysers emit surprisingly few gases.[43]

Just as all other things change, so will the hot springs. As the
chemical-filled waters and the gases etch away more and more of
the subterranean fissures until they become caverns, the deep springs
and geysers will collapse and give way to shallow, turbid springs.
This has not yet happened to any great extent in Yellowstone, but
such a final stage of activity is very noticeable in the New Zealand
thermal areas.[44]

We have discussed fumaroles, steam vents, and hot springs, but
we have yet to explain the action of geysers. The explanation of

this rather complex phenomenon would be difficult in any case, but when we realize that scientists themselves are not satisfied with any of the theories thus far considered, our problem is compounded. We can begin, however, with some basic statements that are applicable to all, or certainly to 98 percent of all geysers. First, they are hot springs of the alkaline type, and their source of energy, their use of meteoric waters, and the relationship between the two are identical to those of ordinary hot springs. They are deep and characteristically have a narrow tube disappearing into the depths, but a geyser may appear to be a depression in a raised cone, a narrow orifice, or a shallow pool up to 50 feet in circumference. Geysers are irregular. Even Old Faithful may vary in the cycle of its eruptions from 33 to 93 minutes, and some geysers will become dormant while new ones erupt. The height and length of the eruption may vary also. Old Faithful varies in height from 110 to 160 feet, and it plays from 2 to 5 minutes. Geysers are also intermittent in their water level. As an eruption comes on, a geyser may rise as a ground swell, decline, rise again, and so on four or more times before the eruption takes place. The water level declines (from a few inches to a few feet) very rapidly immediately after an eruption. Notice Old Faithful. It splashes a few times (that is the swell of the water), then erupts, and then, if the visitor could look into the orifice (which he is not allowed to do), he would see that the water level had declined measurably. Then slowly it will build back up. This behavior is typical of geysers.

But what makes them do all this? Involved in the theories are matters relating to pressure, heat, gases, water circulation, and the subterranean vaults, or cavities that hold the steam and water. In 1811 Sir George Mackenzie envisioned the steam chamber after visiting Iceland. In the 1830s Krug von Nidda postulated that rising steam in the tube forced out water which relieved the pressure so suddenly that an ejection took place; then, the steam pressure being reduced, the water would fall back into the tube and cause a new build-up. Fine — except that the steam supply is supposed to be ever present. If the supply of steam is constant, then, in the manner of steam, will it not fill up all the cavities as the water is forced out? And then will not the continuing steam simply bypass those chambers and pass right on up the tube? And if it did this, would it not form a constantly boiling spring instead of a geyser? Save for this obvious flaw Nidda's concept seemed valid. But the failure to explain this led to another, more widely accepted interpretation.[45]

That altogether too commonly accepted theory is attributed to a nineteenth-century German chemistry professor, Robert Wilhelm Eberhard von Bunsen. A brilliant scientist, he discovered ferric oxide as an antidote for arsenic poisoning, invented the spectroscope and pioneered the field of spectrum analysis, discovered the elements caesium and rubidium, lost an eye from an explosion, and nearly lost his life from arsenic poisoning in the line of duty — but probably did not invent the Bunsen burner, though it is named for him. In the mid-1840s he made a trip to Iceland with a Danish expedition, and from observations there and from subsequent experiments with geyser models in collaboration with the French mineralogist Alfred Descloizeaux, he evolved a theory that somehow stuck. These two men applied their explanation only to the Great Geysir of Iceland, and not necessarily to all geysers, but this fact appears never to have penetrated the popular mind.[46]

Bunsen's theory attempted to explain the difference between constantly boiling springs and springs that boil intermittently. The essential difference, he insisted, lies in the width of the tube. A very narrow tube would heat almost equally from top to bottom, steam bubbles would constantly be rising, and a steadily boiling spring would result. But as anyone who has ever run first hot and then cold water into a bathtub is aware, the circulation of water is a relatively slow process. The toes shiver in the cold water near the faucet, and the posterior turns red as a boiled lobster in the hot water at the other end of the tub. Now if the hot spring has a wide orifice and a long tube, Bunsen theorized, then the water will be much cooler at the opening. Temperature readings of the Great Geysir confirmed this: the water below the surface, being under some pressure, reached a temperature that would have been above boiling at the surface. Bunsen further theorized that the water was closest to the boiling point (considering pressure also) at the midpoint of the tube. Finally, he was convinced that the temperature increased steadily from the initial posteruption stage to the moment before a new eruption began.

With these basic premises, the question still remained: How does the eruption take place? Here Bunsen and Descloizeaux considered the steam, which was presumably rising into the groundwater areas from its magmatic source deep within the earth. In the Great Geysir, these large steam bubbles did not come to the surface steadily, but at intervals. So, they theorized: (1) the water is very hot; (2) a large mass of steam bubbles work up and cause the splashing of the water that precedes an eruption; (3) the steam at this juncture also raises the water level in the geyser by a few meters; (4) this so reduces the hydrostatic pressure below that the hot water boils in the canals and caverns and turns to more steam, which triggers a general ebullition; and (5) the eruption takes place. The eruption will continue until the temperature in the caverns falls below the boiling point. One thing can be said in favor of this theory. It works beautifully in a model, which is probably why it has been so widely accepted.[47]

But it does not explain the problem of intermittent boiling in geysers, and furthermore, a logical conclusion of the Bunsen theory could leave the geyser as not even a hot spring, but a steam jet. As a result of his continued research, Bunsen made a major change in his theory: that cold water, rather than hot, had to enter the chambers, and this would condense the steam, require time for reheating, and thus explain the intermittence. Bunsen's source of such water was simply the water from Geysir's well, flowing back into the tube like water used over and over again in an artificial fountain, but in Yellowstone most of the geysers throw off their water, which then forms streams and joins the Firehole or the Gibbon River. There is no receiving well, so obviously the replenishing waters must come in from below. Moreover, Sapphire, Oblong, and Artimesia geysers are examples in the park of geysers which do not erupt out of a tube at all, but out of a bowl nearly as wide as it is deep, with little temperature difference between surface and bottom. Bunsen's theory cannot explain these geysers. And finally, thermometer readings of Yellowstone geysers do not indicate a steadily rising temperature, but a rise to a certain degree at which the water may remain for hours or even days. The readings also indicate that although temperature increases with depth, the increase is slower than the increase in the boiling point at any given depth, which jeopardizes Bunsen's theory of the rapid boiling and changing to steam of water in the tube.

Yet the theory of Bunsen and Descloizeaux was essentially correct for the functioning of many geysers. They should have included, however, side reservoirs for quantities of water, since the tubes cannot hold more than a very small percentage of the water ejected; and they should have placed more emphasis upon the sources of cooler water in those underground chambers. Fluctuations in the delivery of the steam and water as it filled the chambers after an eruption, and even fluctuations in the temperatures of the water as it did seep in, could all help to account for the irregularity of geysers, the pulsating water levels in the basins, and their eruptions, as the eruption of each geyser has characteristics all its own. Even the temperature and velocity of the wind blowing over the steaming pools, or seasonal variations in rainfall that would affect hydrostatic pressure in the groundwater of Yellowstone's earth, might help to explain the action of such a spouter as the Crater Hills Geyser, eight miles north-north-west of Fishing Bridge, which has a maximum temperature as low as 73°C. and never reaches the boiling point.[48]

The temperature of the Jewel Geyser — in the Upper Geyser Basin about 150 feet from the Sapphire Pool — at whatever depth it is measured in the pool is never boiling, and it drops just before eruptions. Yet it is an active geyser, arising 12–22 feet every 5 or 6 minutes.

These phenomena, which the Bunsen theory does not account for, are explained at least in part by the Icelandic geyser expert, Thorkell Thorkellson. He has found a geyser in his homeland that is a dry fissure among the rocks until eruption. Then a rumbling is heard and shortly it erupts 3–4 meters into the air. When the eruption ends, the water disappears, and as soon as the air dries the rocks, no sign of a hot spring or geyser can be seen. The geyser is just 20 feet above sea level, the water temperature is 99°C. (one degree below boiling), and the water is seawater, although the sea is 1,350 meters away. Clearly, the Bunsen theory will not apply here.[49]

What will apply, and should be valid for many another geyser, is Thorkellson's own theory of geyser action. He insists that every geyser and hot spring will occlude the so-called spring gases, such as nitrogen, argon, and methane. These will rise in the spring to a point where the pressure is such that small gas bubbles will form throughout, just as gas bubbles will form in a quickly uncapped bottle of pop. As the bubbles continue to rise they include increasing amounts of steam, which, being imprisoned there, deprive the water of heat. Soon these bubbles are filling the chambers and the water column. As they rise up the tube they strike cooler water, break, and add their heat to the water. Rapid convection currents will soon make these bubbles displace the water over the rim of the geyser pool; this in turn reduces the hydrostatic pressure in the tube and causes the ebullition to continue downward to a new depth, forcing an upward flow of the water it replaces so that an eruption results. Eventually, as the bubbling extends downward, an equilibrium is achieved, and the eruption ends for lack of water supply and lack of energy.[50]

In criticism of this theory, Allen and Day point out the small amounts of spring gases they have found in the Yellowstone's hot springs, but the rejoinder to their evaluation is that only very small quantities of these gases are necessary (6.9 percent at 2°C. below boiling, at half a degree below boiling only 1.8 percent). These small amounts, it is suggested, make the bubble wall far stronger than it would otherwise be, and in fact make possible bubbles which would otherwise collapse at once.[51]

The Thorkellson explanation for geyser activity might even make a certain Chinese laundryman happy, wherever he may be with his honorable ancestors. The story may well be apocryphal, but Chinese laundrymen were not unknown in the Yellowstone in the early days and, as Bret Harte wrote,

> Which I wish to remark
>   And my language is plain,
> That for ways that are dark
>   And for tricks that are vain,
> The heathen Chinee is peculiar
>   Which the same I would rise to explain.[52]

This oriental entrepreneur's "way that was dark" was to pitch his tent over a hot spring, and his "trick that was vain" was to use that spring as a clothes boiler. All of these proceedings took place, it is said, in the Upper Geyser Basin, somehow eluding the scrutiny of the park officials. All went well until a bar of soap slipped into the pool. Then the quiet hot spring began to change character, shot up in a geyser 20 feet high, wrecked the tent, sent the clothes helter skelter over the sinter, and put the Chinese laundryman out of business. It is still known as Chinaman Spring, and though at present it is dormant, it has been known to erupt to a height of 40 feet.[53]

Why the addition of soap should cause an eruption, and could even occasionally cause a hot spring to become a geyser, was long a matter of conjecture. Now it is known, in line with the Thorkellson theory, that soap "leads to the formation of an insoluble hydrophobic coating of calcium palmitate on the walls" of the bubbles — strengthens them, in other words, thus helping the action that will produce an eruption.[54]

Steam from the magma, circulating groundwater in an area of fissures and cavities, changes in water temperature, spring gases — these appear to be the ingredients of geyser action. The specific actions may and do differ from geyser to geyser, and some questions remain unsolved — for example the problem of the layer of superheated water that is often present at the surface, quiescent and less than a meter deep. "Its quiescence in the face of its metastable condition," write the experts Bloss and Barth, "is difficult to explain." And although dried-up geysers have been found, one in New Zealand and one in Yellowstone, they have helped very little in clearing up the problem, merely indicating a number of small side-openings which may have admitted steam, water, or both, into an otherwise tight sinter-lined chamber.[55]

No one has ever doubted that changes in the earth's crust would affect all this activity, but the great Hebgen earthquake confirmed the supposition and gave geologists an opportunity to study changes firsthand. If the quake had taken place during the day the visitors fortunate enough to have been in the Upper, Middle, or Lower basins would have been witnesses to the greatest geyser display of recorded time. Cracks and crevices appeared like giant spider webs across the basins, fumaroles appeared in new spots for days afterward, and water spilled out of the springs as if "the earthquake had acted like a giant hand which suddenly applied enormous pressure to the rocks beneath the hot springs, forcing water from their conduits in a manner comparable to the squeezing of a sponge."[56]

The water in the hot springs grew hotter, 2.3°F. hotter on the average in 73 geysers (from 192.8° to 195.1°), and in 89 hot springs, an 8.7° increase (from 176.9° to 185.6°). Nearly 300 springs manifested vigorous new activity, of which 160 had no previous history of eruption. And most of the known geysers erupted all at once.

In the Upper Basin, Cascade and Economic geysers, which had been dormant for nearly forty years, erupted; Giantess played for over 100 hours, three times longer than it had ever before been recorded as playing; and only Grant, of the major geysers, appeared to have gone dormant. Sapphire Pool became constant until September 5, when it entered a 2-hour cycle of displays 150 feet high and 200 feet broad; from September 14 to 29 it reverted back into a seething cauldron; then a slight earth tremor once again transformed it into a major geyser.

In the Midway Basin the Grand Prismatic Spring ebbed temporarily and was slightly tilted, Turquoise Pool ebbed 8 feet, but Excelsior Geyser simply changed color from blue to gray. And Morning, Fountain, and Clepsydra geysers in the Lower Basin all erupted at once, which they had never done before; a new "Earthquake Geyser" appeared, paint pots became more active, and other geysers erupted at shorter intervals. It is clear that the earthquake shook things up, changed a lot of the plumbing, and increased hot spring activity.[57]

The hands of our clock sweep through the Upper Basin, with its seventy or more geysers, on through the Middle Basin, the Lower Basin, and down through Gibbon and Norris basins. The hands of our clock have also crossed Madison Canyon and West Yellowstone, the port of entry for visitors entering the park from that direction, and the hands are slipping past the Gallatins — Mount Holmes, Dome Mountain, Quadrant Mountain — and on toward Electric Peak. Closer to the hub of our clock we have passed Roaring Mountain, and then, a few miles farther up the highway, Obsidian Cliff.

To sophisticated twentieth-century folk, Obsidian Cliff is just another cliff. But earlier ages showed more interest in obsidian. Pliny the Elder, the Roman naturalist, said it was named for an Ethiopian of that name or possibly for Opsius, who discovered it. He also says that the ancients made signet rings of obsidian and used it for mirrors in their chambers.[58]

In the United States, stories of a mountain of glass came floating into the eastern part of the country, and people half-believed old Jim Bridger's tale about such a place: how he shot at an elk and it just kept right on grazing, he shot again, nothing happened, and he ran toward the elk to club it to death with his rifle and bumped smack into a wall of glass. Actually, he insisted, the elk was forty miles away. The glass mountain had served as a microscope, making the animal appear to be just a few yards in front of Old Gabe.

Certainly the Indians were attracted to Yellowstone's glass mountain, for the jet black obsidian could be worked into good arrow and spear points with ease. "When broken," the geologist J. P. Iddings said, "it flies into sharp, angular fragments, with razor-like edges which are quite transparent and colorless in the thinnest places."[59]

The approach to the cliff, as one works northward, reveals a long, low bluff. Upon closer examination (if the visitor is curious enough), it proves to be formed of "nearly vertical columns of black obsidian, or volcanic glass, which has resulted from the rapid cooling of a perfectly fused, igneous rock." The loose rocks at the foot of the cliff will readily reward the visitor for pausing. Among the rocks, and embedded in them, are shiny pieces of obsidian, "as true a glass as any artificially produced."[60]

If the visitor is willing to tramp around a bit, he will find that the cliff extends for about half a mile, rising 150–200 feet above Obsidian Creek and declining toward the north. The hard obsidian forms the lower portion of the cliff, while weathered, porous pumice constitutes the upper 50 feet. One-half mile southeast of the cliff J. P. Iddings found an ancient crater, from which he believes the lava flowed to form the obsidian mass. And from jet black the obsidian will vary "from dark to light yellowish brown, purplish brown, and olive green; . . . through the black and red glass are scattered dull, bluish-gray patches and bands and round, gray and pink masses. . . ."[61]

But from here the hands of our clock push rapidly toward high noon. We cross Willow Park, emerge into Swan Lake Flats, pass Bunsen Peak, and descend through Kingman Pass, past Rustic Falls on the Gardner, and through the weirdly shaped travertine deposits which, like Norris's volcanic formation far to the southeast, are called Hoodoos. From there we descend between the Mammoth Hot Springs and Capitol Hill, into the settlement of Mammoth. Thence we go on down to the Gardner River Canyon and north to the northern boundary of the park. Our "noon" stands a little to the east of the hamlet of Gardiner. The Gardner River joins the Yellowstone, which then wends its way through the canyons and valleys to its eventual junction with the Missouri. Our geologic tour of Yellowstone is over.

3

Flora and Fauna

Ages ago, when the rhyolite flows were sweeping over so much of the park, the landscape was barren of all living things. Even when the lava had cooled, the panorama in a broad sweep from south to north was a vision of dry, relatively smooth rock with a few depressions where water might have lain. There was no soil; there were no living things. In the eastern part of the park, where the volcanism was of the more explosive type, there was ash and tufa. From this hardened and inert material, time, working with wind, rain, and chemical actions, had first to create soil, so that plants could grow.

Again we are back to beginnings and to unknown factors and hazily understood processes, but there are sound speculations and confirmed theories which give us at least a partial picture of the beginnings of soil and the early stages of plant life. It is believed that the first plant life in the park was the lichen, lowest of the four divisions of plants; mosses, ferns, and seed plants (in ascending order of structural sophistication) are the other divisions. Lichens are the dried, scaly coverings we see on rocks; when they grow in the moist shade, they are damp and earthy. They are tenacious of life, existing within 235 miles of the South Pole, or on the barren, rocky steppes of the Arctic, or above timberline in the Rockies. In the unfolding drama of plant development, they appear in Act I, Scene 1; without them, the remainder of the drama would be difficult or impossible. Yet much research remains to be done on them.

For the lichen is an anomaly in nature. It is two plants which merge to create a third dissimilar to the parents. The offspring

51

can go on to reproduce itself true to kind. The two plants are the alga, "probably the most widely distributed green plant in the world," and the fungus, such as mold or a mushroom. The alga, a single-celled green plant, becomes enmeshed in the "cotton-like cell of the fungus" and then produces its own plant.[1]

This strange marriage of such minute forms of life began on those flat, hard rhyolite barrens, releasing infinitesimal quantities of acids which worked away at the rock, breaking it, dissolving it, eating away at tiny hairline cracks, which, receiving more acids, plus rainfall, became crevices. And thus, through the slow passage of time, the hard rock began to disintegrate into the beginnings of the soft humus we call soil.

As the lichens covered the rocks with a crusty mat, they caught all manner of wind-blown or water-borne matter, which added still more to the soil cover they were building. Soon the lichen cover may have formed a mat an inch thick. Its own dead matter added to the humus, as did the mosses which flourished at this stage and grew larger as the decades passed. Eventually a soil cover existed of sufficient thickness and richness to support woody, fibrous plants, shrubs, and eventually trees. Now the forest had arrived, and the once barren rhyolite plain, the volcanic debris that covered the eastern part of the park over and over again, was verdant and inviting. How long had the process taken? One authority estimates that in 200 years a mass of lava can develop a sufficient soil cover to permit forest growth.[2]

Through the millennia, with repeated setbacks due to volcanic or climatic action, the flora of Yellowstone developed. Change in nature is constant and infinite, but the speed of change can be as cataclysmic as a volcanic eruption, a forest fire, an earthquake, or a landslide — or it can be so gradual as to appear static in terms of the human life-span, as is the case with the eroding power of a river, the weathering away of volcanic rock, or the sculpturing of strange forms by the wind. Yellowstone had its share of all these forms of change, and the resultant conditions provided different stages of plant development in different parts of the park. In fact, as of today, much of the park has not yet reached the final — or climax — stage of plant development. Moreover, varying environmental conditions (altitudes, dry plateaus, bogs, ponds, and streams) add to the variety of plant life.[3]

There are, then, different types of plant communities in the park. There is the aquatic community, made up of plants which grow in both still and flowing water. These include the deadly poisonous water hemlock, the yellow pond lily with its 3–5 inch blooms, the buttercup, the crowfoot, and watercress. Then there is the sagebrush-grass community, in areas of the park below 7,500 feet, which contains far more plant life than the appearance of such areas from the roadside suggests. Even the sagebrush itself, of which several species grow in the park, has some usefulness. Sheep, deer, and sage grouse eat the foliage, which is rich in protein and fats. Rabbit brush will grow in overgrazed areas, its yellow flowers forming a bright mat in the autumn, and the thistle, the wild buckwheat, the sego lily, the death camas, the wild geranium, the Indian paintbrush, the scarlet gilia, a dozen species of lupine, and the low larkspur are but a few of the wild flowers that may thrive in the sagebrush flats. They are all there, but they must be searched out.

A third plant community is that of alpine and subalpine meadows, the former above timberline (timberline is about 10,000 feet in the park), the latter below it. Here are the fragile flowers of a summer that begins when the snowbanks recede in July and ends with the first snow flurries of August. The short growing season provides no time for superfluous leaves or high-growing stems; only rich, bright colors. There is the little globeflower, just an inch or an inch and a half across; or the heavenly blue alpine forget-me-not; and in the subalpine regions, one may see beds of pink catchfly, blue lungwort, jacob's ladder, carpets of buttercups or white alpine yarrow.[4]

The fourth, fifth, sixth, and seventh plant communities involve forests in the following order: the Douglas fir forest, the lodgepole pine forest, the aspen forest, and the spruce fir forest. About 80 percent of Yellowstone Park is considered to be forest covered.

The Douglas fir forest exists only in the vicinity of Tower Falls, and is of significance only in that it is considered a climax forest. The second of the forest categories (and the fifth of the seven plant communities) interests us the most. This is the lodgepole pine forest, which covers about 75 percent of the park, mostly at altitudes of 7,000–8,500 feet. This forest encompasses the great rhyolite plateau. It is the forest one sees as a great sea of green from the south side of Mount Washburn. The lodgepole pine grows in dense stands, thrives where the soil cover is thin, and sends out a weak root system for its sustenance. Comes the first strong wind, a forest fire, or a heavy snowfall, and over go the pines, falling in the forest like giant jackstraws, to the mule-kicking, cursing frustration of anyone trying to get through. "The autumnal fires sweep among the dense forests," wrote Dr. Ferdinand V. Hayden in 1871, "and the winds then lay them down in every possible direction. Sometimes a perfect network, 6 feet in height, is formed of these tall pines, which are 100 to 150 feet in length, and it was with the utmost difficulty that we could thread our tortuous way among them."[5]

But the most shocking revelation for our generation, taught as we are the horrors of forest fires, is the scientifically established fact that were it not for its self-made fire hazard, the great lodgepole pine forest of Yellowstone Park would cease to exist. For the lodgepole is not a climax tree, but rather exists at an intermediate stage in the flora development of the region. Fire, which destroys its stands two or three times a century, also provides the intense heat necessary to pop open the pine burrs and release the seeds, which germinate, sprout, and start a new lodgepole pine forest. If the fires did not take place, the spruce fir forest would intrude upon the lodgepoles from the upper elevations, as would the Douglas fir from the lower areas. Thus the idealism of the conservationist who wants to maintain "a state of nature" is checked by nature herself, for nature resists a static situation even when man tries to enforce it. If fires were prevented over the logepole forest for fifty or sixty years, the natural lodgepole forest would give way to the Douglas fir and spruce forests, which, on nature's timetable, are not yet ready to occupy that vast section of the park.

While the lodgepole thrives in dry places, the aspen, especially the quaking aspen, fills in the moist, shady places, its light green leaves and white bark presenting a pleasant change from the somber green of the conifers. This tree, whose bark and buds provide food for beaver, elk, deer, and birds, does not need recurring forest fires to start new growth, but sends out new shoots from its roots.

The last and highest plant community is the spruce fir climax forest, of which the section of land from Canyon Village to the Upper Falls is most typical and easily seen. This is an upper-elevation forest, thriving in general above 8,000 feet, the top elevation for the lodgepole pine. The spruce is the Engelmann variety, and is found also at the South Entrance, Keplar Cascades, and Apollinaris Spring. The fir tree, perhaps best known as the balsam fir, also thrives at higher elevations — 7,000 feet on up to timberline.

Other trees in the park are the juniper (often called the cedar), the whitebark, and the limber pine. The willow family is represented by many species along the stream bottoms, but most of the willows are small and rank more as bushes than as trees. The cottonwoods that may be seen at Mammoth are exotics, imported by the United States Army when it policed the park.

Since the retreat of the last ice cover, 8,000–10,000 years ago, the appearance of the Yellowstone country has changed little, and the plant life has remained about the same. Geysers and hot springs have come and gone and been replaced by new steaming pools, spouting jets, and fumaroles. Erosion has been steadily grinding and scouring the floors of the Grand Canyon of the Yellowstone and the other river gorges, canyons, and valleys. Forests have grown to maturity and been reduced to ashes and smoking punk by fires caused by lightning or possibly by the spontaneous combustion of decaying fibrous vegetation, and new growth has started almost at once. The paleontologist or paleobotanist will elaborate on the flora and fauna of other geologic times — how it was once tropical or semitropical here, or how the primitive horse grazed in the primeval meadows — but our interest is focused upon the appearance of Yellowstone today, its plants and animals, its ecology. And for those who will pause, read a little, and do a bit of fieldwork, Yellowstone offers rich rewards. For in the park the rhythm of life continues as if civilized man had never entered the region.

The rhythm includes the turning of the earth and the seasons of the year. In late August or early September, insects and animals, birds and amphibians, begin to prepare for the cold winter when short spans of sunlight will push through the skies from a low southerly angle. There is a sharper crispness now to the always fresh mountain air, a glassy, thin film of ice along the streambanks in early morning, and a rustle of aspen leaves, now no longer green and waxy with life, but yellow, red, and burnt orange, dried and ready to fall to the forest floor. The deeper-blue sky will probably be cloudless, and the noon temperatures warm save for the coolness of the breeze that blows stronger as the autumn comes on.

At dawn of a typical fall day the west wind blows across the dried wheatgrass, bent grass, grama grass, and bluegrasses of the plateau, rustles the pungent sage, waves the cattails along the stream bottoms. It is the moment of day when the stars that moments before spattered the sky now disappear until only the silvery morning star remains. During the night, procreation, cannibalism, digestion, birth, and death have all taken place in the privacy of darkness. Now that the sun is up, insects and animals have retreated to the seclusion of rocky lairs, earthen hiding places, or hollow logs. At this moment in the day, there is silence except for the rustling of the grass. There is no other motion.

Yet, while some creatures hide all day, others will appear again in a few hours to go about their business, aroused by the warmth of the sun. They will be obtaining food, storing it, or eating it, for their metabolism is rapid. This is how the little rodents play their minute roles in Yellowstone's ecology and live out their lives, out of sight and unappreciated. They carry seeds and nuts about, helping to disseminate them, and they keep the soil aerated by their tunneling.

The white-footed mouse is one of the handsomest members of the mouse family, with little feet and lower legs of white, big, bright eyes, large ears, and a tail about as long as his 3–4-inch body, which is gray or brown. He eats seeds and nuts, can climb trees if necessary, and will occasionally make his home in a cabin or a tent. Once in a while he may walk across a sleeping camper's face, and if the flashlight is switched on, the mouse may appear in the beam. The camper should be delighted, for White-Foot is strictly nocturnal and is therefore seldom seen.[6]

The meadow mouse, of which at least four species are found in the park, is common everywhere in North America, procreates litter after litter after litter, and insures good grass-fed food for the jays, crows, ravens, hawks, owls, coyotes, badgers, weasels, minks, martens, bears, and foxes that prey upon it. Meadow mice live wherever there is grass, forming labyrinths of smooth runways on the floors of the meadows, tunneling underground, or building nests of grass above ground. In winter they live in comfort and far more securely than in summer, for nature has provided suitably warm coats for them and they go about their business relatively snug beneath the snow cover, safely out of sight of their enemies. Some of the species, the dwarf meadow mouse and the big-footed meadow mouse, for instance, live near streams and often dive into the cold water. They do not hibernate, and "when the snow disappears in spring a network of trails shows how their tunnels and roads cover the surface of the meadows, and the scattered stems and bits of food indicate how well they have fared."[7]

A notch above the mouse in size, as everyone knows, is the rat, who is also considered more loathsome. But Yellowstone's principal rat is the veritable Beau Brummel of his genus, a gentleman with nocturnal habits who is, probably inadvertently, a businessman. He trades for what he takes, and is often called a pack rat. Call him the gray, or bushy-tailed, wood rat.

He is about fifteen inches long, including his squirrellike tail, and is covered with fairly long fur which becomes handsomest in the autumn. He is a clean little animal who is content to spend untold generations at the same family residence in the crevices of a rocky ledge or cliff. On occasion he will move into an abandoned cabin or barn, but he is not the common barn rat, and his diet consists primarily of grass, foliage, berries, and seed; if man did not have such an abhorrence of the word *rat* he would find this species good eating.

The wood rat is curious, however, and he will enter cabins or raid a campground, opening food packages, boxes, and haversacks, just to see what is inside. He likes to borrow bright and shiny things, such as silverware. As he runs along a kitchen table with a crust of bread in his mouth, if a shiny spoon catches his eye, he drops the bread and takes off with the spoon. Of course, he has not consciously traded anything; he has simply discarded one bit of loot for something better. Watch out for a wristwatch placed on the bureau, especially if the strap is impregnated with salty perspiration. The author lost one down a rathole under those very circumstances.

So much for the mice and rats that do so much for the forest and meadow economy but command so little respect from man. Even smaller are the shrews, three species of which are found in the park. More loathsome to man are the bats, five species of which inhabit the park during the summer and migrate south for the winter. They roost in the Devil's Kitchen, a cave at Mammoth Hot Springs now sealed off from the public, and in the 1920s and 1930s a colony of Yellowstone bats (a special variety given that name) inhabited the attic at Lake Hotel, which the employees dubbed "Bat Alley."

The visitor to Yellowstone will see few if any mice, shrews, or bats, but he will glimpse along the roads many little rodents whose prevalence and conspicuousness demand that they be mentioned here. He will observe the chipmunk, and his children may even feed chipmunks at Tower Falls. Three species are found in the park. They eat nuts and seeds and whatever the tourists may throw to them; what they do not eat immediately they carry off in their cheeks to their storerooms, for future use. They probably do not hibernate. Then there is the drab gray-black Uinta ground squirrel, better known as the picket pin because when he rises up on his hind legs to look about he resembles a stake. Curiosity is his weakness. He and his numerous progeny hibernate more than half the year, stuff their bellies with nuts and seeds, and provide grain-fed morsels for all the park predators. They are especially prized by the badger, who digs after them underground and even ferrets them out of hibernation, until the ground freezes and the badger himself searches out a nook for the long winter's sleep.

Wherever there is detritus, as in the rocky hillside below a road, the woodchuck will certainly be seen. Actually a golden-mantled marmot, he thrives in the park where he still has all his usual enemies, except man-with-a-gun-and-dogs. Over by the streams there are muskrats, which live in chambers in the banks or in sod and mud houses in marshy places. They are excellent swimmers, have beautiful pelts known commercially as Hudson seal, and remain active the year round. They may be seen most often in early morning and evening. Although they are prolific, they have many enemies, who prevent a population explosion. Among these enemies is the mink. Though not as common in Yellowstone as his cousin, the weasel, this voracious hunter sometimes works under the ice in winter, corners the muskrats in their home, and wipes out the whole family. If the muskrats escape the mink they may fall prey to the playful otter, which also inhabits the banks of streams and lakes in the park.

More harmless, though more wild and unapproachable, are the members of the hare family in the park. The smallest of these is the pika, coney, or rock rabbit. This tailless little animal lives among the rock piles, his fur blending with the lichen-covered rocks, and he is so shy that he would almost never be seen or his presence known except for his warning "pip." He is most noted for making haystacks, sometimes equal to a bushel of grass, which he piles among the rocks. Snow will cover the hay, but since it has already cured, the coney has sustenance, deep beneath the protective snows, through the long winter. Once, after fishing at a timberline lake unsuccessfully but silently for some time, I turned my head and saw more than a dozen coneys darting about all over the rocks. One unusual sound, however, and in a twinkling they were gone.

There is also the Rocky Mountain cottontail, which inhabits the sagebrush areas and lives in such constant danger from its enemies that its survival seems miraculous. There is the olympic athlete of the hare family, the whitetail jackrabbit. These running-and-jumping stars bear young fully furred, eyes opened, ears erect, and hind legs ready to leap for safety if danger approaches. It is said that full-grown jackrabbits can jump as far as fifteen feet when necessary.

The most interesting of the Yellowstone rabbits is the snowshoe, also known as the varying hare. Somewhat larger than the cotton-tail, this rabbit bears its young with some fur and the eyes open. The snowshoe fits beautifully into his surroundings, changing from a summer brown that blends with the earth to winter's pure white, save for black ear-tips. His hind toes spread out to form a wide-surfaced "snowshoe," whence his name. He eats buds, bark, and twigs, and as the snow cover thickens, he finds himself able to reach new food.

When C. H. Merriam, who was with the Hayden Survey in 1872, first observed the snowshoe, male specimens appeared to him to have active mammary glands for suckling the young, which gave rise to the theory that the snowshoe was a hermaphrodite![8] It is possible that Merriam, who was only sixteen years old in the summer of 1872, fell victim to some tall tales told around the campfire. Male and female rabbits look identical, and due to the male's anatomy, they mate by facing in opposite directions, "posed like mirror image," and this has led to a persistent theory of rabbit hermaphrodism. But snowshoes, like all other rabbits and hares, are male and female — and very much so. The males will fight over a female like a couple of tomcats, while the female rabbit, not being inclined to monogamy, could not care less.[9]

Another rodent likely to be seen by campers is the yellow-haired porcupine. He leaves oval tracks that give the appearance of having been swept lightly by a broom or a brush. These are the results of this clumsy 15–35-pound rodent's tail swishing along from side to side as he waddles along on his short legs. He also makes sounds, "a combination snort and bark," as he pads through the forest on his solitary way. For Porky is a loner. He reminds us of an obese, overage professor shuffling off to class, mumbling to himself.

The porcupine's enemies have great respect for his armament. He does not throw those quills, but, as many a family dog has discovered, he can slap them from his tail with propulsion enough to go through leather, and because of the barbs, the quills are painful to remove. This is his only defense, and it appears to work well. In the park these rodents go free, for the alleged damage they do to trees is negligible, and they are a part of the forest culture. Stand clear of them, watch them and be amused by them, but do not harm them.[10]

To see the beaver at work is surely one of the thrills of a Yellowstone vacation, for this rodent played a part in the opening of the West matched by no other wild animal. His fur, with a thick buff layer deep below the coarse outer covering, was prized for men's hats, and if not for a change in styles, the beaver might have been exterminated. As it is, some say that the beaver of today is much smaller than his eighteenth-century ancestors.[11] But he is far from extermination, and his presence is quickly evident in Yellowstone, where hardly a stream exists without beaver dams, ponds, and lodges somewhere along its course.

A beaver family looking for a home will send a scout or two ahead to search out likely places for a community; they must consider availability of aspen, willow, and cottonwood, water supply, and perhaps other factors, such as the proximity of man. Once the site is chosen, the beaver arrive and go to work, gnawing round and round a tree with their sharp incisors until it falls, then pulling it along with their teeth, or, on occasion, digging a canal and floating the log to the damsite. There they spot the tree, base upstream, bushy top downstream, and then slap mud on it, using their tails as trowels and shovels. Sticks are added until eventually a leaky earthen dam emerges. Later it will set and become nearly watertight. Then, from some shallow place in the rising pond-waters, the beaver construct their lodge, making sure that the underwater entrance will always be under the deepest winter ice, although the living room will be dry and above the water level. On occasion these animals will have lairs in stream banks instead of stick-and-mud lodges.

Finally the beaver store up their food supply, cutting willow and aspen and cottonwood, the bark of which is their food, and sinking the sticks into the mud of the pond for future use. While working at this during the long days of summer they will eat berries and roots and other green vegetation from the stream or pond banks. When winter comes, they are all set. But spring will find them adding to dam and lodge, recaulking when necessary. And the family, increased by up to four kits, will be giving them aid. Before many years a sizable dam and a large lodge, or several lodges, will be situated there.

In Yellowstone the longest beaver dam, about 1,000 feet in length, is at Beaver Lake, across the road from Obsidian Cliff, but these fascinating workers may also be seen toward evening, busily cutting down trees or carrying them off to the ponds, at many sites in the park.

These forest engineers are not alone in their watery, tree-surrounded homes, however; the muskrat lives nearby, and bears are frequent intruders around the ponds — as well as everywhere else in the park. They may be black bears (brown and cinnamon being variations of the same species) or even old *ursus horribilis,* the grizzly. Probably, at the word *Yellowstone,* more people conjure up visions of bears than of geysers. These bears are exciting, amusing, fascinating, and trouble-making. They are at the garbage pits (where visitors are forbidden to go), the hotels, the campgrounds, along the roads, and out in the trail-veined wilderness. Bruin causes trouble because people refuse to accept the obvious reality that he is a wild animal, strong and unpredictable. His instinct — or more especially hers — reacts faster than conscious reasoning, as anyone who has inadvertently stood between female and cubs is tragically aware. Yet Bruin is human enough to turn into a lazy, slovenly, mangy old moocher, sitting by the roadside all day long waiting for *homo sapiens* to come along and give him free food: potato chips, ham sandwiches, bananas, or a can of beer. Before long Bruin looks like, feels like, and is in fact in about the same shape as a fat office-worker who has watched a pro football doubleheader on television of a Sunday afternoon, fortified with two six-packs of his favorite brew, two packages of cigarettes, a half-dollar's worth of potato chips, and a can of salted peanuts. A steady diet of snacks is good for neither man nor beast.

In about 1920 a bear decided to take his rest in the middle of the road near Fishing Bridge. When a busload of tourists appeared, the bear sat there and someone on the bus, anxious to be on his way, threw a morsel to the bear — a ham sandwich, or something of that sort. The bear gulped down the tidbit and allowed the bus to pass. The next day the bear was there again, and this time he made signs of begging. Again he was thrown some scraps, and the tourists went on their way. News of the begging bear began to spread, until this particular bruin had been named "Jesse James," and one of the high points of the bus tour was being "held up" by Jesse James, the robber bear. Before long the idea had spread to other lazy bruins, aided and abetted by tourists all too willing to feed the bears along the roads, whether the bears wanted food or not. This is how the problem of begging bears originated.[12]

The black bear is the one the visitor usually sees. *Ursus americanus* weighs 200–400 pounds, has one to three — usually two — cubs in January, and emerges with them in April. The bear's hibernation is more of a half sleep than a drugged coma, and if someone comes across his bed, Bruin, like any human being, may take a dim view of things if he is disturbed. He hibernates in caves, under logs, among rocks, or in Yellowstone he may choose a steam-heated lair near the hot springs.

Once in a while the paw tracks along a trail will seem too enormous for a mere black bear. They may be 5 inches or more across and 10 inches long, the marks of the claw tips far ahead of the toes. These are grizzly tracks, and if you see them it would be prudent to start whistling loudly or talking, so that the grizzly will hear you and run into the forest out of sight. The danger is that you will come upon Bruin unexpectedly, and instinct will order him to attack. Should this happen, run for the nearest tree.

Ursus horribilis is easily distinguished by the broad hump at his shoulders, and his great size and weight, which it is believed can reach well over 1,200 pounds. A healthy grizzly is brute magnificence, and proper respect for him will command keeping a healthy distance from where he may be. There is a considerable difference between a grizzly in midsummer and at hibernating time in October. In midsummer his hair is short, dark brown in color with a trace of gray at the tips, which explains why he is sometimes called Silvertip.

He is bone and sinew then, and as he gracefully lumbers over ridge-top, through forest, and across the streams, his muscles ripple rhythmically. Surely he is one of nature's most powerful beasts.

But when autumn comes on, the short hair is replaced by long, as much as 5 inches of fat will have accumulated around his back and shoulders, and he will look a third again as large as he appeared in midsummer. When he stands up on his hind legs, and that snout of his sniffs the air at an upward angle, he may loom over 8 feet high, and all others, including the black bears, give him full leeway.

Bears — black or grizzly — will eat just about everything except glass and tin cans, and they will lick the food from them. As they lope through the woods they will turn over large boulders to eat the insects darting about underneath, tear open rotting logs for the same purpose, pause in a meadow and claw out the mice from their tunnels, snatch fish out of the streams, sniff out a dead elk or deer and feast upon the carrion, tear off the bark from a spruce, balsam, or pine to lick the inner cambrium (a layer of new bark), pause to eat strawberries, serviceberries, and chokecherries; then they will end the day at the Yellowstone garbage dump looking for dessert.

Along the trail one may come across "bear trees." These are often stripped of bark as far up as a bear can reach, or they may be rubbing trees, where the bear stands on his hind legs and scratches, or they may be "blaze trees," on which the foamy saliva he leaves there to penetrate the cut is evidence of the bear's presence. Wahb, Ernest Thompson Seton's morose giant grizzly, left his warning mark all over the areas where he lived.[13] Bruin is also playful. He will occasionally chew up a sign just for pleasure, or bend over a sapling and straddle it to its tip, letting it fly back up while he keeps moving through the forest, or he will walk a narrow log like a schoolboy balancing along a fence on the way home from school. Bears, says one authority, just like to "fool around."

The grizzly will not ordinarily be seen by visitors, and in view of his brute strength and inclination toward action by instinct, this is probably a good thing. Back in the nineteenth century the present grizzly's ancestors did not hesitate to attack white men, but there is a theory that the great beasts soon learned that the light-complected hunters had guns that could kill. So Bruin ceased his aggressiveness toward man and instead decided to stay out of his way. And he does. There are no grizzlies mooching food at the roadsides in Yellowstone, and it is highly unlikely that the ordinary tourist will see that magnificent species of bear.[14]

One of the animals that is sure to slink away when any full-grown bear appears is the coyote. This animal is found in rather large numbers in the park, is heard talking to the moon, and is occasionally seen by tourists, even in the daytime. Often he will be mistaken for a wolf, but there are few if any of the once numerous gray wolves left in the park, and those few, like the cougar, are rarely seen.

The coyote deserves more respect than he receives. A canine, looking like a buff-yellow undernourished shepherd dog, he shows signs of intelligence and of the desire for human companionship that, millennia ago, brought his near relative into man's house to rest by the hearth while the winds whistled outside. In his lonely yet social way (for the coyote is a family beast, with the father accepting parental responsibility over long periods of the year), in his singing at the big yellow moon in the enormous canopy of the western sky, in his slyness and shrewdness at keeping alive in a world full of enemies, this predator is a four-footed epitome of the western experience. Listen to the coyote again, you civilized people in your campers, trailers, and tents. Listen to him, as J. Frank Dobie would have had you do, "carrying whoever listens to 'old, unhappy, far-off things' and to the elemental tragedy of life."[15]

The coyote sings, perhaps for joy as well as for mating or warnings, and the outdoorsman comes to like the sound and finds it comforting. The animals themselves are the subjects of thousands of stories dating back to the Indians, who rather revered them. In Yellowstone the coyote goes free. Neither lead nor steel nor poison is used against him, and he can eat his fill of rodents and feast on winter-killed antelope, deer, and elk without fear of man. Perhaps he lets the badger do his digging for him and then grabs the fleeing picket pin, or he shares carrion with a magpie, or in winter he follows the snowplows, looking for rodents whose wintry protection has been removed, or he attacks sickly or weakened ungulates. Today, it is believed that, in the park at least, he does more good than harm. Still misunderstood and distrusted, the coyote is nevertheless an intelligent canine who is well worth watching.[16]

One of the most interesting animals in the Yellowstone country, a frequent visitor to the slopes of Mount Washburn, is the bighorn or Rocky Mountain sheep. A big fellow, well above a yard in height at the shoulder and nearly 2 yards long, with massive horns, this shy fellow bears watching for his mountain-climbing agility, darting and climbing and jumping over crags and cliffs and rocky eminences in a style that no human mountain-climber could ever duplicate. Or one may watch the lambs actually playing games of tag in such places. To see a stately ram peering down from some eminence is a thrilling sight, a fleeting glimpse into a more primitive time.

The bighorns, which, as game animals, have been virtually exterminated in most places outside the park, appear to be declining in number in the park also; perhaps no more than 150 or 200 of them live there.

It is in the autumn that the antics of these denizens of the high country become most amusing. During the rutting season a jealous male, herding a harem of four to seven females, may defend his property by waging combat with an insistent rival. For as long as twenty minutes the two may stand beside each other, but facing opposite directions, kicking sidewise. Then they walk 20 to 30 feet apart and at almost the same instant turn, stand on their hind legs, and run toward each other. When they are almost together they drop again to all fours, lower their heads, and crash into each other's skulls, the clap of their collision reverberating through the crags and canyons, clearly discernible a mile away. The impact sends shock waves ripping all the way through their bodies. The antagonists pause a few moments, dazed, then run back, face each other again, and repeat the procedure. They may do this for two hours, then come to some "'animal's agreement," and walk away side by side. The ewes, incidentally, are in such demand that they may hide in the most dangerous places from the rams, who chase after them mercilessly until the season is over.[17]

More frequently seen is the pronghorn antelope, which is native to North America. It is the sole representative here of the family *antilo capridae,* and is not a true antelope at all. It is between a goat and a deer, having horns like a goat but shedding them as a deer sheds antlers, though in a different way. This gentle animal, just a bit larger than a bighorn, has long been considered prime hunting because it is so difficult to approach. Its playfulness, speed, grace, litheness, curiosity, as well as its signal system, have attracted the interest of amateur as well as professional naturalists.

The pronghorn sheds the outer covering of its horns, known as the horn sheath, annually, leaving a bony covering with the black, hairy beginnings of the new sheath cone, which grows and hardens downward from the tip. For better than half the year these horns are useless, and even when they are hardened and formed they are used more as weapons in the antelope's mating warfare than as armament against predators. For protection against its enemies, the pronghorn uses its hoofs, which have no dewclaws (that topmost claw on a dog's paw) and can do as much damage as the spiked heels of a woman's shoes. These hoofs have a cartilaginous padding that forms a resilient cushion, and "being without nerves the pronghorns suffer little from tender feet even though they run continuously on abrasive outcrops." Their legs, the lower joints of which are comparable in structure to the human ankle, are of marvelous design. Along with strong tendons and a covering of short hair that withstands the abrasions of rocks and sagebrush, these remarkable animals are superbly fitted to their environment. Their respiratory system includes a heart almost twice the size of that of a domestic sheep of the same body weight, and they have a windpipe 1.6 inches in diameter, as compared with an adult human male's 0.76-inch windpipe.[18]

Antelope have some other physical features that help them in their eternal struggle for survival. Their vision is excellent, and stories told around campfires defy truth unless the visual capacities of antelope are understood. Their large eyes (one and a half inches for the eyeball) are set deep, for safety, in sockets which protrude slightly from the skull, giving the beasts wide-angle vision, though not of a complete 360°. They catch sight of every moving thing, every change in their wide domain (in their natural state they may range more widely than any other animal except the cougar) that prompts movement. A naturalist using binoculars and searching for what the antelope sees will often make out a slinking coyote or a blowing piece of paper 3–4 miles away.[19] Yet the antelope will have seen it. And, in due time, his ears, 5 inches high and 3 inches wide, will have heard it. By this time he is bounding away. The pronghorn is known for his graceful and noticeable rump, which has a large white girdle about it. But the girdle does not act to contain him; instead it serves as a heliographic signal flag. When danger threatens, the muscles raise the hairs until they become glistening white rosettes which can be seen in the rarified western air when the rest of the animal is blended completely with the terrain. At the same time, glands in these muscles release a strong musk odor which even human beings can detect from several hundred yards away.[20]

The antelope always rests with his feet out in front, so that he springs up to run like a track star at the sound of the gun. The pronghorn can run nearly a mile a minute for very short spells and at half that speed for substantial periods. He likes to race an automobile and then in a burst of energy cross its path. At play he will race through patterns like an end on a football team. The pronghorn's one great weakness is curiosity. He will watch anything unusual, such as earthmoving machinery at work, by the hour.[21]

There are between 200 and 1,000 antelope in the park and a quarter of a million within the United States. Once, they may have been as numerous as the buffalo, or even more so. But they are now controlled and can be legally hunted outside the park without danger of extermination. Many westerners consider antelope meat the most palatable of all wild game. Watch for Yellowstone's protected ones between Gardiner and Mammoth, out toward Tower Falls and eastward into the Lamar Valley. Stop the car and observe their antics, their grace, and their feminine litheness. They are fascinating animals.

It is possible to miss the antelope, the coyote, the beaver, and even the bear, but to drive through Yellowstone on a typical three-day trip and not see some member of the deer family is unusual indeed. Most likely the tourist will see the elk, but with luck he may glimpse a magnificent moose, and, as an added experience, a mule deer might cross the road in front of him. All three varieties of the deer family are present in the reservation.

The mule deer, of which there are from 600 to 1,200 in the park, are the largest of the common American deer. A mule deer weighs 150–200 pounds, is less than 6 feet long and about 3½ feet high at the shoulder. Their large mulelike ears explain their name. Although they are also called blacktails (and in truth the tips of their tails are black), they are not strictly speaking of that variety, which is found in the forests of the Pacific Coast states.[22] The white-tailed deer, which are the most common in the United States, once inhabited Yellowstone but have apparently departed. The larger mule deer, the elk, the moose, and the antelope deprived them of forage and forced them to leave the park and its environs, or starve.

But the most prevalent member of the deer family in the park is the elk, or wapiti (pronounced as in "hippity-hoppity there goes the wapiti"). *Wapiti* is the more accurate name, *elk* being the name given originally to the European moose. In this country, however, both designations, elk and wapiti, are acceptable.[23] Since the near extermination of the elk in the nineteenth century, the Yellowstone and Teton areas have become the cradle of the American elk population. From the overstocked Teton and Yellowstone ranges, these stately animals, largest of the family save for the moose, have been sent all over the nation in hopes of restocking areas long since abandoned by elk.

Elk are great game. The massive antlers, grown anew each year by the male, are prized by hunters and admired by naturalists. A single elk-antler may weigh 10 pounds, almost all of it lime calcium salts. Where the elk gets such quantities of the chemical is unknown.[24] The bull begins to grow new antlers in the spring, and by late summer, when he is fat and saucy, they will be "in the velvet." This refers to the velvety covering of the antlers, which may add to their magnificence for a short time but will quickly be rubbed off on tree trunks or fence posts, leaving a hard, polished, beautiful set of antlers.

With these the males will go forth early in the fall when the rutting season begins. Various changes take place in their anatomy, they become cranky and quarrelsome and antisocial to any man who may be in their way, and they blow forth their bugling calls and set out to collect their harems. The bull elk collects all the cows he can get — as many as sixty or more — and watches over them with a jealous eye.[25]

When another bull challenges his domain, a fight may ensue; on occasion necks are broken or antlers locked, and both beasts perish. Usually, however, one will give up and go trotting off. Meanwhile, other bulls have come along and run off with the harem, leaving both victor and vanquished without cows.

Then, in due time, the rutting season ends and the bulls lose interest in the cows. Now bulls, cows, and calves gather in herds and begin working their way down from the high country; Yellowstone elk, if ranches and fences did not intervene, would go far down the Yellowstone Valley. If nature were not interfered with, the elk would work back up to high meadows come summer, and many of them would gain refuge from insects by staying on the ridges where the cold winds would tend to keep the pests away. Cows look after their calves until they are yearlings, at which time the mother's interest wanes as the time approaches for her to drop another calf or two, or, rarely, three. Coyotes lurk on the periphery of the grazing grounds, and bears will crisscross such an area searching for the little helpless calves which lie flattened out in the grass, nearly odorless and so camouflaged as to fool many a shortsighted bear.

More primeval in appearance then the elk, and weighing 900–1,400 pounds compared with an elk's 700–1,000, is the Yellowstone moose, the Shiras moose. It is slightly smaller than the variety that inhabits the region east of the Rockies, and it has "a wash of rusty brown over the neck and back, and . . . grayer ears and smaller feet and antlers."[26] The tourist will hardly note the difference, however, for this animal is so big, grotesque, and powerful that he thrills people by his mere presence. He seems to belong in an earlier age.

The moose is in fact the largest antlered animal that ever trod the earth. Those broad-bladed hat-racks that the bull carries around above his head, and which he grows anew each year, may spread 6 feet or more across. He may stand 7½ feet high at the shoulders. His head, with its great mealy muzzle, and the bell, or tassel, hanging down from his neck, conjure up hazy reflections of the primitive environment of early man.[27]

Yet the moose seems well equipped for his life on earth. He can get down on his knees and go along eating new grass, or rise up on his hind legs to reach foliage as high as 12 feet from the ground. He likes pond lilies and other aquatic plants, and goes slopping through bogs and ponds, his muzzle buried in the water; then up comes his head, the mouth full of green sprigs, water dripping from that strange bell. He is an excellent swimmer.

His mate is smaller, has no antlers, and looks rather awkward and ungainly. The bull does not gather a harem as does the elk, but merely visits one cow after another, each for about ten days, like a sailor with a girl in every port. At the end of rutting season small groups of bulls, cows, and calves will gather and stay in a rather small area such as Swan Lake Flats, or between Fishing Bridge and Sylvan Pass. At Willow Park, between Swan Lake Flats and Norris, the Park Service has erected a moose exhibit that is a model of factual presentation.

Another strange-looking animal that inhabits Yellowstone is the buffalo, or, to be more strictly correct, the bison. From his ridiculous scorpion-shaped tail through his great hump and woolly foreparts, to his beady little eyes and billy-goat mustache, this topheavy creature out of a more primitive age was, like the moose, perfectly formed for his habitat.

The Yellowstone bison herds have a complex and fascinating history, and some of the finest specimens of the beast are today roaming the park.[28] But they avoid people, and head for the quiet places and the uplands where the insects are not so bad and where few tourists go. There they graze and live out their lives, their basic social unit being a family with a cow the center of the organization, several calves of varying ages around, and a more or less loyal bull. But some buffalo are individualists, and some old bulls get literally kicked out of the herd — probably because they were molesting the calves — and they dare not return. They may be found almost anywhere: a huge buffalo wallow is evidence of their presence, as are "rubbing trees," which will be lighter colored in the area of contact. It is quite possible almost to walk into one of the buffalo, as the author once discovered while out in the woods by the Lower Geyser Basin.

They really are big creatures, bulls attaining a length of 11 feet and standing nearly 6 feet high at the shoulders. A skull from the Yellowstone herd, now in the Mammoth Museum, has a spread between the horns of 35⅜ inches.[29] To see a Yellowstone herd is a thrilling experience, for it is in its natural state, with no bars or barbed wire to restrain it.

And so, from the shrew to the bison, the animals live in the Yellowstone, surprisingly close to their timeless primitive ways. They are born, live, and die nearly as if men — 2 million a year — were not around. The animals hunt, kill and get killed, contract diseases and become infested with ticks, and wallow in the mud to combat deer flies, gnats, and mosquitoes. They are totally unaware, of course, of the precariousness of their existence, for infringing civilization is making the flora and fauna of Yellowstone more and more of an anomaly in the nation at large, and the pressure of population may eliminate them within a generation or two. Let us hope not.

Yellowstone also has fish, both the eight exotic strains introduced by man, such as the rainbow and the brown, or Lock Leven, trout, and the native species, thirteen in all, of which the best known is the splendid fighting native, or cutthroat trout. It is the only trout in the Yellowstone Lake and is also found in both the Snake River and Yellowstone River drainages (this incidently, is one of the facts supporting the theory that in all probability the Yellowstone Lake at one time drained out through the Snake River). The only other significant natives are the whitefish, of which there are two varieties in the park, and the spunky grayling. There are some suckers and some small fish which are usually just called minnows, although they do have a scientific name just like all other identified fish.[30]

No Eden would be complete without its serpents, but Yellowstone is not a snake-infested region. Except in the country north of Mammoth down the Gardner River Canyon, the likelihood of meeting up with the poisonous prairie rattlesnake is remote in the extreme, and the other serpents — the Rocky Mountain rubber boa, the bullsnake, and the wandering garter snake — do nothing but good. There are also frogs and toads. An unusual amphibian in the park is the blotched tiger salamander. A full-grown salamander will be 9 inches long, but this secretive, harmless creature, black with olive-green or yellowish-green spots, will have devoted two years to attaining maturity. Hatched from eggs in a small pond, he looks like a tadpole, developing arms and legs but retaining gills and a dorsal and ventral fin. By autumn, however, he breathes through his lungs, has lost the fins, and looks like the adult, except that he is only about half its size. He spends that winter in the mud at the bottom of the pond, and the next spring he emerges as a regular salamander, growing rapidly to his full length. He lives under logs and the like, close to the water, and feeds on insects. On occasion, hundreds or even thousands will migrate, sometimes covering a highway for a brief space of time. Occasionally they will make a damp cellar their home: leave them alone, for they are harmless and eat the insects.[31]

Over the park soar birds — millions of them, from the predatory bald and golden eagles down to the tiny calliope hummingbirds, smallest in the United States. Aquatic birds range from the rare, graceful trumpeter and whistling swans, sandhill cranes, almost all kinds of ducks, white pelicans roosting at Molly Island in the lake, California gulls, and the common loon, down to the screeching ospreys, trying to get the fish to the nest before an eagle or a hawk makes them drop it, to the water ouzels, king-fishers and grebes. Such game birds as Richardson's grouse (often called "fool-hens"), sage grouse, and sharp-tailed grouse wend their way through field and forest with chicks following after. There are the western great horned owl and the Rocky Mountain screech owl, woodpeckers, sapsuckers, jays, finches, and the western meadow-larks.

One day it had to happen: the odor was strange, the gait was awkward, and the soaring hawks overhead, the bear and the deer in the forest, and the beaver in his pond, paused to stare and then slunk off or scampered underground. Perhaps the strange one was at the lake, walking along the shore. After he had passed, a coyote trotted out from the dried grass to investigate, and stopped and sniffed at the tracks. They were different from any other: long and narrow, with a strange lingering odor.

Man had come to Yellowstone.

PART II

Wanderers and Explorers

4

The Wanderers

The wanderers crossed on land, over an isthmus that is now the Bering Strait. They roved far and wide, probably in small groups, living by the hunt, but moving predominantly southeastward. They left just enough artifacts to make it clear that they were present and to pose problems and create mysteries for civilized, modern, inquisitive man — enough to conjecture by, enough to formulate riddles, but not enough to solve them. They are shadowy figures, the first trespassers upon this virgin continent. Who were they? What did they look like. How did they communicate? What was their social organization? We must shrug our shoulders. We can and will speculate, but we will never know for sure.

Even our theories about the time of man's arrival in North America are disparate, as are our ideas of the routes he traveled. However, evidence confirmed by radiocarbon dating indicates that man was living in the southern part of the continent "as early as twelve or fifteen thousand years ago, and perhaps as much as twenty-five thousand years ago; and [that he] had reached the southern tip of South America, more than ten thousand miles from the port of entry [Bearing Strait] by eight thousand years ago." Some authorities estimate that man has been here 40,000–60,000 years.[1]

It is logical to assume that the wanderers came "prior to the last glacial age of the Wisconsin period, probably 15,000 to 20,000 years ago, [for] only at this time is it likely that a land bridge existed between Siberia and the Alaskan peninsula." Ice-free corridors also appeared, down which the wanderers could trek, and, when the last glacial advance began and the game migrated southward, man, dependent upon that game for his sustenance, certainly followed it.[2]

75

From this knowledge archaeologists can piece together a few obvious facts about the most ancient man in America. Even if he traveled in an interglacial period, the climate was rigorous, so he must have been familiar with fire and have had some knowledge of the making of clothing and the building of shelter. Since he was certainly a hunter, he must have used spears, and he must have utilized some kind of butchering tools and scrapers. Had he domesticated any animals? No evidence has been found that he had even the friendship of the dog. Only a few stone artifacts and a few caves and rock shelters give us evidence of his presence,[3] and they create as many mysteries as they solve.

Assuming that man entered North America at the Bering Strait and wandered southeastward until he reached Tierra del Fuego, then suppositions must arise about the routes he followed. Only generalizations are agreed upon, since northwestern America even in today's climate would pose formidable problems for such a wanderer, and the meteorological conditions in any other age were probably worse. But he probably followed two principal routes, one southward through the interior of what is now British Columbia and the other farther eastward, along the east base of the Rockies where the Alaska Highway runs today.[4] Man hunted down the western intermountain "highway" that bordered on the west, the plateaus and mountains protecting the Yellowstone country, and also down the trail that ran south along the front ranges of the Rockies.[5] Between these two routes, high but not unattainable, lay Yellowstone.

Conjecturally, we can assume that early man came into Yellowstone for the simple reason that there was nothing to prevent him from doing so: if he was drifting southward on both sides of the great mountain rampart, what would have kept him from coming in? It is true that the earliest points from primitive weapons which have been found, the so-called Folsom points (named for the town in New Mexico near which they were first discovered), have never shown up within the boundaries of the park, but they have been found close enough to it at the MacHaffie site near Helena, for example, to indicate that these primitive hunters surely roamed within the boundaries of the park. And those strangely fluted Folsom points are believed to be up to 11,000 years old.[6] They have been discovered in many parts of North America, and especially "from Alberta and Saskatchewan in the north to New Mexico in the south, skirting the eastern slopes of the Rockies,"[7] bearing witness to the widespread meanderings of the early inhabitants of the New World.

Recent discoveries may substantiate these theories about early men — early hunters, the anthropologists call them — in Yellowstone. A Forest Service fire watcher, Richard W. Klukus, spent his spare time hunting for artifacts along the ridges between the Hellroaring and Slough creek drainages, and he found chips and broken points, indicating that ancient man had lived there perhaps 9,000 years ago. At elevations of nearly 10,000 feet, in "hanging valleys" — those high shelves where watercourses head — definite signs of campsites were found. If the artifacts are being interpreted correctly, then early man was tough indeed, for all about him were glaciers, and only the tundra-covered, windswept ridges remained free. Here Pleistocene man must have roamed, searching for mammoths or primitive bison and somehow withstanding the intense cold.[8]

Gradually the climate improved. The massive glaciers began to recede, and the pluvial or anathermal period, a soggy, cold span of many centuries, set in, with the temperature gradually warming. In these years, 9,000–5,000 years ago, all of the northern plains were inhabited by big-game hunters who left few traces of their existence save some scrapers, chopping tools, and weapon points. They appear to have roamed at will, and to have remained at no one place for any length of time. It is assumed that their hunts also took them into the area of the park.[9]

The warming trend continued long after man would have been pleased to have had it level off. Five or six thousand years ago it got so hot and arid that the lakes dried up and the game disappeared, dying off or retreating to the few relatively humid areas such as the uplands and the high mountain valleys. For about 2,000 years this dry, hot era, called the altithermal, continued, and then a gradual cooling set in, accompanied by an increase in humidity, bringing us to the climate, and the flora and fauna, that we have today.[10]

It is during these middle and recent prehistoric periods that evidence accumulates of the presence of man in Yellowstone. At Shelf Lake, far in the northwest corner of the park, chips, five broken projectile points, and four parts of hand tools have been found. "The location," writes Aubrey Haines, "is a pleasant one for summer habitation and may have been even more so during the great altithermal."[11]

A more recent ancient people, whom archaeologists call foragers, appear to have been in the park over a consistent period of time from 6,000 to 500 B.C. Their occupation sites, usually on terraces by the rivers and along the lake shores, are the most prevalent signs of their habitation. There are also strong indications that they inhabited the thermal areas, probably because of the prevalence of game in the proximity of the hot waters and steam. A University of Montana team which made an archaeological survey of the park found about 150 specimens of projectile points representing "all phases of human occupation in the Great Plains except Early Man remains."[12]

During the altithermal era, Yellowstone, with its high, mountain-rimmed plateau, offered pleasant pastures to the game which found its way there from the hot, parched high plains, and man, stalking the game, was not far behind. Such a man, or family group, or assemblage of hunters, built campfires near the present Corwin Springs on the Yellowstone River, 4,600–5,200 years ago. A few years ago a fisherman noticed some symmetrically arranged stones in a bluff, examined them more closely and realized that they looked like part of an ancient hearth. Systematic professional investigation of this Rigler Bluffs site, as it is called, revealed an almost perfect campfire site, with sufficient amounts of wood charcoal to run a radiocarbon half-life check. The statistics tell the story of its situation: 90 feet from the river, 25 feet above it at low water, 6 feet above the drainage bottom of the gully in which it was found, and 22 feet below the level of the hay field above. The hearth was about 27 inches wide; it rested on silt layers, with very fine silt extending about 8 feet above it.

When the geologists were called in, the presence of the fire site was explained. They found evidence that about 5,000 years ago a landslide similar to the one in Madison Valley in 1959 blocked the Yellowstone across Yankee Jim Canyon and backed up a lake almost to the present site of Gardiner. The foragers had camped along its banks, searching for berries, edible roots, fish, and game.[13]

The foragers, who ate anything that grew, crawled, flew, or walked, are believed to have centered around the Yellowstone Lake and northward, along the Gallatin, Madison, and Yellowstone rivers. An abundance of their materials have been found by archaeologists around Yellowstone Lake.[14] We wish we knew more about them, living on the Yellowstone Plateau or along the north-flowing rivers, aware of the dusty, parched, hot plains far to the east, watching the erupting geysers with awe, enjoying the luxury of a hot bath, shaking with fright at the feel of an earth tremor, gazing at the purples and blues and pinks and reds of the Aurora Borealis, watching the sun rise over the eastern mountains and set over the western ones, huddling together around their fires in the damp coolness of the night. Here were rational beings: hunters, foragers, makers of fire, tanners of hides, and manufacturers of clothing, people with remarkable resistance to cold and physical discomfort. What kind of human specimens were they? Our knowledge of their environment makes us respect them, but of their physical features, their society, their language, their ways of doing things, we know virtually nothing.

When the climate changed, beginning about 1,000 B.C., with conditions well on the way to what they are at present by 500 B.C., the foragers of this middle prehistoric period gave way to the hunters of the late prehistoric period, 1,400 B.C.–1,700 A.D. Although the animals they hunted may have been larger than those of today (the bison was probably larger, for example), their flora and fauna were essentially the same as those we know. In that sense we can identify with them. And a little more evidence of their presence has been found. Of the 170 sites examined by the Montana archaeologists, some clearly indicate the presence of the late hunters. On the Lamar River drainage there is an ancient hunting corral used by communal hunters, and "a peculiar rock wall in the vicinity" is believed to have some connection with the ancient corral.

Projectile points and chips of obsidian are found in numerous places in the park, and some of them indicate workmanship of 1,800 or more years ago. These are surface finds, however, which reduces their value, since they could have arrived at their present locations in any number of ways. The value of these projectiles is determined by typology: the early hunters, the foragers, and the late hunters used points varying in shape, form, and material. Obsidian, especially black obsidian, is prevalent in its natural state in Yellowstone, but, rather surprisingly, jasper and flint projectiles have also been found. One final note: the artifacts indicate that different groups of Indians occupied the plateau south and north of the lake.[15]

About 500 A.D. the late hunters learned of the bow and arrow, which was a great improvement over the spear and the extended spear (the atlatl). But it must be kept in mind that they were still unmounted wanderers following the game, especially the bison that populated the Great Plains. Possibly some of those unexplained circles of rocks, called teepee rings (of which there are a number in the park) are attributable to these pre-Columbian inhabitants; possibly not. In any event, we do know that beginning about 600 years ago, some mass folk movements began which, when they had run their course, left the Indian tribes of the Great Plains in the approximate geographical areas that they occupied when they first met the white man. By that time most of them were mounted, mobile hunters, foraging within a loosely defined area which they considered theirs, or else marauding far and wide.

The tribes that play roles in the history of the Yellowstone country, like all Indian tribes, defy generalization. Not only did Indians differ greatly in looks, customs, and language, but they differed in their social and economic conditions — almost from decade to decade following the white man's appearance. The stereotyped Indian is about as real as the wooden Indian that used to stand outside the cigar store.

In the 1830s the tribes of the Upper Missouri could only be described as prosperous. They were, wrote the painter George Catlin, "the finest looking, best equipped, and most beautifully costumed of any on the Continent. They live in a country well stocked with buffaloes and wild horses, which furnish them an excellent and easy living; their atmosphere is pure, which produces good health and long life; and they are the most independent and the happiest races of Indian I have met with: they are all entirely in a state of primitive rudeness and wildness, and consequently are picturesque and handsome, almost beyond description."[16]

These tribes would have included the Crow, the several groups of the Blackfeet, and possibly some of the Shoshone. Add to the list the tall, lithe, warriors of the Bannock tribe, who lived southwest of the park in southern Idaho, the Nez Perces and some northern Paiutes and Flatheads located rather northwest of the Yellowstone, and most of the Indians who have been involved in Yellowstone history since the coming of the white man have been mentioned. Of these tribes the most numerous and the one that made a permanent settlement in the park was the Shoshone.

These "stocky-built, dark-skinned, full-featured highlanders" came, according to their tradition, from "the land beyond the setting sun," and they roamed from the Sierras and Cascades east to the northern plains beyond the eastern front of the Rockies and south to Mexico. When a general reshuffling of the Plains Indians began in about 1700, their brothers the Comanches migrated to the southern plains and the Shoshone concentrated in eastern Idaho, northern Utah, and later in western Wyoming and Montana and even into Canada. Other segments of the tribe remained in Nevada and Oregon and western Idaho.[17]

In the early years of the eighteenth century, at about the time of the shifting of the tribes, the Shoshone obtained horses, probably from their Comanche brothers to the south, and this placed them at an advantage over their enemies, especially the Blackfeet, until that tribe obtained guns from white trappers coming overland from the east. Add the scourge of smallpox to the changing advantages that the possession of the horse and the gun were giving the various nomadic peoples, and a situation of great instability and fluidity arises. As a result the Shoshone were apparently pushed into the mountain and plateau regions, including Yellowstone Park, Idaho, Utah, and southern Wyoming. When Meriwether Lewis first made contact with a Shoshone warrior (August 10, 1805), the Indian kept his distance and finally spurred his horse and disappeared. It was three more days until Lewis came upon an old squaw and a twelve-year-old girl who, feeling themselves too close to him to make good their escape, sat down and lowered their heads in anticipation of a death blow. They believed that the strangers from the great buffalo plains to the east had come to war upon and destroy the people of the mountains.[18]

Even though the Shoshonean people had been pushed into the highlands or had remained in the wastes of the Great Basin, they were nevertheless numerous and widespread, divided into several segments often bearing the name of their principal food or their mode of obtaining sustenance. Thus there were the Hukandikas ("dust eaters" of the deserts); Kamodikas (eaters of black-tailed jackrabbits); Pengwidikas (fish eaters); Kucundikas (buffalo eaters), and, of course, the Tukarikas, or Sheep Eaters. [19]

Some of their names had geographical meanings, and some had ludicrous origins. Included in the latter designation would be "Snakes," the name given the portions of the tribe inhabiting southern Idaho and northern Utah, centering around old Fort Hall. The name was probably due to a misunderstanding by white men of the meaning of their wiggling finger sign of identification, which really meant "basket weaver" but was misinterpreted. Even the name "Snakes" was restricted, however, applying only to those who possessed horses. Without horses they were probably called "Diggers," a name that embraced all the little groups of wandering aborigines who trod the deserts of the Great Basin and ate almost anything that lived. The Diggers were, however, of Shoshone stock. Other portions of the tribe were referred to as the Northern Shoshone, who might be found hunting around Henry's Lake, or west of the park in general, and occasionally within its future boundaries. There were Western Shoshone, or Shoshokoes, along the Humboldt; Southern Shoshone in the Great Basin who might be called Diggers or Gosiutes; and there were Green River Shoshone in the area the name implies.[20]

Perhaps the least numerous of the Shoshone segments were the shadowy people who resided permanently in the deepest recesses of the northern Rockies. These were the Tukarikas, or eaters of the bighorn sheep — the Sheep Eaters. Most of them never possessed horses and never ventured out onto the buffalo plains; they retained in a pure form the ancestral culture of the Great Basin whence their ancestors had come. They were peaceful, solitary, and puzzling even to their brethren on the plains, with whom they occasionally intermarried. Their culture was certainly stagnant, their mode of life highly specialized. They adjusted to an existence in the vast high mountain area which includes parts of Idaho, southwestern Montana, and northwestern Wyoming.

With their dogs, to which they attached travois, thus making them beasts of burden, and their squaws, their children, and their papooses, they wandered within the park, down around the Grand Tetons, in the narrow defiles of the Absarokas, and in the Wind River Mountains down to South Pass. As time went on some intermarriage and amalgamation took place, so that some of the Tukarika were descendants of the walkers of the Great Basin, while some were plains Shoshone who had suffered reverses, lost their horses, and retreated to the mountains; some were Panaiti Toyani (Bannock mountaindwellers) in whose blood coursed fully or partly the blood of unrelated Bannocks. And occasionally, to add to the confusion, small parties of them did gain horses and hunt on the Green River plains, but they were nevertheless identified by their plains brethren as

Tukarika and were so called. But most of them remained unmounted mountain wanderers.[21]

Because they did not own horses, and were therefore considered lower in status than the proud horsemen of the plains, and also because most white men did not come in contact with them until the 1860s and 1870s when they, like all the Indian tribes, were in rapid decline, the myth has arisen that the Sheep Eaters were a despicable, cowardly, and miserable people. Historically this is certainly not true. Osborne Russell, one of the most literate of the mountain men, described some of these mountain dwellers as he saw them in the Lamar Valley in 1835. "They were all neatly clothed in dressed deer and sheep skins of the best quality and seemed to be perfectly contented and happy," he wrote. The six men, seven women, and eight or ten children, "the only inhabitants of this lonely and secluded spot," had fled to the heights but came down and camped with the trappers when they were persuaded of the white man's peaceful intentions. While their personal property was scant, consisting of an old butcher knife, a couple of nearly useless fusees, and a small stone pot, they had about thirty dogs and good, primitive weapons. "They were well armed with bows and arrows pointed with obsidian," Russell said. "The bows were beautifully wrought from Sheep, Buffalo and Elk horns secured with Deer and Elk sinews and ornamented with porcupine quills and generally 3 feet long."[22]

Such a description hardly evokes the squalor and destitution usually associated with them. It is more accurate to present the Tukarikas as a small group of Shoshone, without horses, who adapted well and lived in comfort by aboriginal standards. They hunted the bighorn mountain sheep, a most edible and useful beast of prey, and they became so associated with these beasts that they were given its Indian name. They also hunted deer, elk, antelope, bear, groundhogs, and other rodents; they fished in the streams and the high mountain lakes and knew every palatable berry, herb, and root in the high country. They used bows and arrows to kill their game, had fire to cook it with, tanned the hides for clothing, and constructed conical brush or bark wickiups or occupied caves for shelter. Clothing, shelter, and a full belly constituted peace and contentment in Tukarika life, and they seem to have enjoyed enough of all three.[23]

Because they did not have horses, and because the economics of their hunting would allow them to exist only in very small groups, they did try to avoid confrontations with the wild and warlike Sioux tribes and the Blackfeet who occasionally did enter their mountain bastions for hunting and warring purposes. If questionable authority can be accepted on the basis of the factual results, then massacres by plains tribes plus the decimations wrought by a smallpox epidemic reduced the Tukarika numbers from hundreds to mere dozens. One writer tells of a tradition that their chief, Red Eagle, won a great victory over the Sioux by releasing boulders down upon the enemy as they worked up a narrow defile; a better authority attributes their near demise to a smallpox epidemic.[24]

Because they were identified as the only permanent human inhabitants of the park, every rotting wickiup or other indication of Indian habitation was attributed to these people, although hunters from other tribes, especially the Crow, could just as easily have done the work. Philetus W. Norris, the second superintendent of the park, thus called one such location of rotting wickiups Sheepeater Cliffs, a name which is still in use.[25]

That they were seen by subsequent white men and that by the 1860s and 1870s they were unattractive — at least some of them — is beyond contradiction. In 1869 David Folsom described an old woman as follows: "Her gray hair hung from her low, narrow forehead in elf-locks over bleared eyes; the rheum from their cavernous depths and the drivel from her toothless mouth ran down the gutters of her withered cheek and fallen jaw; her skinny arms were begrimed with dirt, her claw-shaped hands were stained with the juice of [choke]cherries and the rags, reeking with filth, which served her for clothing, revealed rather than concealed the hideousness of her form . . . [they] had no bedding except the rags upon which the cherries were spread, not a single utensil for cooking was anywhere to be seen and, so far as we could discover the cherries were their only means of subsistence. . . . "[26]

Other Sheep Eaters revealed sufficient intelligence to be employed as guides by the early explorers. Captain William Jones, who made a reconnaissance into the park in 1873 northward from Camp Brown (now Lander, Wyoming), hired a group of Shoshone as guides, only to discover that just one of them knew the mountains. This fellow took advantage of his newfound power, much to the captain's chagrin. "When all ready for the start it was discovered that he was enjoying all the comforts of home," the captain recorded in his journal, "taking a quiet smoke after having been told to get ready an hour before." And the very next morning: "The Indian difficulty came up early. The fellow after being told to get ready in time to start with us, went off up the stream to trap for beaver." The poor captain was in a dilemma; Togwotee (for that was the Indian's name) must be chastised, but not too severely, for he alone assured them a safe trip back to Camp Brown. Captain Jones explained the situation to the two Indians whom he sent after Togwotee, and they soon returned with Togwotee, who was now a cheerful guide and caused the captain no more trouble. Exactly what the two Indians said to Togwotee is not known. "He belongs to a band of Shoshones called 'Sheep-eaters,' " the captain recorded in his journal, "who have been forced to live for a number of years in the mountains away from the tribe." Later Jones named the pass at the head of Wind River, southeast of Yellowstone Lake, after Togwotee, not in the Indian's honor, but in accord with a policy of giving geographical sites Indian names.[27]

In his hunting and fishing trip into the park in 1881 General Sheridan used five Sheep Eaters as guides, who surprised the party by professing ignorance of the geyser basins, although they had lived for years about Mounts Sheridan and Hancock and the high mountains southeast of Yellowstone Lake. Sheridan explained that of late these Sheep Eaters had begun trading with Chief Washakie's Shoshone. "'Finally,'" the general wrote, "when the Geyser Basins were discovered, and the whites commenced to render their habitations, high up as they were, insecure, they were persuaded by the old chief, Washakie, to abandon their mountain homes and come into the reservation at Fort Washakie, on Wind River."[28]

The Tukarikas were always glad to get back into their old mountain hunting-grounds, however, and when President Arthur came up into the park in 1883, Togwotee and several of his Indian friends went along as guides.[29]

Living east of the man-made park boundaries were the Crow, frequent visitors to the park, who in times past had broken off from their brethren the Hidatsas (also known as Gros Ventres or Minnetarees) and had traveled west to the Rocky Mountains. There, south of the Yellowstone to the North Platte, and including the headwaters of the Powder, Wind, and Bighorn rivers, these people had established their homes. In their Siouxan language they called them-

selves *Ap sar roo kai* (hence the Absaroka Mountains), meaning
"anything that flies"; the origin of the name *Crow* is unknown.[30]

They loved their country, which, east of the mountains, was
described as "perhaps the best game country in the world." It was
also a land with a geographical personality. As early as the 1850s
white traders knew of the volcanic origin of several of the ranges.
Such landmarks as "large towers of melted sand 20 or 30 feet high,"
or grotesque formations similar to the Mauvaises Terres of the Sioux
country, were known to be within the Crow domains, as were such
thermal phenomena near the head of the Yellowstone as bituminous
springs, "sending forth a substance like tar, which is inflammable,
while others were sulfurous, "and one or two boiling."[31]

Certainly the Crows wandered the mountains throughout the
park, trading for horses at the upper reaches of the Yellowstone with
Nez Perces and Shoshone who had come from the west to meet and
trade. The Crow warriors were handsome and proud and owned
horses in abundance; they were in continual warfare with the Blackfeet and the Sioux, and occasionally they fought bitter battles with
the Shoshone. The Crows only gave up their southern lands in the
Wind River area to the Shoshone after the battle of Crow Heart
Butte, probably in 1858 or early 1859.[32]

In some ways, the park deserves, like old Kentucky, to be called
the "dark and bloody ground," for Indians hunting about the lake
and the river were as interested in two-footed game as in the four-
footed varieties. The Blackfeet, those far-wandering thieves and killers
from above the Missouri, were frequent warlike intruders. Sheep
Eaters, Shoshone, Bannocks, Flatheads, Nez Perces, Crows — the
Blackfeet treated them all alike. All these tribes were fair game, and
all were victims of the sinister ambush that marked the Blackfoot
attack. So were the white men.

There were three tribes of Blackfeet — the Piegans, the Bloods,
and the Northern Blackfeet — and they were in close alliance with
the Gros Ventres and the Sarcees. All of these tribes spoke an Algon-
quian dialect, which affiliated them with the numerous woodland
tribes east of the Great Plains. As for the origin of the name Blackfeet, it is indeterminate at this late date.[33]

They were proud, warlike, and hardy, perfectly adjusted to
hunting the northern plains buffalo, weathering the harsh winters,
meeting the competition of other tribes, making horse-stealing forays

as far as 600 miles from their home encampments. If fighting and bloodshed ensued in the process, the Blackfeet usually gave more than they received. And since they were usually the aggressors, their name became symbolic of a human scourge on the northern plains; evidence of their presence struck terror into the hearts of red men and white men alike. Their expeditions took them to the lands of the Flatheads, Nez Perces, Shoshone, Bannocks, and Crows, and often led them into the park and its environs. If it had not been for the Blackfeet, the park would probably have been known to the white man several decades earlier than it was. Meriwether Lewis encountered the Piegans in July 1806, on his reconnaissance of the Marias River, and killed one of them in the horse-stealing attempt that followed. They were hostile to the white man from then on.[34]

John Colter, who left the Lewis and Clark Expedition at the Mandan villages in 1806 and returned to the mountains, may have experienced Blackfoot violence twice before he left the wild country to settle down as a farmer in Missouri. The first time was in 1807, when he and his Crow companions were attacked and he received a severe leg wound. The next year he and his partner John Potts were trapping near the Jefferson when the Blackfeet killed his companion, stripped Colter naked, and made him run for his life. Attempts in 1810 by Andrew Henry and Pierre Menard to maintain a fort at the Three Forks of the Missouri, in the heart of Piegan country, were unsuccessful, and when Wilson Price Hunt and his Astorians went West in 1811, they detoured south of the Lewis and Clark route in order to steer clear of the Blackfeet. In 1839 the trapper Osborne Russell and his party were victims of a Blackfoot attack while in camp near the northeast shore of Yellowstone Lake. Finally, it was a band of Piegans, the Blackfoot band that traditionally lived closest to the park, that guided the Jesuit Father Kuppens into the park in 1865.[35]

Still another aggressive tribe whose members traversed the park and were acquainted with it was the Bannock. Tall, slim, and sinewy, dignified astride their horses, these Indians vied with the Blackfeet in their hatred of the white man.

The Bannocks, about 2,000 strong, were a branch of the Northern Paiutes who had migrated in historic times at least 200 miles southeast from their original homeland and had established themselves in the vicinity of what was later Fort Hall in eastern Idaho.

Here they had lived in a situation of necessary tolerance with the Shoshone who were already there, not intermarrying extensively until historic times, and noticeably distinguishable from their stockier, shorter, darker-complected Shoshone neighbors.[36]

Although they had apparently migrated from eastern Oregon, and even in the Fort Hall area were still far removed from the great buffalo plains rolling eastward from the front ranges of the Rockies, these Indians appear to have adapted readily to the plains-buffalo culture. Tradition says that they left Oregon when the buffalo disappeared from there, and it is certain that they were early possessors of the horse and accomplished horse-thieves. When the white man arrived, with his horses and his roads and his demands for grazing land, clashes were inevitable. Bannock resistance and pride made the tribe the scourge of the West in a wide belt from Fort Bridger and the Big Hole westward to the Humboldt and the Oregon country.[37]

Just as the buffalo had disappeared from eastern Oregon, so, by about 1840, had they disappeared from the Upper Snake country inhabited by the Bannocks.[38] But these Indians — boastful of their horse-and-buffalo economy that contrasted so favorably with the scrounging search for food of their Shoshone neighbors — refused to abandon their proud livelihood. It was true that they had two means of sustenance, including salmon fishing in the Snake River and its tributaries and the digging of camas roots from the Camas Prairie in Idaho, in addition to hunting buffalo, but surely the buffalo hunt was their prideful occupation. Seasonally, it followed the food-gathering customs of the previous two.[39] As autumn came on, preparations were completed, salmon and roots were stored or packed, and the longest and most adventurous of their annual pere-grinations began. Knowledge of the mountains to the east of them, and of the buffalo plains on the other side, had come to the people as gradually and steadily as the change of the seasons, and the ex-periences and guidance of brave warriors eventually resulted in a single trail — albeit one often dividing into two or more parts for fairly long distances — which came to be known as the Great Ban-nock Trail. In the late 1940s and early 1950s, a park ranger traced the length of it, and for those who know what to look for, parts of it may still be seen from today's Yellowstone highways.[40]

Although the Bannock Trail passed through the heart of the

high country, it had two virtues over other routes. It was relatively clear of tribal enemies, which was not true of the easier route that led up to the Three Forks of the Missouri, where the hostile Blackfeet roamed, and then went onto the buffalo plains; or the trail north and east of South Pass, where the Bannocks might encounter their enemies the Utes; or the route out from the Tetons, where clashes with the Crows were likely. So the Bannocks chose the high road. Since numbers increased their safety, they often united with the Nez Perces, the Flatheads, and segments of the Shoshone. Risk was still present, for the Blackfeet were a menace even in the Yellowstone country, to say nothing of possible Crow and Sioux marauders likely to steal their horses during the hunting days on the eastern plains. Squaws packed the horse and dog travois, one stick of which always extended farther back than the other to alleviate some of the jouncing for the sake of the babies who were carried in a basketry cradle along with small children on the travois; the older children walked alongside or enjoyed a few proud hours riding horseback behind the father. Someone was responsible for carrying a "bark bundle slow match" — tightly wrapped sagebrush about three inches in diameter and three or four feet long — that would smolder for a long time and then readily start a fire at the evening campsite. On the way the squaws and children would gather pine nuts and cache them for use on the return journey.[41]

From Henry's Lake, teeming with waterfowl and fish, mysterious with its floating islands,[42] the Indians followed their trail north through semi-tree-covered country over Targhee Pass (which crests at 7,078 feet) into the valley of the upper Madison near Horse Butte. They made their way on northward to the Great Spring (now Cory Spring), 8 miles north and 2 west of West Yellowstone. Here they established a rendezvous camp where they waited for elements from down the Madison and Gallatin, and then they headed for the buffalo plains to the east.[43] Just north of Duck Creek and just inside Yellowstone's west boundary, the trail enters the park, and the view from northeast to southeast enhances our respect for the Indian pathfinders. Standing on a sagebrush plain one sees an enormous tree-covered plateau rising gradually toward the forbidding Gallatin Range that looms in the distance. Between the sagebrush plain and the other side of those mountains lay swamps, forests, streams, and lakes. Could anyone find a passage through here that families with horses and travois could penetrate?

Through trial and error the Indians discovered a route: southward nearly to Cougar Creek, then abruptly northward, over the Gallatins north and a little west of Mount Holmes and eastward down into the Indian Creek drainage, which brought the hunters to the Gardner River. Often the Bannocks camped in this vicinity, and the men made side trips to Obsidian Cliff to fetch pieces of the volcanic glass to work into arrow and spear points.

The main trail appears to have run north through Swan Lake Flats, then slightly west to work down through Snow Pass into the nearby Mammoth Hot Springs area, then east, downward and across the Gardner, and so upstream in a southeast-by-south direction toward and beyond the mouth of Lava Creek along its east banks. At Mammoth this trail was met by a trail coming up the Gardner from the Yellowstone, so that an Indian who dared take the risk could go down this trail and do his hunting in the upper Yellowstone Valley. An alternate route did not pass through Mammoth at all, but descended eastward to the south of Bunsen Peak and rejoined the main trail near the spot where the high bridge over the Gardner now stands.

From the approximate site of the Lava Creek bridge and campground, the trail crossed to Blacktail Deer Creek, and was joined there by two minor Indian trails, one from the mouth of the Gardner and the other from a ford across the Yellowstone below Oxbow Creek. It continued along essentially the same route as the old Tower Falls road, through "the Gut" and around the south side of Crescent Hill, descended to Yancey's, crossed Pleasant Valley to the Yellowstone, surmounted Overhanging Cliff, and crossed Tower Creek at about the site of the present campground. Below this site, where it crossed Antelope Creek, the trail is still visible from the road; at that point an Indian trail joined it from the western flank of Mount Washburn and the canyon area.[44]

The Bannock Trail now descended to the Yellowstone to a point called the Sulphur Beds, the site of one of the few fords across the river. Here the Indians crossed the river and then climbed out of the Yellowstone Valley, heading northeast into the Lamar Valley holding close to the base of Specimen Ridge and Amethyst Mountain.

A minor trace branched off at the mouth of Slough Creek, working up that stream and eventually reaching the Stillwater and

Rosebud drainages. At the junction of Soda Butte with the Lamar, another Indian trail began, this one leading to the upper Lamar and Shoshone rivers, from the latter of which a wanderer could have made his way eastward to the buffalo plains.

At this same junction, where Soda Butte Creek joins the Lamar, the main Bannock Trail split into two branches. One followed Soda Butte Creek up over Cooke Pass, paralleling and in some places being incorporated into what is now the highway, until it reached the Clarks Fork, which the trail then followed to the plains.

The other branch — perhaps the more used — headed southeast for the divide between Cache and Calfee creeks, and then straddled the divide for 15 or 20 miles, surrounded by the magnificent Absaroka Mountains. Then the trail dropped down to Canoe Lake, just inside the park boundary (it drains westward into the park). But a few paces eastward the trail met Timber Creek, which drains eastward into the Clarks Fork, and the Bannock Trail thus followed it until it reached the buffalo plains.

The mileage involved in the annual buffalo hunt is difficult to determine, one obvious reason being that there is no way of knowing how far the Bannocks penetrated the buffalo plains. Surely the round trip covered 300 miles of rugged terrain, and possibly twice that much.[45]

Such an arduous annual migration, with women and children, horses and provisions, tells us much about these fierce, warlike hunters. Digging roots and catching salmon were necessary for survival, but the buffalo hunt made the Bannocks proud, aggressive, and wealthy in terms of the material possessions desired by the red man. Tradition said they had left eastern Oregon when the buffalo disappeared, and when the Snake River Plains became barren of the beasts, the Bannocks had forged a trail in the direction of the rising sun over the mountains to the plains. The annual hunting expeditions probably dated from about 1840.

Until the coming of the white man into the Northwest in the early 1860s, the hunt had probably been consistently successful. But then the deluge of the white man's migration advancing into the new mining regions of Montana and Idaho, or through South Pass and into the Great Basin, or northwest from there into the valleys of the Snake and the Columbia, threatened and ultimately halted the great range of the Bannocks, who were found from the Big Hole to the

Humboldt River, and also went east by way of the Bannock Trail.[46]

As would be expected of so proud and independent a people, they reacted with violence to the white man's advance until, at the Battle of Bear River, fought January 29, 1863, Colonel Patrick Connor and his California Volunteers soundly defeated them. For the remainder of the decade they were relatively quiescent, settling down to reservation life centered at Fort Hall, but some still made the annual trek over the Bannock Trail. "I am willing to go upon a reservation, but I want the privilege of hunting the buffalo for a few years," Chief Targhee told an Indian agent in 1867. "When they are all gone far away we hunt no more; perhaps one year, perhaps two or three years; then we stay on the reservation all the time."[47] In fact the Indians continued to use the trail, though avoiding the miners at Cooke City by taking the route that straddled the Cache Creek–Calfee Creek Divide through the Absarokas, until the Bannock War of 1878; and they hunted to the south, in the Teton country of Wyoming, until 1895.[48]

These were the Indians, then, who knew of the park: Bannocks, Nez Perces, Flatheads, Blackfeet, Crows, and Shoshonean groups including the Sheep Eaters, who actually lived there. As was evident elsewhere in the West, the terrain of the Yellowstone country, far from being the "trackless waste" so often pictured by romantic fictioneers, was crisscrossed with trails used by animals and by men. Yellowstone had its share of both.

5

The First White Men

Until the nineteenth century, virtually no white men had been to the Yellowstone country. True, French Canadian, Scotch, Welsh, or English explorers had forged into the austere, windswept northern plains prior to 1800. Baron de Lahontan narrated a trip up a mysterious "Long River" in the late 1680s and told of a Salt Lake to the west.[1] As early as 1742 two of the sons of the Frenchman Le Vérendrye had pushed southwest from the Mandan villages, located along the Missouri in what is now North Dakota, searching for the western sea. At their point of farthest penetration, they had seen mountains to the west of them. Because they described their journey with irritating vagueness, where they stood and what mountains they saw have since been topics of controversy. Logical deductions, plus the discovery in 1913 of a lead plate left by them in the neighborhood of Pierre, South Dakota, point to the Black Hills as the range in question, or, according to another set of deductions, they may have seen the Bighorns.[2]

David Thompson, a famous British explorer, collected information at the Mandan villages in 1797 and 1798 and concluded that the Yellowstone River had its source at 43°39′45″ north latitude and 109°43′17″ west longitude, which placed the source of the river just 21 miles from its actual location. Thompson was also the first white man to use the words *Yellow Stone* for the name of the river.[3]

Spain, concerned over British intrusions from Canada, encouraged one Jacques D'Eglise to go up the Missouri from St. Louis, and by 1790 that adventurer had reached the Mandan villages, where, he reported, a Frenchman named Menard had been living for fourteen years. In the 1790s, James Mackay, a Scotchman, and John

Evans, a Welshman, likewise explored the Mandan villages and traded with the Indians. They had a map showing the Yellowstone River; one of their maps fell into the hands of Thomas Jefferson.[4] If, by 1800, the white man had not actually penetrated much to the west of the Big Bend of the Missouri, at least he knew something of the land there. "The Country from the Mandaines [sic] to the Rocky Mountains is well watered by different Rivers that empty themselves in the Missouri, particularly from the South West," John Evans wrote in his journal in 1797, mentioning several rivers, including the Rivière des Roches Jaunes.[5]

But had they heard anything of the wonders of the Yellow-stone? Logic tells us that if men had seen or heard of geographical features and Indian tribes farther West, then they would have heard of the unusual phenomena of the Upper Yellowstone too. Lewis and Clark were curious men and "the writingest explorers of their time,"[6] and indeed they hinted of what they heard, but they refused to be explicit. Possibly this was because they desperately wanted to be believed, and if they had related tall tales which they could not themselves verify, they might have harmed the reception of the journals they hoped to publish. Just how close they did come to recording some of the tales they heard is amply demonstrated in the following passage, written by Clark on June 20, 1805, on the outward journey, in the vicinity of the Great Falls of the Missouri, some 300 miles from Mammoth Hot Springs (the spelling and punctuation are Clark's):

> Dureing the time of my being on the Plains and above the falls I as also all my party repeatedly heard a nois which proceeded from a Direction a little to the N. of West, a loud [noise] and resembling precisely the discharge of a piece of ordinance of 6 pounds at the distance of 5 or six miles. I was informed of it several times by the men: J. Fields particularly before I paid any attention to it, thinking it was thunder most probably which they had mistaken. at length walking in the plains yesterday near the most extreem S. E. bend of the River above the falls I heard this *nois* very distinctly, it was perfectly calm, clear and not a cloud to be seen, I halted and listened attentively about two hour[s] dureing which time I heard two other discharges, and took the direction of the

sound with my pocked compass which was nearly West from me as I could estimate from the sound. I have no doubt but if I had leisure I could find from whence it issued. I have thought it probable that it might be caused by running water in some of the caverns of those emence mountains, on the principle of the blowing caverns; but in such case the sounds would be periodical and regular, which is not the case with this, being sometimes heard once only and at other times several discharges in quick succession. it is heard also at different times of the day and night. I am at a great loss to account for this Phenomenon. I well recollect the Minitarees say that those Rocky Mountains make a great noise but they could not tell me the cause, neither could they inform me of any remarkable substance or situation in those mountains which would autherise a conjecture of a probabl cause of this noise. it is probable that the large river just above those Great falls which heads in the direction of the noise had taken its name *Medicine river* from this unaccountable rumbling sound, which like all unaccountable thing[s] with the Indians of the Missouri is called *Medicine*.

The Ricaras inform us of the black mountains makeing a simalar noise etc. etc. and maney other wonderfull tales of those Rocky mountains and those great falls.[7]

On their outward journey Lewis and Clark were never within 150 miles of the future boundaries of the park, and on the return trip Clark, scrambling over Bozeman Pass and reaching the Yellowstone River at the approximate site of Livingston, was still 60 miles or so from the Mammoth Hot Springs. But several references make it clear that they were curious about the river and its headwaters. In a letter from Lewis to Jefferson, dated "Fort Mandan, April 7, 1805," he wrote, "On our return we shall probably pass down the yellow stone river, which from Indian informations, waters one of the fairest portions of this continent."[8] And in Biddle's notes of his interviews with Clark, there is the statement, "on the head of the Roche jaune [Yellowstone] live the Yepi pi band of Snakes of 200 men,"[9] which could refer to the Sheep Eaters.

Notwithstanding the reluctance of Lewis and Clark to indulge in rumors, tales of volcanic phenomena at the headwaters of the

Missouri or its southwest tributaries (such as the Kaw, the Platte, and the Teton) were spreading throughout the States even before the two explorers returned to civilization. To understand the reasons for this, the reader must probably readjust somewhat his concept of the western wilderness. Wild and open, it was inhabited, though sparsely, by human beings who possessed intelligence although they were "barbarians." The land was free and attractive to the white man, who was represented by trappers or traders. They penetrated the land as a stream of water will make its way down a dry, gradual incline, creeping ahead here, halting there, but eventually engulfing the whole. White men unknown to history saw more new things than did those whose names became part of the chronicles of mankind. It was from these unknown ones, as well as from the known, that the rumors spread.

For example, in 1805, while Lewis and Clark were climbing the Rockies, making contact with the Shoshone, the Flatheads, and the Nez Perces as their route led to the Pacific, a trapper named François Antoine Laroque was exploring from the Assiniboine to the Yellowstone, passing north of the Bighorn Mountains, eventually working west to Pryor's Fork, floating down it to the Yellowstone and from there home.[10]

And in that same year Governor James Wilkinson of the Louisiana Territory was writing to the secretary of war that he had "equipt a Perogue . . . to ascend the Missouri and enter the River Piere jaune, or Yellowstone, called by the natives, Unicorn River, the same by which Capt. Lewis I since find expects to return and which my informants tell me is filled with wonders . . . ." Barely six weeks later he sent President Jefferson "a few natural productions of this Territory, to amuse a leisure moment, and also a savage delineation of a Buffalo Pelt, of the Missouri and its South Western Branches, including the Platte and Lycorne or Pierre jaune, this Rude Sketch without Scale or Compass 'et replie de Fantaisies ridicules' is not destitute of interest, as it exposes the location of several important Objects . . . among other things a little incredible, a volcano is distinctly described on Yellow Stone River. . . . "[11]

When an earthquake was felt in Nashville late in 1811 or early in 1812, it was blamed, said a local newspaper, the *Clarion,* upon a concussion from an eruption "of the volcano to the west mentioned by Lewis and Clark."[12]

One man who added to these rumors by telling tall tales he insisted were true had arrived in the St. Louis area from up the Missouri sometime in the fall of 1810. The single extant description of this frontiersman described him as "about thirty-five years of age [as of 1809], five feet ten inches in height," with "an open, ingenious and pleasing countenance of the Daniel Boone stamp." The same author adds that "his veracity was never questioned among us and his character was that of a true American backwoodsman." His name was John Colter. He was one of the "nine young men" enlisted by Lewis at least by the time that explorer had arrived at the Falls of the Ohio in 1803; some evidence indicates he may have joined at Maysville, Kentucky.[13] He was merely an army private with the expedition of discovery; he got into trouble and was tried for his misbehavior on Thursday, April 29, 1803, along with privates Shields and Frasure. The next day he is recorded as having "asked the forgiveness etc. etc. and promised to do better in the future. . . ."[14] Gradually, his abilities came to the fore, and his biographers proudly point to occasions when their hero was given responsible and dangerous assignments. By the time the expedition was approaching the Mandan villages on the return trip, and Colter, drawn to the northwest country by some magnetic influence, had requested his discharge, the two leaders were willing to grant it. They had met two American trappers, Joseph Dixon and Forest Hancock, who had made an attractive offer to Colter to return west with them. "As we were disposed to be of service to anyone of our party who had performed their duty as well as Colter had done, we agreed to allow him the privilage provided no one of the party would ask or expect a Similar permission . . . ," Clark noted in his journal, August 15, 1806, writing the following day that they had "Settled and discharged Colter," and noting the next day that he and the two trappers had departed upstream.[15]

Thus did John Colter begin his four years in the Rockies. He may have wintered with his two companions where the Clarks Fork emerges from the Absarokas; he may have explored the Sunlight Basin, east of the park; in any event, he set out for home in the spring of 1807.[16] When he reached the Platte he met Manuel Lisa's trapping and trading party and was persuaded to return upstream with them. Another three years went by, and in 1810 John Colter finally reappeared in Missouri, there to give information to his old commander, William Clark, who was making a map of the north-west country. He married, settled down, and died of jaundice at an early age.

It is within this four year span, 1806–10, that Colter may or may not have witnessed Yellowstone's thermal phenomena. He certainly ranged from Lisa's Fort (Fort Manuel), at the junction of the Bighorn with the Yellowstone, to the Three Forks of the Missouri, west and just slightly south, 170–200 miles away; southwest into the Crow country, possibly 200 miles from Fort Manuel; west from the Crow country possibly as far as Teton Basin, 100–150 miles; and north again to the Three Forks, another 175–200 miles. These routes form a rough triangle, Fort Manuel southwest to the Teton Basin (known then as Pierre's Hole), due north to the Three Forks, due east (and a little north) back to Fort Manuel again. The Yellowstone Park would lie in the narrowing lower third of this triangle.

Although much has been written about John Colter, almost all we know in any detail comes from a single source: Thomas James's narration in his *Three Years Among the Indians and the Mexicans*. Here is the story of the battle between the Flatheads and Crows, who were with Colter, and the Blackfeet; here also is the story of Colter's terrible run for his life.[17] But in none of these original sources is there any mention of "Colter's Hell," or of hot springs, or of any unusual thermal phenomena.

Yet when the Biddle edition of the Lewis and Clark journals was published in 1814, there, lo and behold, was a map which has intrigued and bothered historians to this day. It has a dotted line marked "Colter's Route" leading southwest from Pryor's Fork to the Stinkingwater (now Shoshone), then on southwest, looping north and past "Lake Biddle" and "Lake Eustis" and back down east to Pryor's Fork again! There are no arrows to indicate which way Colter followed this route, so that we cannot tell for certain whether he was going north or south, east or west, on a journey to or from the mountains.[18]

What is known is that in making this map Clark received help from George Drouillard (one of the members of the expedition), from some of the returned Astorians, and probably from John Colter himself. Clark had never seen the land in question, and his interviews did not establish accuracy for the western half of the map, though the eastern half is fairly correct. Other than indicating that he knew there were lakes somewhere there, the placing of Lakes Eustis and Biddle was based upon knowledge little more reliable than that of a blindfolded child pinning the tail on the donkey. We will have more to say about this map.

The term "Colter's Hell" did not in fact appear in print until Washington Irving in 1835 published *The Rocky Mountains,* later called *The Adventures of Captain Bonneville.* In a paragraph describing the Crow Indian country and a "Burning Mountain" there, Irving went on to say:

> A volcanic tract of similar character is found on Stinking River, one of the tributaries of the Bighorn, which takes its unhappy name from the odor derived from sulphurous springs and streams. This last mentioned place was first discovered by Colter, a hunter belonging to Lewis and Clark's exploring party, who came upon it in the course of his lonely wanderings, and gave such an account of its gloomy terrors, its hidden fires, smoking pits, noxious streams, and the all-prevading "smell of brimstone," that it received, and has ever since retained among trappers, the name of "Colter's Hell!"[19]

Colter could have seen, and undoubtedly did see, the springs along the Shoshone River just outside Cody, Wyoming. The Clark map has "Colter's route" along the Stinkingwater, and nothing at all is said or implied about any other springs or geysers, mud pots or volcanoes.

But Hiram Martin Chittenden, in his *Yellowstone National Park* (1895), took Colter into the Yellowstone Park, and there, owing to man's fondness for myths and legends, Colter has remained ever since. Although there is substantial proof that he saw the springs along the Stinkingwater, there is no proof that he saw the Yellowstone area. Speaking historically it cannot be said absolutely that Yellowstone was "Colter's Hell."

Is there room for speculation? Could Colter have possibly seen Yellowstone?

Yes. In spite of the geographical errors in the Clark map, one could interpret Colter's route as taking him ultimately north to the Yellowstone Lake, down the west banks of the river either to the

ford at the Mud Volcano (the Nez Perces' ford), or to the one below
Tower Falls, out into the Lamar Valley, and via an Indian path
that later became a part of the Bannock Trail, down the Clarks
Fork and back onto the high plains. Crow Indians could have told
Colter of this route, he could have said, "show me," and they could
have guided him on a primitive package tour. It could have been
as simple as that, and if he did get into the Yellowstone, that was
probably how it came about.

Such a theory is further confirmed by the knowledge that there
was a vast parkland known as the Buffalo Pasture in the mountains
south of the Stinkingwater River. Here the Shoshone drove the
bison and then kept them there as food on the hoof until needed.
The Indians would have been present in the Stinkingwater area,
then, and from contact with them Colter could easily have obtained
guides to take him into the Yellowstone country.[20]

Merrill D. Beale offers an intriguing argument for Colter's trek
through the park: he interprets a mysterious mountain range that
appears on the Clark map as, instead, the shoreline of the South
Arm of the Yellowstone Lake. If Colter traveled into Yellowstone
as Professor Beale thinks, then the South Arm and the Thumb would
have been all the trapper ever saw of the lake.

In actual fact, this replacing of a mountain range with the
shoreline does create an outline similar to that of the South Arm,
but it also forces the professor into wide-ranging conjectures concerning the motivations of William Clark and his cartographer, Samuel
Lewis, for disguising as a mountain range the lake they had been
informed was really there. A common supposition is that if they had
shown it, they would not have been believed, and they desperately
wanted the world to believe them. But even in 1814, educated people
knew of the geysers of Iceland and volcanic phenomena all over the
world, and as we have seen, the rumors of volcanic disturbances far
up the Missouri were wafted around the United States as early as
1805. Thus, to show a great high-altitude lake and volcanic phenomena on the map of the virtually unknown northwest would hardly
have resulted in ridicule. Yet Professor Beale argues that it was this
fear that prompted the tampering with the map.[21]

Unless new material is discovered no one will ever have an
answer to this riddle. But, once again, let it be emphasized that there
is no historical proof that Colter was ever inside the park.

From John Colter's return in 1810 until 1826 there were trail blazers on all sides of the Yellowstone — trappers and traders such as Andrew Henry and his men, who abandoned their fort at the mouth of the Bighorn to go to the Henrys Fork of the Snake River. There were the Astorians, sent out in 1811 by the fur trader John Jacob Astor to help establish Astoria at the mouth of the Columbia. The overland party, led by Wilson Price Hunt, traversed present-day South Dakota, Wyoming, the Rockies, and finally arrived at the half-completed post in early 1812. There were Canadian trappers in the employ of the North West Company, which engaged in a vicious trade war with the Hudson's Bay Company until the two merged in 1821. Someone, not identified, carved "J.O.R. Aug. 29, 1819" on a tree above the upper falls of the Yellowstone. The possibility is strong that some of these wanderers traversed the park area, but the absolute proof is missing.[22]

The first individual to have reached the park and left evidence to prove it was a trapper named Daniel T. Potts. He was a member of the 1822 Ashley–Henry fur-trading expedition from St. Louis to the Rockies and, it was hoped, the Columbia, by way of the three forks area of western Montana. Daniel certainly found the West a monstrous lion's den. He nearly starved, and he tells of men eating the singed, roasted hides of dogs; he was shot through both knees with a wiping rod; he was pursued by the Blackfeet and, he says, "narrowly made my escape by hiding in a little bush and they came [so] close that I could see the very whites of their eyes which was within five yards." He froze his feet and lost "two toes entire and two others in part." He adds that "a man in this Country is not safe neither day nor night, and hardly ever expect to get back."[23]

Daniel stood up to the lion's den, however, and three years later was writing from Sweet Lake (Bear Lake in northern Utah). He tells of crossing the Tetons into Jackson's Hole and veering north up a river (the Snake) "to its source which separates the water of the Atlantic from the Pacific." He describes the Yellowstone Lake as "a fresh water lake . . . which is about one hundred by fourty Miles in diameter and clear as Crystal on the South borders of this Lake is a number of hot and boiling springs some of waters and others of most beautiful fine clay and resembles that of a mushpot and threw its particles to the immense height of from twenty to thirty feet. . . . " The thermal areas he describes are those at the

West Thumb, and it would seem that those phenomena were much more active 150 years ago than they are today.[24]

One source says that a free trapper named Baptiste Ducharne worked the headwaters of the Snake and Yellowstone in the fall of 1824, going down the Firehole to the Madison and thence west to the prairie. In 1826 he is supposed to have returned to the area, taking nearly the same route.[25]

Another wanderer who almost certainly traversed portions of the park was Joseph L. Meek, a Virginia-born adventurer. In 1829 he enlisted with William Sublette's expedition, worked up into the area west of the park, then northeast over the Madison Range to the Yellowstone. There, somewhere between the places that are now Gardiner and Livingston, the party was attacked by Blackfeet. Nineteen-year-old Joseph was separated from his companions, and his best chance to save himself, he judged, was to make for the Wind River, far to the southeast in Crow Country. Here a winter encampment of mountain men had been scheduled.

His narration of the trip invites speculation. He crossed the Yellowstone and headed southeast. On the fifth morning of his journey, "he ascended a low mountain in the neighborhood of his camp — and behold! The whole country beyond was smoking with the vapor from boiling springs, and burning with gases, issuing from small craters, each of which was emitting a sharp, whistling sound. . . . The morning being clear, with a sharp frost, he thought himself reminded of the city of Pittsburgh. . . . " Joe found the warmth of the place most delightful, after the freezing cold of the mountains, and he remarked to himself that "if it war hell, it war a more agreeable climate then he had been in for some time." A little later he stumbled upon two of his companions, and they forged through to the Bighorn, passing the springs on the Stinkingwater (Colter's Hell) on the way.[26]

Again, a study of the literature on the fur trade and the mountain men demands an educated conclusion that the Yellowstone region was traversed in the period 1825–40 by a number of individuals or even parties, but the natural reticence of these men, their general illiteracy, and the absence of chroniclers to collect their stories have combined to deny us the factual accounts we need.

There is sufficient evidence to list one Johnson Gardner as having been in the park area in 1831–32, and the halcyon Gardner's

Hole, northwest of Swan Lake Flats, and the Gardner River derive their names from him.[27]

When did Jim Bridger first see the geysers? His most respected biographer (although this biography of "Old Gabe" is by now somewhat outdated) mentions the possibility that Bridger came into the park area from Jackson's Hole over Two Ocean Pass in 1825 but adds that "the fabric of fact ravels out into a thread of uncertain strength without the support of corroboration." Joe Meek's first biographer places Bridger in the park in 1831. It is, in sum, quite evident that Old Gabe was there several times before 1840.[28]

Finally, two literate mountain men saw Yellowstone and lived to tell about it: their descriptions leave no doubt of their veracity. The first of these men was Warren Angus Ferris, an employee of the American Fur Company, a New Yorker who died a Texan, and a man endowed with a sufficient sense of history to keep a diary during those years of his western wanderings, 1830–35.[29]

Ferris first mentions a brigade leader named Manuel Álvarez, who, with about forty men, worked up Henrys Fork, over to the Yellowstone, and down to the Green, in the spring and summer of 1833. Ferris's narration implies that the Álvarez men had seen the Yellowstone wonders "on the source of the Madison" that very spring, that he had talked with them and "the accounts they gave, were so very astonishing, that I determined to examine them myself, before recording their description, though I had the united testimony of more than twenty men on the subject."[30]

He got his chance in the middle of May of the following year, when he was about 40 miles due west of the Madison headwaters. With two Pend d'Oreilles, he set out on horseback and camped for the night in what must have been the Upper Geyser Basin. "When I arose in the morning," he wrote, "clouds of vapor seemed like a dense fog to overhang the springs, from which frequent reports or explosions of different loudness, constantly assailed our ears. . . . From the surface of a rocky plain or table, burst forth columns of water, of various dimensions, projected high in the air. . . . The largest of these wonderful fountains, projects a column of boiling water several feet in diameter, to the height of more than one hundred and fifty feet. . . . These wonderful productions of nature, are situated near the centre of a small valley, surrounded by pine-covered hills, through which a small fork of the Madison flows."[31]

Ferris also left a map showing the Yellowstone Lake, the "Burnt Hole" and "Volcanoes," the Madison and Gallatin rivers, and other features that demonstrated his thorough knowledge of the region. In fact, if exact latitude and longitude are ignored (since Ferris possessed no cartographic instruments), the proportions of this map are remarkable. He drew it in 1836, when he had returned from the Rockies and was still a young man of twenty-six years.[32]

Another literate trapper was the Maine-born Yankee, Osborne Russell, who spent nine years (1834–43) in the Rockies. He enlisted with Nathaniel Wyeth's Columbia Fishing and Trading Company at Independence, Missouri, on April 4, 1834. He was not quite twenty years old at the time, but already he had been to sea and had worked for a fur company in Wisconsin and Minnesota. Nevertheless he still had much to learn about a trapper's life on the plains and in the Rockies — such as how to shoot a buffalo, and never to plunge into a thicket after a wounded grizzly bear.[33]

Russell first saw Yellowstone during the "Fall Hunt" out from Fort Hall in 1835 — although the months were actually July and August. "It was the intention of our leader to proceed to Yellow Stone Lake and hunt the country which lay in the vicinity of our route," the young man wrote in his journal. One man was drowned in crossing the Snake River; the party was attacked by Blackfeet at Pierre's Hole, and their progress was slowed by the pain of a wounded man, "balls in 3 places in the right and one in the left leg below the knee. . . . " They crossed Teton Pass into Jackson's Hole, forded the Snake again, and plunged into the maze of mountains southeast of the park. There they floundered for nearly two weeks, at one time on the Stinkingwater, at other times high in the Absarokas where "thousands of mountain Sheep were scattered up and down feeding on the short grass which grew among the cliffs and crevices: some so high that it required a telescope to see them." Finally, trekking in a northwesterly direction, they "encamped in a small prairie about a mile in circumference" through which flowed a north-running stream "which all agreed in believing to be a branch of the Yellow Stone." Fifteen miles on down they "came to a beautiful valley about 8 Mls. long and 3 or 4 wide surrounded by dark and lofty mountains" — the Lamar Valley of Yellowstone National Park.

There, in a paradise of pine and aspen, fresh water and succulent grasses, the trappers met some Indians: '6 men 7 women and 8 or

10 children who were the only inhabitants of this secluded spot."
These were the Sheep Eaters, already mentioned above.

These simple people of the mountains drew the trappers a map
on a white elk-skin with a piece of charcoal. They explained that the
outlet of the Yellowstone Lake was a day's travel to the southwest
and that the stream along which they were encamped joined the
Yellowstone a half-day's travel down it in a westerly direction. "The
river," one of the Indians further explained, "then ran a long distance
thro a tremendous cut in the mountain in the same direction and
emerged into a large plain the extent of which was beyond his geographical knowledge or conception."

Russell found the pastoral Lamar Valley a paradise. "We
stopped at this place and for my own part I almost wished I could
spend the remainder of my days in a place like this where happiness
and contentment seemed to reign in a wild romantic splendor surrounded by majestic battlements which seemed to support the heavens
and shut out all hostile intruders," he wrote. This is still a perfect
description of the valley in summertime.

On August 2 they forded the Yellowstone at the well-known
Indian crossing due east of Tower Falls, headed south, and after
about three miles emerged into high, open country. They headed
west, traveled that direction all the next day, and on the night of
August 3 were encamped in Gardner's Hole.[34]

By August 31, Russell's party had passed over into the Gallatin
River Valley and, after considerable wandering in search of beaver,
had come into the upper Madison area. Here they found a valley
"surrounded by low spurs of pine-covered mountains, mountains
which are the sources of [a] great number of streams which by
uniting in this valley form the Madison fork." In place of Hebgen
Lake and Dam, visualize a grassy valley laced with streams coming
from the pine-covered mountains. Then have a fire destroy the grass
and the pines. Such a scene led trappers to name that part of the
Madison the "Burnt Hole." It is several miles west of the park
boundary, and although not many miles removed from the thermal
phenomena along the Firehole River to the east, it should not be
confused with them.

Russell's first trip through Yellowstone thus came to an end.
He had not seen the thermal regions nor does he mention the Grand
Canyon of the Yellowstone, but he had traversed much of the country,

crossing from west to east below the southern boundaries, scrambling northward around the Absarokas and finally west down into the Lamar Valley, then west to the Yellowstone, across it at the ford below Tower Falls, then west to Gardner's Hole and beyond, across the Gallatins and into the river valley of the same name, then up the Madison to the Burnt Hole, and then, following harrowing adventures and great hardships, to Fort Hall.[35]

When July 1836 approached and the time came for the next Fall Hunt, Russell was at the annual trappers' rendezvous at Horse Creek, a tributary of the Green. With a party of about fifteen in the employ of Jim Bridger, Russell headed for the Yellowstone Lake, there to await the arrival of Old Gabe and the remainder of the trapper brigade, probably about forty-five men. They worked up the east shore of Jackson Lake and continued northward when, Russell noted in his journal, "we came to a smooth prairie about 2 Mls long and half a Ml. wide lying east and west surrounded by pines. On the South side about midway of the prarie stands a high snowy peak from whence issues a Stream of water which after entering the plain it divides equally one half running West and the other East thus bidding adieu to each other one bound for the Pacific and the other for the Atlantic ocean." "Here," he adds, "a trout of 12 inches in length may cross the mountains in safety." He was at famed Two Ocean Pass.[36]

From there they went to the swampy "thorofare" of the Upper Yellowstone and followed it to the inlet of the lake; when Bridger came up the whole brigade moved down the east shore of the lake to the outlet, now Fishing Bridge. Near where they camped there were thermal phenomena, but Russell is remarkably unemotional in his description: "Near where we encamped were several hot springs which boil perpetually." He also mentions a loud steam vent. The next day as they worked eastward they followed an elk trail over a thermal area where "the treading of our horses sounded like travelling on a plank platform covering an immense cavity in the earth whilst the hot water and steam were spouting and hissing around us in all directions." That night was silent as the men bedded down, "except for the occasional howling of the solitary wolf on the neighboring mountain whose senses are attracted by the flavors of roasted meat but fearing to approach nearer he sits upon a rock and bewails his calamites in piteous moans which are reechoed among the mountains."

The next day's march took them to the Secluded Valley (Russell's name for the Lamar River region) where they traded with the Sheep Eaters. The young New Englander never forgot the beauty of the place. "There is something in the wild romantic scenery of this valley which I cannot nor will I, attempt to describe but the impressions made upon my mind while gazing from a high eminence on the surrounding landscape one evening as the sun was gently gliding behind the western mountain and casting its gigantic shadows across the vale were such as time can never efface from my memory." From there they progressed to the Gardner River and Gardner's Hole, thence east a short distance to the Yellowstone and down it, and thus once again out of the park area, having traversed it entirely from south to north.

Russell also traveled in the Yellowstone area in 1837 and 1838. He wandered to the remotest corners of the park, and his journal is full of explicit descriptions of the many wonders. Then, on June 26, 1839, Russell left with a small party for his last hunt in the Yellowstone region. On July 4 they were encamped at Jackson Lake. "I caught about 20 very fine salmon trout which together with fat mutton buffalo beef and coffee and the manner in which it was served up constituted a dinner that out [sic] to be considered independent by Britons," he recorded. Three days later, working north of Jackson Lake, they came to the junction of the Lewis and Snake rivers, just above and slightly east of the present South Entrance into the park. They took the west (Lewis) fork and became reacquainted with that pesky Yellowstone phenomenon, the deadened lodgepole pine forest — "in many places so much fallen timber that we frequently had to make circles of a quarter of a mile to gain a few rods ahead . . . " — but by evening they had reached Lewis Lake; the next day they followed the shoreline to the inlet on the west side "and came to another Lake about the same size" — Shoshone Lake (actually larger than Lewis Lake). The next day, following the shoreline, they came to the Shoshone Geyser Basin northwest of the lake, where they "found about 50 springs of boiling hot water." They tarried there several hours and were shown an "hour Spring" which erupted once an hour and was studied by one of Russell's comrades who had been through there the year before. Though no longer identifiable, the spring certainly could have existed. But their journey continued after a few hours, north over a mountain for a distance of about seven miles, which brought them to the Upper Geyser Basin along the Firehole River.

In this area they set their beaver traps and remained four days. From Russell's descriptions of the snow-white geyser cones among the deep green pines, it is apparent that time and too many men have made of the geyser basins a mutilated and broken-down remnant of their original splendor. "Some of these spiral cones are 20 ft. in diameter at the base and not more than 12 inches at the top, the whole being covered with small irregular semicircular ridges about the size of a mans finger having the appearance of carving in bass relief formed I suppose by the waters running over it for ages unknown . . . , " he wrote. "Standing upon an eminence and superficially viewing these natural monuments one is half inclined to believe himself in the neighborhood of the ruins of some Ancients City whose temples had been constructed of the whitest marble." Black-tailed deer grazed in the area, apparently accustomed to the steam and noise: "a buck," Russell wrote, "may be found carelessly sleeping where the noise will exceed that of 3 or 4 engines in operation."

Beauty did not prevent a practical man from using the lower cones for cooking, however, "for here his kettle is always ready and boiling his meat being suspended in the water by a string is soon prepared for his meal without further trouble."

By July 15 they were passing down the Firehole and gaping in admiration at the Grand Prismatic Spring:

> At length we came to a boiling Lake about 300 ft. in diameter forming nearly a complete circle as we approached on the South side The tsream [*sic*] which arose from it was of three distinct Colors from the west side for one third the diameter it was white, in the middle it was pale red, and the remaining third on the east light sky blue Whether it was something peculiar in the state of the atmosphere the day being cloudy or whether it was some Chemical properties contained in the water which produced this phenomenon I am unable to say and shall leave the explanation to some scientific tourist who may have the Curiosity to visit this place at some future period — The

water was of deep indigo blue boiling like an imense cauldron running over the white rock which had formed [round] edges to the height of 4 or 5 feet from the surface of the earth sloping gradually 60 or 70 feet.

From here they continued to the Madison Junction where the Firehole and Gibbon unite, which, he said, with the uncanny accuracy of the woodsman, "runs in a NW direction about 40 Mls before reaching the Burnt hole." They then traveled up the Gibbon, over a spur of mountains and down into the Hayden Valley, bounded on the east by the river, which they followed up to the outlet of Yellowstone Lake. There they set their traps for beaver. But they did not tarry there for long. Of course Russell had to go over into his favorite "Secluded Valley"; then they worked Clarks Fork, then trudged northwest and worked Hellroaring Creek and, against his advice, some of the men went out onto the plains to get buffalo.

When the buffalo hunters returned after a successful hunt they told of seeing "where a village of 3 or 400 lodges of Blackfeet had left the Yellowstone in a NW direction but 3 or 4 days previous." But they saw no Indians as they worked up to Gardner's Hole and then to Hayden Valley. By August 27 they had set their traps along Pelican Creek, which runs into Yellowstone Lake near the outlet on the northeast side, just north of where the present highway east from Fishing Bridge crosses it.

Oh, for the life of a trapper! On August 28, after servicing his traps, Russell returned to camp for an hour or two, shouldered his rifle, sauntered through the groves of pines, took a leisurely bath in the lake, and returned to camp about four o'clock. Two of his comrades went elk hunting, the remaining one lay asleep, and Russell went off thirty or forty feet to a bale of dried meat spread in the sun. "Here," he wrote, "I pulled off my powder horn and bullet pouch laid them on a log drew my butcher knife and began to cut." The camp was on a bend of land about twenty feet above the stream bottom, which he described as being about a quarter of a mile wide. They were on the southeast side, on the bench, with thick pines and fallen timber at their backs and, he wrote:

After eating a few [minutes] I arose and kindled a fire filled my tobacco pipe and sat down to smoke My comrade whose name was White was still sleeping. Presently I cast my eyes

towards the horses which were feeding in the Valley and discovered the heads of some Indians who were gliding round under the bench within 30 steps of me I jumped to my rifle and
aroused White and looking towards my powder horn and bullet
pouch it was already in the hands of an Indian and we were
completely surrounded We cocked our rifles and started thro.
the ranks into the woods which seemed to be completely filled
with Blackfeet who rent the air with their horrid yells. on presenting our rifles they opened a space about 20 ft. wide thro.
which we plunged about the fourth jump an arrow struck
White on the right hip joint I hastily told him to pull it out
and [as] I spoke another arrow struck me in the same place but
they did not retard our progress At length another arrow striking
thro. my right leg above the knee benumbed the flesh so that I
fell with my breast accross a log. The Indian who shot me was
within 8 ft and made a Spring towards me with his uplifted
battle axe: I made a leap and avoided the blow and kept
hopping from log to log thro. a shower of arrows which flew
around us like hail, lodging in the pines and logs. . . .

Indians passed within twenty or thirty paces of the two besieged
and wounded men, who had determined to shoot at the first Indians
that saw them, and then die like men. But miraculously, the savages
did not discover them, and passed on. The trappers limped to the
lake and quenched their thirst, which was maddening from the
exercise, terror, and loss of blood. "Oh dear we shall die here, we
shall never get out of these mountains," whimpered White, but Russell's reply shows what kind of man he was: "Well said I if you
presist in thinking so you will die but I can crawl from this place
upon my hands and one knee and Kill 2 or 3 Elk and make a shelter
of the skins dry the meat until we get able to travel."

The determined mountaineer bolstered the spirits of his younger
companion, and they proceeded to make themselves as comfortable
as possible, under the circumstances. White fetched a couple of
sticks for crutches, and the next morning, after helping Russell get
up, they hobbled to a grove of pines where they had to hide from
the reappearance of the Indians. Then they made their way to the
remains of their camp, which had been totally destroyed, found one
more of their companions (so that now just one, Elbridge, was miss-

ing), spent another miserable night by the lake, and then made a raft of dry timbers, crossed the outlet, and in a nearby pine grove passed another day. Here Russell continued to nurse his wounds methodically, making a salve of beaver oil and castoreum (a grainy substance from beaver sex-glands) which "drew out the swelling in a great measure." When they killed a doe elk they cut the meat slices thin and smoked them over the fire, then packed them into bundles to carry on their backs. They reached Heart Lake, noted the geyser basin there, and headed south, eventually reaching the junction of the Lewis and Snake rivers via the Snake. As Russell pointed out, they had worked up the Lewis and had been at the forks on July 9 "in good health and spirits," in sad contrast to their "weary limbs and sorrowful countenances" now (August 31). From here they advanced south to Jackson Lake, over the mountains to the junction of Henrys Fork with Falls River; from there they hobbled the 90 miles southwest to Fort Hall. After ten days of nursing his wounds, Russell was sufficiently recovered to be out setting traps for beaver again — a testament to the man's physical fitness.[37]

Thus ended Osborne Russell's trips through Yellowstone. Three years after his last escapade, he abandoned trapping and accompanied a wagon train to Oregon. In the fall of 1842 he settled at Willamette Falls, the present site of Oregon City. There he lost his right eye in an explosion, but in spite of this accident he went on to become a lawyer, a judge, and a prominent politician. At one time, after moving to California, he held court for the vigilantes in Placerville. He died in that town on August 26, 1892, and is buried in an unmarked grave. He never married.[38]

If there was one man who was an authority on the Yellowstone country prior to 1870, it was not Jim Bridger or John Colter, but this quiet Yankee, Osborne Russell, whose trapping expeditions developed into annual journeys that led him eventually to see far more of the park than is covered by all but the most ambitious rangers even today. From Soda Creek up by the Beartooth Plateau, southwest to the Cascade Corner; from Sylvan Pass to Gardner's Hole and west over the Gallatins; from the Hoodoo Basin, where the Lamar River originates, to Yellowstone Lake and the Gibbon and Firehole rivers; and from the Yellowstone River, above the North Entrance, south to the Snake running southward out of the park, this man knew Yellowstone — and he loved it.

There is some evidence that in the year 1838 (but possibly in 1844), forty trappers started north up the Snake and traveled past Jackson Lake, over the divide to the headwaters of the upper Yellowstone, and down to Yellowstone Lake. On a small prairie at the north end they built a defensive corral and were besieged there for two days by Piegans (Blackfeet) before the Indians gave up and left. Five of the trappers were killed and a number wounded, and the Indians too certainly suffered a number of casualties. The trappers' brigade then trekked west to the Madison and on out of the region. During their sojourn they were said to have seen the mud geysers, the "Sulphur Mountain" which was Mammoth Hot Springs, and the geysers along the Firehole River.[39]

The last trappers' rendezvous was held along Horse Creek in 1840; the demise of the beaver hat, which went out of style, along with the near extermination of the beaver, brought the brief but romantic era of the trappers to an end. If they had continued in their calling, they would have been forced to adjust to changing times and changing demands, and in fact the trade did continue to the Civil War. But that glorious era when free whites trapped prime beaver — while in turn being stalked by Blackfeet, Bannocks, Crows, or even Shoshone — in a vast land with no government or authority but the rifle, was to end by about 1840. The great migrations to Oregon and California were already beginning, the Indian was losing ground, and the long arm of the United States — represented by army men, territorial officials, and Indian agents — was making its appearance. By 1840, the golden age of the trapper was over.[40]

How many white men had seen the geysers, the lake, the mud pots, the Grand Canyon of the Yellowstone, or Mammoth Hot Springs by 1840? There is really no way of knowing. We do not have the names of all the American trappers, let alone the French Canadian, Iroquois, and half-breed packers and camp men who accompanied them. Furthermore, whether they were free trappers or employees of the companies, these people got lost, strayed, went their own ways alone or with a comrade or two. Some men totally unknown to posterity must have been through Yellowstone.

It is a little easier to state who did *not* get to Yellowstone. The Astorians under Wilson Price Hunt did not; Father de Smet, though he knew of the Yellowstone, never saw it; neither did Captain Bonneville. Jim Bridger saw it, of course, but the year of his first penetration into the wonderland is a matter of speculation.

So too, it is impossible to make more than an educated guess about the years from 1840 to 1860. However, with the decline of the fur trade, probably fewer white men visited Yellowstone than in the two decades preceding 1840. Old Bill Williams, who is said to have heard of the geysers in campfire sessions in which William T. Hamilton was present, is credited by George Frederick Ruxton with having been there.[41]

One of Ruxton's St. Louis "Pilgrims," young William Clark Kennerly, states in his memoirs, published more than a century after the event, that the party had camped in "the region now known as Yellowstone National Park," and he vaguely described some of the phenomena, including a geyser with a ten-minute cycle which the young man tried unsuccessfully to suppress. It is difficult to believe his story; whatever he saw, it was not Yellowstone.[42]

Kennerly's statements constitute the slight evidence that the Scotch sportsman Sir William Drummond Stewart camped in the geyser regions in 1843. However, neither of Stewart's books of fiction — *Altowon: or Incidents of Life and Adventure in the Rocky Mountains,* and *Edward Warren* — contain anything on the thermal phenomena. Yet they do speak of the Snake River, the Tetons, and Jackson's Hole. It would seem that a romantically inclined fictioneer like Stewart would have written about Yellowstone if he had seen it.[43]

The decade of the 1850s is significant in Yellowstone history as a period of gradual dispersal of knowledge about the region. In a general way, the information that was sifting out was correct. It whetted the curiosity of — and may have entered into the plans for — the Raynolds expedition at the end of the decade. This was the first government party to plan consciously to enter the area and determine what was really there.

It was in this later period that Jim Bridger — who remained in the high country as trader, trapper, and guide after most of the other mountain men had died or gone to more civilized places — emerged as an authority on the Yellowstone. He appears to have been there at least twice after the demise of the fur trade, once in 1846 and again in 1850.[44]

Old Gabe was certainly the greatest early disseminator of information about Yellowstone. Illiterate though he was, he must have been an intelligent old cuss, and certainly he was a wanderer for most of his days. "His graphic sketches are delightful romances," Captain Gunnison wrote. "With a buffalo-skin and piece of charcoal, he will map out any portion of this immense region, and delineate mountains, streams, and circular valleys called 'holes,' with wonderful accuracy. . . . He gives a picture, most romantic and enticing, of the head-waters of the Yellow Stone." Bridger told of a lake 60 miles long, of the sloping plain to the west, the hollow sound as the horses trod the ground, geysers 70 feet high, waterfalls, and "Great Springs, so hot that meat is readily cooked in them, and as they descend on the successive terraces, afford at length delightful baths."[45]

In 1856 Colonel R. T. Van Horn, the editor of the *Kansas City Journal,* interviewed Old Gabe, who told him all about the place "where hell bubbled up," but because the colonel had been warned of Bridger's Munchausen ways, he decided not to print the information.[46] Meanwhile a vigorous missionary-explorer, the Jesuit Father Pierre Jean de Smet, listened to Bridger and in a letter dated "St. Louis, January 18, 1852," with uncanny geographical perception, placed this "extraordinary spot . . . in the very heart of the Rocky Mountains between the forty-third and forty-fifth degrees of latitude and 109th and 111th degrees longitude, that is, between the sources of the Madison and Yellowstone" — a very close approximation of the park's actual boundaries save in the south where, if de Smet's estimate had been followed, the Tetons would be a part of the park today. Actually the missionary's descriptions of the Yellowstone country clearly reveal that he had never been there, for he appears to envision a "volcanic pile," a great mountain rather than the plateau that is the reality. He does mention a "mountain of sulphur" near Gardner's River, and attributes this information to "Captain Bridger, who is familiar with every one of these mountains, having passed thirty years of his life near them."[47]

Father de Smet, quite probably with Bridger's crude cartographic help, drew many maps, of which five are significant for their details in the area of Yellowstone. The fourth one — the so-called Bridger map — especially "depicts that remarkable twisted region of the Rocky Mountains where the headwaters of the Yellowstone, the Wind, the Green, the Snake, and the Missouri Rivers unwind before rolling to their respective oceans." Although there are distortions, the Yellowstone region begins to take form on this map, and the

1. Soda Butte Creek. *National Park Service Photo.*

2. Black Sand Basin. *Photo courtesy Los Angeles County Museum of Natural History.*

3. Crater of Giant Geyser. *Photo courtesy Los Angeles County Museum of Natural History.*

4. Monad in Hayden Valley. *National Park Service Photo.*

5. Seismic geyser developed from crack caused by Hebgen earthquake, 1959. *U.S. Geological Survey Photo.*

J. R. Stacy

6. Air view of Madison Canyon slide from over Earthquake Lake. *U.S. Geological Survey Photo.*

7. Mammoth Hot Springs. *Photo courtesy Los Angeles County Museum of Natural History.*

David Condon

8. Beaver. *National Park Service Photo.*

9. Grizzly bear. *National Park Service Photo.*

William S. Keller

10. Bighorn sheep.
National Park Service Photo.

11. Pronghorn antelope. *National Park Service Photo.*

William S. Keller

12. Wapiti.
National Park Service Photo.

Cecil W. Stoughton

13. Bison. *National Park Service Photo.*

William S. Keller

14. Young cormorants on nest, Molly Islands, in Southeast Arm of Yellowstone Lake. *National Park Service Photo.*

15. Swans at nesting site, Floating Island Lake. *National Park Service Photo.*

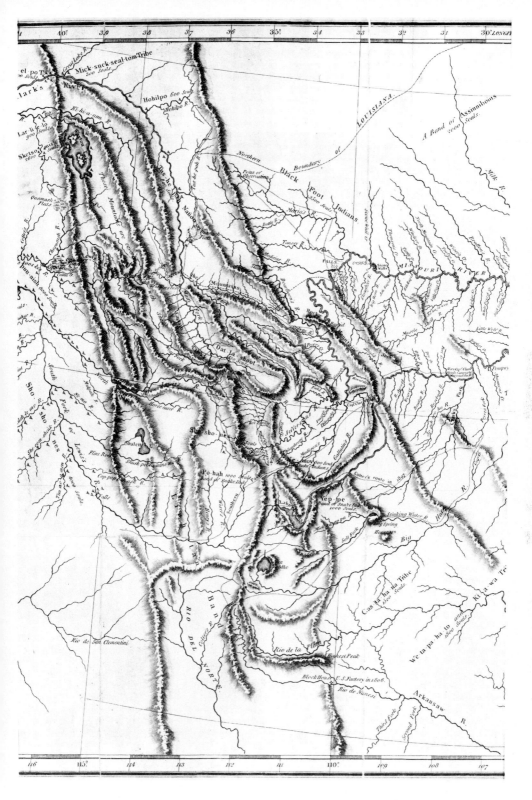

16. Clark's map, made after the Lewis and Clark expedition, shows Colter's route as well as that of Lewis and Clark. *From the collections of the Geography and Map Division, Library of Congress.*

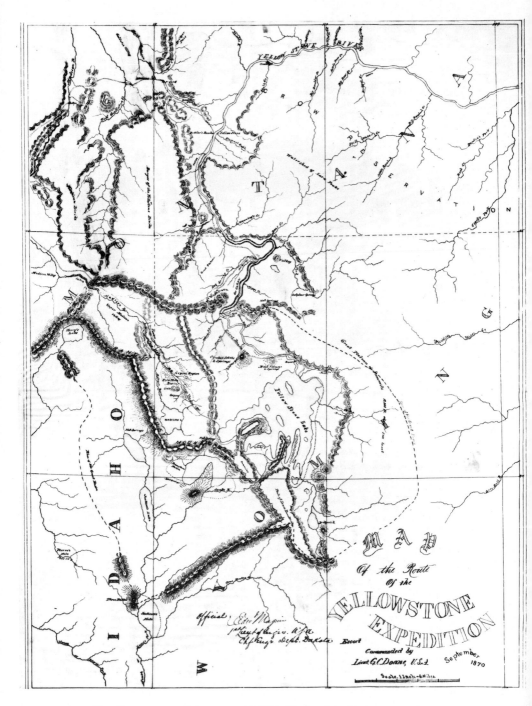

17. Doane expedition map (1870). *National Archives.*

18. Thomas Moran seated at the water's edge of the Second Canyon, 1871. *U.S. Geological Survey Photo.*

19. The *Anna,* the first boat ever launched on Yellowstone Lake, 1871. *U.S. Geological Survey Photo.*

20. Hayden Survey camp on Yellowstone Lake, 1871. *U.S. Geological Survey Photo.*

21. Hayden Survey, Lower Geyser Basin, 1871. Ferdinand V. Hayden is seated, third from left, holding plate. *Bancroft Library.*

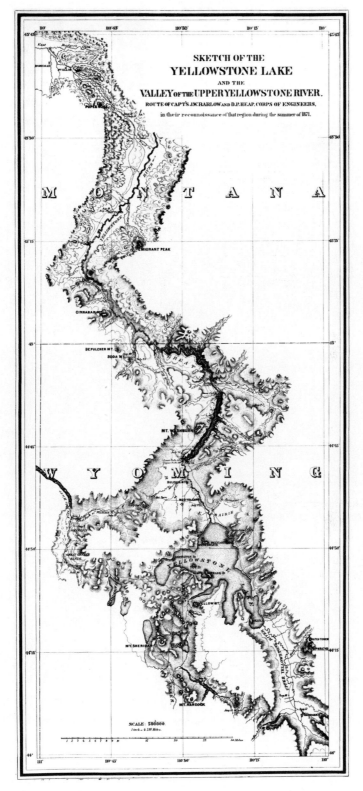

22. Barlow and Heap expedition map of the valley of the Upper Yellowstone and Yellowstone Lake (1871). *National Archives.*

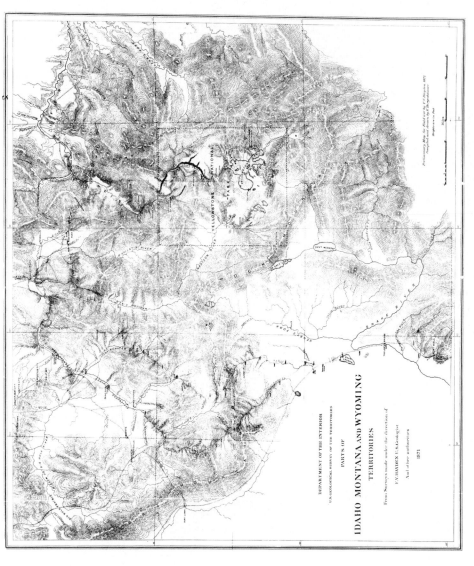

23. Hayden Survey map of Yellowstone area showing the new Yellowstone National Park. *National Archives.*

24.   Hayden Survey, 1872. *Smithsonian Institution.*

25.   Hayden Survey, 1872. Photographer W. H. Jackson is second from right. *Smithsonian Institution.*

26. Crater of Lone Star Geyser, 1883. Geologist Arnold Hague and an assistant are on the summit of the cone, probably lowering a sounding line to measure the depth of geyser pipe. *U.S. Geological Survey Photo.*

knowledge is included on a fifth de Smet map of the western United States, drawn in 1851 or 1852.[48]

Finally, Jim Bridger hired on as guide to an official government expedition which was to explore the headwaters of the Yellowstone and the Missouri and to determine feasible routes across the mountains from the Yellowstone south to South Pass, and from the Bitter Root Valley of western Montana to Fort Laramie, far to the southeast. This territory would embrace the rumored wonderland of the Yellowstone, and if the expedition was successful, it would fill in a gaping hole on the maps of the Northwest.

The reconnaissance was placed under the command of Captain W. F. Raynolds of the Topographical Engineers, whose previous assignment had been in southern Florida; his second-in-command would be Lieutenant H. E. Maynadier. A young geologist would also be along: his name was Ferdinand Vandiveer Hayden. He had been in the northern plains with a previous exploring expedition under the command of Lieutenant Gouverneur K. Warren in 1856, and, his intellectual appetite whetted, had sought this assignment.

Raynolds spent 1859 on the plains and did not get farther west than the Bighorn River. He wintered at Deer Creek, along the Platte, and in the spring of 1860 set out for terra incognita. He sent one party under Lieutenant Maynadier north and then west of the Three Forks of the Missouri, along a route that was similar to the future Bozeman Trail. Raynolds, with Bridger as guide, proposed to head to the source of the Wind River, and from there to cross to the headwaters of the Yellowstone. This river was in turn to be traced out onto the plains to where it bends east, at which point Raynolds would head northwest for the Three Forks, where he would rendezvous again with Maynadier.

Lieutenant Maynadier achieved his mission satisfactorily, but Captain Raynolds, after crossing the divide at Union Pass (named by him), failed in the last days of May — very early in the season to be in that region — to penetrate the snow-covered bastion separating him from the Two Ocean area to the northwest. With a heavy heart he let Bridger guide him along the Gros Ventre, down into Jackson's Hole, over Teton Pass to Pierre's Hole, north over the pass which bears Raynolds's name today, to the Madison, and down that river to the Three Forks.

The Raynolds expedition had circled Yellowstone but had not penetrated it. Captain Raynolds had to forego the exploration of the wonderland, where Old Gabe said there were a stream cold at the top and hot at the bottom, a mountain of glass, geysers, and bubbling springs. Raynolds returned to the States and to the Civil War; his report was not published until 1868.[49]

6

The Prospectors

Between 1800 and 1890 the Great West was transformed from a hunter's barbaric paradise to a settled country. Even by 1840, men felt that the West was becoming a wasteland. They wrote of the beaver, nearly extinct. A few farsighted outdoorsmen knew that the buffalo were less prevalent than they had been; men spoke of the bleached buffalo bones dotting the prairies, of the disappearing signs of once-great Indian encampments. The young Indian galloping on his mount free as the wind over the high plains was becoming just a memory.

Meanwhile the white man came — to California, Nevada, Arizona, Colorado, Oregon — and finally to Montana and Idaho, to Alder Gulch (Virginia City) and Last Chance Gulch (Helena) and more than a thousand other western nooks and crannies where gold might be found.

If the changes of 1800–1860 were traumatic, then the *coup de grâce* took place between 1860 and 1890. There was a West after that — there still is today — but not the West of the buffalo or the free Indian or the free trapper. And Yellowstone, as part of the West, could remain unknown only a little longer.

The transformation of the vast areas surrounding the Upper Yellowstone from an anarchistic no-man's-land, a howling wilderness visited by nomadic Indians and predatory whites, to a sparsely settled, relatively peaceful land of ranches and mines, all took place within less than three decades. The anomaly of the situation was apparent in the territorial newspapers, which often carried alarming stories about Indian depredations, actual or rumored ("Terrible Massacre by Indians in Gallatin Valley!") alongside advertisements for

117

patent farm machinery, miner's equipment for sale at a local hardware store, or patent medicines "good for man or beast."

The search for precious metals was the primary cause of settlement, but not the only one. It should be kept in mind that not only had the hunt for gold created settlements at unlikely places all over the West, but the more prosaic desire for land, and the incentives of agriculture, had brought in thousands of emigrants to the Oregon country, while the persecution of a religious faith had prompted its adherents to settle near the arid Great Salt Lake. Given these facts, it was clear that the country that would one day embrace Wyoming, Montana, and Idaho was not going to remain terra incognita for long. Because humanity is both curious and mercenary, the lands surrounding the upper Yellowstone would be explored and settled.

The exact date and the specific persons involved in the discovery of gold in Montana are conjectural. The enormous expanse of land that California argonauts in the 1850s and 1860s called "the northern mines" or "the northern interior" was developed between 1854 and 1865. It included today's eastern Washington and Oregon, southern British Columbia, all of Idaho, and western Montana. At Colville (in eastern Washington) and along the Salmon River in central Idaho, substantial strikes were made, and the whole vast area was prospected by the ubiquitous gold seekers. The Idaho diggings, opened in 1861–62, were especially important for attracting miners from south, east, and west, and these migrations brought the men who opened the first big placers in Montana.[1]

In getting to the northern mines, many of the prospectors followed a new route. They came across Dakota from Minnesota or took a steamboat up the Missouri to near Fort Benton, where by 1862 Mullan's Road, a military highway named for its builder, had just been completed. This road, leading all the way to Fort Walla Walla in eastern Washington, practically crossed Montana from east to west, and many a traveler was enticed to pan its streams for "color" along the way. Others were mindful of the possibilities for grazing and agriculture, and, recognizing that miners must eat, staked out productive lands rather than pay-dirt claims. It all helped to bring settlement to Montana. Other goldhunters left the Oregon Trail in northeastern Utah and worked northward to the same Mullan Road as it snaked its way across western Montana, giving easy access to the Idaho mines. Some of those who went north chose to prospect the Montana country, especially around Deer Lodge, for new strikes.[2]

And, inevitably, the strikes came: at Alder Gulch, later known as Virginia City, in May 1863; at Last Chance Gulch (Helena), in July 1864; and from time to time through the decade all over the Montana Rockies. There were strikes at Bear Gulch and Crevice Gulch north of the park, and in 1868 at Clarks Fork, northeast of the park boundaries. Thus the area that would become Yellowstone Park was bounded on the west, north, and northeast by gold strikes. The prospectors also searched the Tetons to the south and, as we shall see, they traversed the park itself in pursuit of gold.

It is true that mining is an extractive industry that leaves waste and ugliness in its wake, but at the same time it brings large concentrations of humanity to isolated places. These people must be fed and clothed; they must be protected, they need transportation facilities, and, whether they get it or not, they need religion. Some people drift away from mining but fall in love with the country and settle down, as we have seen, to some other way of making a living. And so, the mining strikes brought other settlers to Montana.

There were the cattlemen, who discovered that their stock could feed as well in the lush valleys of western Montana as they could hundreds of miles farther south. Farmers settled in the fertile Gallatin Valley. Control of the Blackfeet, Flatheads, Crows, and Sioux was aided by the United States Army, which housed its men in about a dozen lonely military posts scattered through the region. Yellowstone was of particular interest to the three to five companies stationed at Fort Ellis, 3 miles east of Bozeman. The fort was established in 1867, five years prior to the creation of the park, to protect the beautiful, fertile Gallatin Valley from the Indians; Bozeman at the time was just three years old. The town and the fort became the principal outfitting bases for excursions to Yellowstone, while the soldiers watched over the Crows, whose vast reservation, established in 1868, was due east of there.[3]

Religion entered into the settlement of the region too. The Jesuits had manifested an interest in the Northwest Indians from the days of Father de Smet, and in the 1860s their determination to convert the Blackfeet brought the Holy Fathers to the Upper Missouri, the Marias, and the Sun rivers.[4]

Because Montana did not constitute a political entity in 1860, we can make no useful estimate of its population at that time. Eastern Montana from 1854 to 1861 was a part of Nebraska Territory, and from 1861 until 1863 it was part of Dakota Territory. Montana west of the Continental Divide was part of Washington Territory in 1860; when Idaho Territory was created in 1863, all of Montana was included. Mining settlement resulted in the drive for a new political status, and on May 26, 1864, the Territory of Montana was formed.[5]

The census of 1870 gave the territory a population of 39,895, of whom 19,457 were Indians. Gallatin County, north of Yellowstone, whose principal town was Bozeman, had a population of 1,578; in Madison County, northwest of Yellowstone, with Virginia City as the largest community, 2,684 people resided.

While Montana displayed the greatest interest toward Yellowstone in the early years and still manifests the most sincere concern of all the states surrounding it, the fact remains that most of Yellowstone Park is within the confines of Wyoming, with very small strips of land in eastern Idaho and southern Montana. Idaho Territory had a population of 20,583 in 1870, of whom 5,631 were Indians, while Wyoming Territory, south and east of the Upper Yellowstone, had 11,518 inhabitants in that year, of whom 2,466 were Indians. Idaho had achieved territorial status in 1863. In 1868 Wyoming was organized as a territory made up of portions of the neighboring territories of Utah, Idaho, and Dakota.[6]

Thus Montana, Idaho, and Wyoming, the territories which surrounded the park-to-be, were organized prior to the creation of the park. They would show varying degrees of interest in the reservation and the policies followed toward it, and they would often register their interests through their delegates to Congress. When they became states (Montana in 1889, Wyoming and Idaho in 1890), their congressmen and senators voiced their opinions.

Such, then, was the nature of the settlements in the great northwest surrounding Yellowstone. The few white inhabitants were mostly males; they were prevailingly optimistic and ambitious, searching for the rich strike or the big deal. They were all newcomers to the region, with careers, fortunes, reputations, and estates to establish. They called each other by their nicknames, formed vigilante committees or fire companies or raised posses to chase the Indians, waged hot political contests, and drew up laws that revealed their feelings about home, hearth, and bed: at the mining camp of Yellowstone City it was written into the laws that a man could be hanged for insulting a woman.[7]

One other attitude of these frontiersmen should be stressed. They tried to buy or lay claim to every bit of real estate that showed even the most remote chance of realizing some profit. Their sense of property was as keen as that of a robber baron, and often as careless of social needs. Again and again this selfishness shows itself in the history of Yellowstone.

By the summer of 1863 the Alder Gulch (Virginia City) boom was at its height. All the land was staked out, and restless drifting men sought new discoveries far afield. Some of them, whose names are unknown to us, prospected alone or in twos and threes; but most of them joined substantial, fairly well-organized parties that anticipated long journeys, possible Indian skirmishes, great discoveries, and lucrative results. Fortunately, one of these parties is well chronicled, thanks to the literate frontiersman, Walter W. De Lacy, who was its leader.

Perhaps De Lacy was a little older than the typical miner — he was forty-four years old in 1863 — and certainly he was better educated than most American frontiersmen. After attending Mount St. Mary's Catholic College in Maryland, where he excelled in mathematics and languages, this Virginian had followed a varied career which included the teaching of foreign languages at West Point and then in the navy, where he taught aboard ship. Then he went west, making his living as a surveyor, enlisting in the Mexican War, working on railroad surveys in southern New Mexico, West Texas, and Arizona, and then working his way to Puget Sound. There he continued as a surveyor and also participated in the Indian Wars that plagued Washington Territory in the 1850s. He experienced many narrow escapes and incredible hardships during those years. In 1859 De Lacy became an engineer with Captain Mullan, and worked with him on Mullan's Road until 1862. Then he did some prospecting, drifted into Virginia City, and there joined the party with which we are here concerned.[8]

De Lacy heard a rumor that a party was assembling over on the Beaverhead River, west from Virginia City, "for the purpose," he later wrote, "of ascending the South branch of Snake river to its head." One of the men had been part way up the Snake and had reportedly seen gold. The rumor carried a mercenary appeal to an ambitious man adrift, and it also inspired his curiosity. "As the country was unknown, distant, and dangerous," he wrote, "it possessed all the elements which combine, in the eye of a frontiersman, 'to lend enchantment to the view.' "[9]

On his way to the Beaverhead he had an accident of the kind that makes all of us but the most romantically inclined consider the automobile a great improvement over the horse. While he was dismounted and checking on his packhorse — "an independent animal" — his riding horse, probably "Muggins," whose one black and one blue eye symbolized a schizophrenic character, began capering and got a rope across the lock of De Lacy's gun, which then went off, aimed directly at the surveyor. The ball passed just over De Lacy's head. He reflected that he should feel very thankful that the horse had not fired the other barrel, for it was loaded with buckshot.

By August 6, joined on the way by drifters, De Lacy had found the main party. All told, there were twenty-seven men, of whom he knew two. One of them, the guide Hillerman, was later to be banished by Montana's vigilantes. Most of the party was totally ignorant of the terrain, having arrived recently from California, Colorado, and elsewhere. The main source of information about where they were going was a faulty map owned by De Lacy. On August 7, he was elected captain, because, he later wrote, nobody knew him, and on the 8th the party started. On that day they were joined by another group, bringing their number to forty-two. They were a wild bunch; De Lacy often called them "the forty thieves."

On the 15th the party had reached the forks of the Snake River. This is where the real Snake is joined by Henrys Fork. The men started up the Snake. De Lacy kept a journal of each day's march, and using his surveyor's training, made rough sketches of the country through which they passed. He was restricted in any topographical work, however, by the absence of even rudimentary instruments from the group's equipment; he had a pocket compass, but no one possessed a telescope and, he said, "there was hardly a watch in the whole party." By the 20th they had reached the Grand Canyon of the Snake River (Irving's "Mad River," through which the Astorians clawed their way in 1811), and they found an old trail running about 100 feet above the river, by which they were able to get through most of the canyon before darkness set in.

Now the river had turned a near 180° and ran north, and, a little later, northwest. The guide informed them that now he was himself in new country. But they kept on, prospecting and hunting along the way, with little success at either, and on the 24th they saw "the white, outlying spurs of the Teton range, on the other side of the river." On the 25th they entered Jackson's Hole. They had made a great U, going down west of the Tetons and up east of them.

Shortly thereafter they camped near (but not at) Jackson Lake, drew up some mining regulations, separated into several parties, and prospected the streams in the vicinity. "They found plenty of gravel but no pay," De Lacey reported. Completely discouraged, some of the party decided to return to Virginia City via the route they had come by. But "about twenty-seven . . . resolved to try and reach Virginia City by going north. I knew," he added, "that we could not miss it, and that we would pass through a new and unexplored territory."

Starting on September 2, they followed a north-northwest course, "at first along the lake [Jackson Lake], but afterward through timber and small prairies out of sight of it." They laid over one day to prospect, but then continued up a narrow canyon and on September 5 reached the fork of the stream — the place where the Snake River comes from the east and joins the Lewis River (which De Lacy called the South Snake), just above and east of the present South Entrance to the park. "There were hot springs with cones four or five feet high near the junction," De Lacy reported. (They are still there.)

The twisted masses of fallen timber, so characteristic of Yellowstone, prompted the party to leave the Lewis River and climb to the west, where they soon "reached a large open prairie, apparently along the summit, where there were two small lakes, of a beautiful blue, and small streams in opposite directions." These were Beula and Hering lakes, where they paused for dinner. There, another section of the party departed to investigate some quartz outcroppings, leaving De Lacy with thirteen men.

After dinner De Lacy's party continued in a northwesterly direction, coming down into a canyon with a northeasterly flowing creek running through it. The next morning they followed the stream (probably Moose Creek) down the canyon and to everyone's sur- prise came to a large lake. Following the shore line for three or four miles, they came to a south-running outlet out of which flowed a stream larger than either the Lewis or the Snake rivers, which they had seen the day before. How, they all asked, could this be?

They did not find the answer until they returned to the settle- ments and De Lacy talked with one of the men who had been in the other party — the group that had departed at Beula and Hering Lakes. While De Lacy's group had discovered Shoshone Lake (known for several years, and with good reason, as De Lacy Lake) the other party had come upon Lewis Lake, south-southeast of Sho- shone Lake. They had then followed the stream that links the two bodies of water up to the outlet, where they found the remains of the DeLacy camp. A surveyor would now conclude correctly that the stream connecting the two lakes carried more water than the Lewis River contains as it flows out of Lewis Lake. Incidentally, the split-off party passed up the west side of Shoshone Lake, while De Lacy and his men went up the east side, so that the split-offs discovered the Shoshone Geyser Basin.

The De Lacy party went up the east side, and by evening had left the lake and pushed on to a small dry prairie, where they camped. All day they had seen many game trails and many signs of the woods buffalo, but they had not seen the beast in the flesh. Since it rained the next day, they remained in camp, being troubled by nothing ex- cept a migration of black lizards which committed suicide by running into the campfires and irritated the men by getting into their blankets.

On September 9 they continued their journey, struck a stream of hot water, "and soon entered a valley or basin, through which the stream meandered, and which was occupied on every side by hot springs." They dismounted, and, as they led their horses, gaped in awe at the sights. "The ground sounded hollow beneath our feet, and we were in great fear of breaking through, and proceeded with great caution," De Lacy wrote. "The water of these springs was intensely hot, of a beautiful ultra-marine blue, some boiling up in the middle, and many of them of very large size, being at least twenty feet in diameter and as deep." They were marching through the Lower Geyser Basin, and the small stream they were following(pro-

bably White Creek) would soon join a larger, north-running river —
the Firehole River.

That night they camped at the forks where the Gibbon and the
Firehole join to form the Madison. Strangely, the discussion that
night was not about the phenomena they had witnessed, but instead
dealt with the question of where they were, since De Lacy's map
was totally inaccurate. In the days following, the party advanced
northwest until it struck the Gallatin, from there made its way
to the Madison again, and, after fifty-one days, returned to Virginia
City. The first man they met gave them the news of Gettysburg.

Among those who were with De Lacy was a young fellow named
John C. Davis. Years later, from the comfort of Alexander's Hotel
in Louisville, Kentucky, he related his story to a reporter. "When
we first came in sight [of the geyser basin]," he said "we thought
the steam from the geysers was the smoke from a large Indian camp."
Even after they found their fears groundless, they were unimpressed.
"[We] never dreamed that we were on the threshold of a great discovery," said Davis. "We left after a few hours without any of the
party paying attention to the surroundings."[10]

De Lacy's skill as a surveyor and topographer resulted in his
appointment by the Montana legislature, in 1864–65, to make a map
of the territory, dividing it into counties. Four different but very
similar copies of this "first map of Montana" have been discovered,
and they establish their author as an excellent map maker. Nevertheless the map in all the variations is full of discrepancies, since much
of the area was known only by hearsay; but it does include "Colter's
Hell" down on the Stinkingwater and does show an unnamed lake
as the source of the South Snake (Lewis) River. (De Lacy wanted
to name the lake after himself, but he lived to see F. V. Hayden
dub it Shoshone Lake.) He appears to have indicated the Shoshone
Geyser Basin as "Hot Springs" and listed a "Hot Springs Valley"
at the point in the Lower Geyser Basin through which he passed.[11]

In 1867, while working as a draftsman in the United States
Surveyor General's office in Helena, De Lacy made another map,
and in this one, which we assume was at least similar to the one
published in 1870, he placed his name on the lake he had discovered.
In listing his "Sources of Information" he included "Exploration of
Messrs. Cook and Folsom to Yellowstone Lake in 1869"; in later

issues of this same basic map he included the route of the Washburn–Langford–Doane expedition of 1870.[12]

De Lacy was aware of Hayden's thievery of his lake and wrote that gentleman about it, but he never received the satisfaction of seeing his name restored to the lake. "I never claimed that my map was correct in all particulars," he wrote. "I put down what I considered the best, hoping to be able to improve the map every year, and make it thoroughly correct finally. . . . I have seen every kind of map which has been published in the last thirty-five years, and I have never seen one which has a correct representation of this region or of the Yellowstone, while at the same time, there is enough to put down to show that some one had been there, and was acquainted with the main features of the country."[13]

He was also the first of many persons to suggest a railroad into the Yellowstone region. De Lacy had been asked about a possible route for a linking track between the proposed Northern Pacific and the Union Pacific. In reply he described a route north up the Green River from the Union Pacific crossing, then across a water divide to one of the rivers flowing into the South Snake, up such a river to where the Snake turns from north to southwest, then up the Snake to the lake at its head, over the mountains in a northwesterly direction, and then "down the south branch of the Madison [the Firehole] and the Madison itself, to the three forks of the Missouri." " . . . It offers," he added, "the most direct and practicable solution of the problem that I know of. . . . The river heads in a large lake some 12 or 15 miles long, and flows into another lake called Jackson's lake, of about the same length." In a separate paragraph he added, "At the head of the South Snake, and also on the south fork of the Madison [Firehole] there are hundreds of hot springs, many of them 'geysers.' "[14]

While it is obvious that the De Lacy party was thinking only of gold as it went through a part of the Yellowstone in 1863, there also can be no doubt that their leader comprehended something of the exotic beauty of the country, and desired to have his name identified with the park.[15]

Another 1863 prospecting party, led by a man named Austin and consisting of about thirty men, went up the Yellowstone to the East Fork (Lamar) and up the valley "to the first creek coming in from the left above Soda Butte creek," thence up that creek to its head, where they were attacked by Arapahoes and their stock driven off — all save one miserable pack-donkey. "The boys," writes the chronicler, "not being ready to go back, cached their things and, packing the jackass heavily and themselves lightly, went over the divide to Clark's Fork." In due time they returned, retrieved their most valuable articles from the cache, and struck for Virginia City via the Upper Yellowstone, finding gold at a creek on the east side of the river, which they named Bear Gulch for a hairless cub they found there.[16]

In the following year the flood tide of prospecting out of Virginia City resulted in the founding of a number of small communities along the upper Yellowstone, below the future northern boundary of the park and above a much-used ford across the Yellowstone. This was known after 1867 as Benson's Landing until the city of Livingston arose close to it in 1882–83. Emigrant Gulch was discovered and Yellowstone City established at its mouth with 300 male and 15 female inhabitants. Flour was $100 a barrel and bacon $1.00 a pound. N. P. Langford, later of national park fame, was one of the founders of the Broad Gauge Company, which was given a telegraph and stage franchise from Virginia City to Emigrant Gulch and down the Yellowstone to its mouth. The territorial legislature also franchised the "Red Streak Mountain Coal Co.," named for Cinnabar Mountain and Devil's Slide, which were close by. Civilization was obviously encroaching on the north and west sides of the park.[17]

John C. Davis, the one other person to leave an account of the De Lacy expedition, was also in Yellowstone the following year, 1864. His narrative is full of discrepancies and, quite possibly, the exaggerations of a boastful man whose imagination supplied details in place of forgotten facts, two decades after the events had taken place. In February he had joined an expedition led by James Stuart which prospected along the Bighorn and the Stinkingwater rivers.[18]

When the men failed to find gold, the party, which had initially numbered about seventy, split up. Stuart and about half the prospectors returned to Virginia City, while the remainder splintered and resplintered into isolated groups of twos and threes and half-dozens. Davis lived quite an odyssey that winter and spring, if his story can be believed. First he prospected the Sweetwater by way of South Pass, then worked into the Green River country, and finally hit the Snake, "where," he related, "I and two others left for the headwaters of the Upper Yellowstone. Gaining this river, we went down it to the lake which we reached on the northeast side."[19]

Davis says that they "came into the park just above the lake," and that "the boiling springs and geysers were all around us." He also says that he "had visited this place in the previous year," but this must have been an approximation since the De Lacy party was considerably west of Yellowstone Lake. Conceivably Davis in 1864 could have seen the thermal activity of the Brimstone Basin and Signal Hills, on the southeast side of the lake. Then his narrative indicates that after wandering "along the shore for awhile," they left it and went toward the Grand Canyon of the Yellowstone; that they camped a mile and a half above the falls; that they crossed the river on their ponies and followed along the crest of the canyon for a short distance. He then suggests that he christened Pelican Creek, which flows into Yellowstone Lake northeast of the Fishing Bridge. He also comments on seeing Indian signs but no Indians, and leaves off there, assuming that the reader is aware that he got out of the park safely.

As for discrepancies, Davis says that he "and two others" left the party of six on the Snake River to search for the headwaters of the Yellowstone; yet two paragraphs later he states that this party of three split up, two men returning to Virginia City but apparently remaining with Davis in spirit, since he continues to use the pronoun we. Crossing the Yellowstone above the falls is not as simple as he indicates, the safest place being at the Nez Perce ford some ten miles above the Mud Volcano. He was probably there in the early summer, and the river is swollen then, making the fording hazardous.

The balance of the evidence, however, is in favor of John C. Davis. He probably did pass through Yellowstone in 1864, and may indeed have seen the falls and a good many other things; his imagination supplied some of the rest, and time depleted his memory so that his true itinerary cannot be reconstructed. He is mentioned because he is symbolic of the numerous prospectors of the 1860s who saw phenomena within the present confines of the park but never recorded their travels and are thus unknown to us now. That the rugged, acquisitive frontier society had not yet focused its attention on the park is a fact; that it was *unknown* until the late 1860s is, of course, a fallacy.

We have definite information about another prospecting party that went into the area two years later, in 1866. It consisted of six men, of whom one, George Huston, would later be of some importance in the Yellowstone story. This party left Virginia City, went up the Madison to the Forks, and up the Firehole to the geysers. Then they crossed the divide and came down to the Mud Volcano, where they struck a trail made by horse thieves. They followed the trail around Yellowstone Lake to Heart Lake, where they left it and headed down the east shores of Yellowstone Lake, on down the river to below the falls, across to the East Fork, and then on down the Yellowstone to Emigrant, where, after giving their story to a correspondent of the *Omaha Herald,* they dispersed.[20]

In June 1866, with one Jeff Standifer as captain and Bart Henderson as lieutenant, a group of about 100 men trekked southeast from Blackfoot, Montana, northwest of Great Falls, to the Stinking-water by way of Stillwater Creek. Again in 1867 the same Jeff Standifer probably set out with a party for the Wind River on a prospecting trip. This time he "went up the Yellowstone to its source, and over to the head of and then down the Wind River," where the party's activities were disrupted by an Arapaho attack.[21]

In the late summer of 1867 a group of men got together at Deer Lodge, far to the northwest of the park, and set out on a prospecting trip to the headwaters of the Snake, the Wind River, and, as the diarist called it, "the Yellow." Members of the party were one John W. Powell [no relation to the Colorado River Powell], a Captain Bracey, a William Allen, and the diarist, A. Bart Henderson. He would be a character around Yellowstone from this time until 1877, when the Nez Perces burned his ranch west of Gardiner. After that, he took to roving and disappeared from history.[22]

The boys were all set for a fling. "We left town at noon, two sheets in the wind and the third fluttering in the breeze," Henderson began his entry for August 12, "and with 2 bottles of whiskey in our cantinas. We took the first road we saw, which proved to be the Silver Bow and Virginia road." When they sobered up — for two bottles of whiskey can last only so long — they got down to business, headed for the Snake below Henrys Fork, and followed it down, around, and up to the Gros Ventre fork, which led them to the Continental Divide at Two Ocean Pass. More than two weeks had elapsed, and the entry of September 29 takes them up Atlantic Creek to a campsite close to Bridger Lake, which is just south of the park boundary.[23]

On August 30 the men looked down upon a lake that lay "about fifteen miles to the northwest. We were at a very great loss to know what it was," wrote Henderson. "Captain Bracey said he would soon settle that question and let us know the facts. He soon had Captain De Lacy's map spread on the grass, tracing out the different rivers that he found marked on the map."

On De Lacy's map Yellowstone Lake appears as a long, narrow finger of water, about fifteen miles long and five miles wide. It did not look at all like the lake the Henderson party was looking down upon. "After examining the map and scratching his head several times John [Powell] remarked that the body of water that we could see was nothing more nor less than the Pacific Ocean and that neither Captain Bracey or Captain De Lacy knew anything about the country. That Capt. Bracey had better go back to sea and Capt. De Lacy go home. He would lose anyone that would travel by his map."

They concluded that it was Yellowstone Lake, as indeed it was, and on August 31 they trekked down and worked along the eastern shore, now along the beach, now forced inland by a barrier such as Lake Butte, so that they encountered Yellowstone's terrible jungles of fallen timbers. Camp was finally made below Butte Springs, not far from Sedge Creek, whose dark waters were unfit for cooking purposes. Powell caught some trout and made the usual discovery that many of the fish were wormy.

The next day and night it rained and then snowed, but the following day they found a trail "of about 80 barefooted tracks, freshly made. We pronounced them Blackfeet and they meant no good to those they met," Henderson wrote, adding that his party then changed its course and headed for the river, crossing to the west side near the mouth of Otter Creek, far north of the outlet of the lake. The horses had to swim, and a man who had joined them at the upper end of the lake, whose name was John Bull or Jack Jones, "said he would drown as he could not swim. However Powell told him to dry up, and take his horse by the tail, and he would lead him safe. . . . They landed all right."

Here they made camp, and Henderson shouldered his rifle and strolled down to the river, "but a short distance below where we swam the river . . . I walked out on a rock and made two steps at the same time, one forward, the other backward." He had come upon the Upper Falls.

On September 3, with the weather cloudy and cool, they followed the river around Mount Washburn, noticed the hot springs on its south side, and picked their way along the edge of the Grand Canyon of the Yellowstone, with the river looking "like a white ribbon laid at the bottom." Then they turned west, climbed over the mountain, and came down into the forested basin between Carrelian and Tower creeks, where four inches of snow was interlaced with bear tracks running in all directions, "some so fresh that they smoked." They camped for the night near Tower Falls — "the most beautiful falls I ever saw," Henderson wrote in his diary. The next day they followed the Yellowstone, passed the mouth of the East Fork, and noticed that the terrain gave indications of being mineral country — "the first indications since leaving Snake River." On September 5 they struck the Gardner. "West up the creek we could see a heavy smoke, or steam raising [*sic*] from a cluster of white hills, just such hills as we saw on the Upper Yellowstone. So we pronounced them a cluster of hot springs." This was of course Mammoth Hot Springs.

By September 6 they were making their way down the canyons north of the park. The following day they would meet miners from Emigrant, and on September 8 they would work west over Bozeman Pass and come down safely into Bozeman, "a one horse town," where, the diarist says, "we arrived safe and sound."[24]

In this same year, 1867, one Lou Anderson, who may have visited the geysers as early as 1850, and men named Hubble, Reese, Caldwell, "and another man," went up the river on the east side. They found gold in a crevice and named the stream Crevice Creek. The next day Hubble went on ahead, and when queried about the streams, he replied that the next one was "a hell roarer"; asked a similar question about a further creek a couple of days later, he answered, "Twas but a slough." The names have stuck. The first two streams flow into the Yellowstone just south of the boundary, and the last flows into the Lamar about three miles above its junction: Crevice Creek, Hellroaring Creek, and Slough Creek.[25]

The first prospectors to work into the rugged Beartooth country southeast of Benson's Landing and north and east of the Lamar River

would find gold, start a stampede, establish two mining districts —
the New World (Cooke City) and the Sunlight — and in so doing
create a problem when the park was established, one that remains
something of a nuisance to this day.

And our friend A. Bart Henderson was among them, keeping
his salty, ungrammatical diary that is so full of the flavor of the times.
We also have a short statement by James Gourley, another member
of the party, to help us fit the pieces together and trace the group's
movements, probably with considerable accuracy.[26]

The two other members of the party were Adam Miller and
Ed. Hibbard; they also brought a pet dog along. They started immediately after a heavy late spring snowstorm, with Henderson's
first entry dated June 6 at the Crow Agency, about ten miles east
of Genson's Landing. "Left this place at 10 o'clock for a prospecting
tour to the headwaters of Wind River, East Fork and Clark's Fork
of the Yellowstone," the diary tells us, making no mention this time
of whiskey. Perhaps they had learned their lesson.

The streams were swollen with snow-water, and they crossed
Bear Creek by felling a huge pine, three feet in circumference, which
served as a bridge for men and horses. They paused at the mining
camp of Independence, which Gourley said he had been interested in
back in '66.

For about two weeks they prospected in the mountain regions
bordering the park east of the Yellowstone and well north of the
East Fork, at one time coming down into Hellroaring Creek, then
onto "a beautiful flat" (the Buffalo Plateau) where they "found thousands of buffalo quietly grazing" along with an abundance of other
game — elk, black-tailed deer, bear, and moose. Then they worked
north again above the park to Boulder Pass, and apparently all was
serene until June 28, when Henderson reported: "Buffalo bull run
thro the tent, while all hands in bed."

Again, on June 29, they were attacked by a buffalo near Slough
Creek. "Fired one shot, he ran over me and attacked the horses.
Finally killed him," Henderson recorded with frontiersman's brevity.
They camped that day on Slough Creek, about three miles north of
the park boundary, and there saw the "first indications of gold" and
"several [prospecting] holes sunk in the Middle fork" (of Slough
Creek, which is joined near there by French Creek from the west
and Wolverine Creek from the east — the latter of which they

named). "Mosquitoes and flies plenty."

They worked east along Abundance Creek to Lake Abundance, which is just a little over a mile north of the northeast boundary of the park. Henderson described this mountain jewel as "one of the finest lakes in the mountains, . . . full of the finest trout in the world." But not only had they come upon a beautiful lake, they had finally struck the fringes of what became known as the "New World mining district," of which Cooke City became the population center. "Here we found the first gold of the trip — gold in every gulch and sag," Henderson wrote, adding, "Snow in patches, grass just starting. Thousands of bear, elk, buffalo and deer. We camped on the east side, and discovered several quartz lodes in the afternoon." And again, still in camp on July 3: "Everybody excited. Found gold in paying quantities in several places. Gourley got five cents to the pan." Moreover, according to Henderson, they had found gold in quartz, inviting hard-rock operations as well as placers.

For two weeks they prospected, fished, hunted, and fought one round after another with *ursus horribilis,* for the grizzlies were abundant and crotchety. Finally they packed up and trekked southeast to the Broadwater River, which they followed downstream until it joined the Clarks Fork. By July 18 they were camped in the shadow of Pilot Peak. Henderson noted the geologic change: "country lava and concrete."

Gourley's descriptions of this phase of their explorations are brief and less optimistic. From Lake Abundance, where, he says, "we found gold but no diggins," he jumps three or four miles southeast to Henderson Mountain from which, with a clear sky above him, he "witnest a thunder storm looking down on it." Close to the nearby Chimney Rocks he found some lead silver ore "which," he said, "destroyed all our prospect for gold."

It must have been at about this juncture that Gourley and Adam Miller, "finding no placer diggins in the Cooke City country," packed across the mountains to the northeast. They found no gold, but they did find Grasshopper Glacier, which they named. "We found a fisher [fissure] in the smooth ice sixteen or eighteen inches wide and looking down in the fisher we saw two layers of grasshoppers, the upper one seemingly about ten inches and the lower one about five inches," he said. "We crossed it holding on with one hand and having to chop foot holds in the ice. . . . It was some forty or fifty

feet across and our dog could not make it across and left us there."
They then lowered themselves with ropes to the Stillwater River, and
returned to the base camp.

It appears that the full party then turned southwest by west up
Pilot Creek, camped near Republic Pass right on the park boundary,
and then continued west along Cache Creek, coming out into rolling
hill country teeming with buffalo, elk, deer, and bear — the elk
"so tame that they only moved a little distance to the side of us."
They camped at the forks of the streams, about two miles below the
present Cache Creek patrol cabin.

On the 23d they emerged in open country on the East Fork of
the Yellowstone. "Here," wrote the diarist, "we found thousands of
hot or boiling springs. . . . Just opposite camp a small creek empties
into the river. One mile up this creek is a very singular butte, some
40 feet high, which has been formed by soda water. We gave the
cone the name of Soda Butte, and the creek the name of Soda Butte
Creek." They also found "thousands of antelope and flies."[27] Henderson's diary continues:

Sunday, July 24, 1870.
Clear and warm. Raised camp early, followed down river
on south side [in a] west direction 10 miles. Came to junction
with main Yellowstone.
Here we turned south, followed the divide between the
two rivers [and] camped near summit 15 miles north of the
Great Falls of the Yellowstone.

They then followed the divide east for some twelve miles, along
Specimen Ridge and the Mirror Plateau, coming down Flint Creek
onto the East Fork again. By the 27th they were advancing up the
Middle Fork (the Little Lamar), then crossed some excessively rough
terrain, working northward to the North Fork (Lamar River). On
the 29th they "camped on N side of N fork, near summit. Fine
grass." They were west of the Sunlight Basin, in the high country
where several rivers, including, they believed, the Stinkingwater,
originated. On the 30th, Henderson and Ed. Hibbard "left camp
for the purpose of hunting a way to get down on the N. Stinking
River." About six miles east of the camp the country changed, and
they found "a granite and quartz mountain. . . . we started back to
camp in great glee, as we was now near the place where we had

no doubt there was rich placer and quartz mines." This was, of course, the Sunlight mining district.

Gourley says they were camped "near the divide at the head of the north fork of Shoshone and Crandall creek. . . . " On their way back to his place on Saturday, July 30, Henderson and Hibbard "heard several shots in the direction of camp," but then the firing ceased, only to begin again when they were within half a mile of their destination, "and this time there was no mistaking its meaning. The camp was beyond a doubt attacked by Indians."

Gourley was thirty yards from camp when the attack began, and he found himself surrounded by the red men. "I got to camp as the outfit passed and called to Miller not to unload his rifle except to kill sure," he recalled. He fired as the Indian leader turned toward camp. "I do not know that I hit him, but he flattened down on his horses neck," he added.

It was at about this stage that Henderson and Hibbard reached a point at which they could survey the whole scene. "We saw at a single glance," Henderson wrote, "that the camp was surrounded by Indians who already had our horses in their possession." The two men "picked a safe locality and joined in the action." They fired just one volley, for the Indians now felt that *they* were surrounded, and beat a hasty retreat.

Henderson and Hibbard rejoined their companions, and they now prepared for a siege, being certain that the Indians would return. The camp was in a clump of nut pine with large logs about. "I dug a breastwork which Miller told the others when they got in, was a foot in bed rock before I knew it," said Gourley, "but I said I would bet that he could not lift one end of a log that he picked up like a stick of cordwood and laid down."

After the breastwork was completed, and the long, agonizing wait had begun, Gourley flushed four warriors from behind a low ridge where they had been hiding. It overlooked a deep coulee. Obviously, the Indians had planned to force the men out of their fortifications; if this happened the logical place for the white men to run was for the coulee, and the Indians were prepared to pick them off when they did so. Since plans were now upset, the Indians gave up. Night fell and there was no attack.

Thus ended the prospecting, for the Indians had indeed stolen the horses. The men destroyed what they could not carry on their backs, or else abandoned it. Twenty-one traps and twenty-seven bearskins were left behind. The first day they traveled through dead timber that horses could not penetrate, trying not to leave a trail, and spending the first night in a place where the Indians could not find them. On the second day, according to Henderson, they cached some of their property, and thus gave Cache Creek its name.[28] Tempers were short: "Ed. and Horn quarreled about a dog [and] drew guns and knives. I cocked my gun and told them to stop quareling," said Henderson.

By the evening of August 4 they were at Soda Butte Creek; the next day they turned north, saw Indians approaching their camp, fired, and then went on another three miles and spent the night hiding in the brush. On August 6 they reached Slough Creek and destroyed their excess powder by blowing it up. They worked their way up the creek, over Buffalo Fork, then to Hellroaring Creek, the Boulder River, and so back to the Crow Agency, where they arrived on August 13.

Gourley says that they destroyed all their meat, thinking that they could kill game on the way, but it was "flying time and game was high on the mountains." For one night and two days they had nothing but tea; then they gorged on trout, which led to "serious results for some of us."[29]

They tentatively identified the marauders as the same Arapaho Indians who had killed Lieutanant Stambaugh early in May, far down in the South Pass country, not far from Atlantic City. Gourley said the Indians had two Springfield carbines with them. This same war party probably murdered Crandall and Finley, two of a party of five that had prospected from Crevice Gulch southeastward to the Clarks Fork. Crandall Creek is named for one of the men. Gourley and a partner, Bill Cameron, found the bones exposed in 1871 and buried them deeper; several years later he and his partner "made some repairs on the graves of these two men."[30]

Henderson, Gourley, Hibbard, and Miller talked up their discoveries at the Crow Agency and over at Bozeman. There all the group save Henderson made immediate preparations to return. Among their acquisitions were seven Springfields and 1,000 rounds of ammunition which, Gourley later wrote, "would have been criminal under any other circumstances." They found the trail of the Indians who had followed them, since some of the horse tracks revealed a horse shod only in front — a perfect identification of one of Gourley's stolen mounts which had the habit of kicking other horses and had therefore been denied the luxury of having his rear hooves shod. They had no Indian troubles, however, and they sank a shaft thirty feet deep before early autumnal snows forced them to give up for the winter. Bozeman's newspaper, *The Pick and Plow*, gave the new diggings a big play, and drifters began arriving early, portending the stampede that would come when spring arrived.[31]

Where did these argonauts come from? From everywhere. They were a part of the army of drifters who rode the rails where they existed, and trudged along dusty roads all over America in the decades following the Civil War. They were a phenomenon of the years between 1865 and 1914, these lonely, ill-dressed, ill-fed, shabby — but not always lazy — men. Many were rootless but were searching for rich soil where they could put down roots; many searched all their lives for the one big chance. Most of them were part-time workers, in an age before unemployment insurance, when to lose a laborer's job meant the end of regular meals. So they drifted from a gold or silver strike to a logging job to a construction job, and so on. And they heard of new jobs, or strikes, or easy places to spend a summer or a winter, and, as if from nowhere, they were suddenly there.

Although Bart Henderson had not returned with his partners to the diggings in the early fall of 1870, he had not abandoned his hope of striking it rich in the new area. When spring arrived he made his preparations, and his diary picks up again on May 13, 1871, with the terse comment, "Left this morning for Clark's Fork, Camped at Bottler's ranch. River very high."[32]

By May 18, Henderson had "crossed the high bench country" and come down to Hellroaring River, which was swollen with snow water, "80 feet wide, rapid and deep, with large boulders in it — very dangerous fording." On this same day his party "overtook the Duke of Hamilton and party."[33]

By the 20th they had crossed Slough Creek three miles above its mouth — "70 feet wide, sluggish and deep. . . . Camped on south side." Here Henderson found seventy-four men encamped, waiting for the snow to melt before continuing to the diggings. On the 21st Jeff Standifer came up, and everyone, including the cooks, went on a spree. (Such binges in camp, rather than in town, were unusual. The diarist does not say whether liquor was consumed.) It was soon made clear that the Standifer party had been awaiting Henderson's arrival, since he obviously knew the country. But anyway, the snow was still deep, and the spree continued on May 22. Deer and elk were prevalent, and the men ate well.

By the 29th they were camped three miles above the mouth of Soda Butte Creek, where the large party remained for a few days, since there was "good wood, water, and grass"; the diary entries indicate that there was good hunting too. On June 1 Henderson and two of his companions, "Dutch and Bill," left camp early and went up Soda Butte Creek. "Good trail," Henderson noted, "wide bottom, high cement mountains on both sides, which rise several thousand feet high, and thousands of little streams come rippling down the side and from the tops of the mountains. Camped in the diggings. Snow several feet deep. Rain and snow all night, no tent."

Henderson had followed the approximate route of the highway to the Northeast Entrance. In the late spring, the mountains turn into splendid walls of crystal snow-water, splashing cold and clear over the cliffs: Druid Peak, Mount Hornaday, Barronette Peak, on the north, and Mount Norris, the Thunderer, and Abiathar Peak on the south or southeast side of the canyon. Most tourists do not look for it, but by the side of the highway is Icebox Canyon, so narrow that the snow never leaves it — an indication of the long winters and brief summers in that part of the country.

By June 5 everyone was at the diggings. Snow was still deep, there was a shortage of forage for horses, and the men had gone on another spree the day before. At this stage American democracy took over. Someone called a meeting, and a committee (what would Americans do if they could not have some committees?) was appointed "to draw up a code of laws to govern the new district." Jeff Standifer, Horn Miller, James Gourley, William Hamilton, and Henderson were the members; they were to report the next day. Even this was not soon enough, for on June 6, a clear, cold, late spring day, Henderson recorded, "Great excitement. Stampede last night for the different gulches. Several of the outfit got lost and the rest disgusted."

But on the 7th, clear and cold again, another meeting was

called. "Read the laws," Henderson noted tersely. "Elected Maj. Farrow Recorder. Great confusion in camp, grub failing. Snow deep, no bare ground in the diggings, no grass for the horses. All these things combined had the desired effect on the stampeders." Then he added, in a short, succinct paragraph, "There was no one in the outfit that can say he was invited to come to this place before July."

By June 8 the grumbling was getting serious. "Lively times in camp. Some of the men threatened to take Miller and myself out and compel us to show them our diggings, which we had positively refused to do before the snow disappeared. We would then take them to our prospect holes." But Miller and Henderson were not to be browbeaten or threatened. "We told them that the first man that made a move toward forcing us would fall a martyr to his foul and rash undertaking. This," he stated simply, "put a stop to further threats." And then he added:

> The camp soon after busted. In a few hours parties could have been seen outfitting for all parts of the world. Snake River, Idaho, Salt Lake, New York, San Francisco.
>
> Our honorable recorder made a short speech and gave back the diggings to the discoverers, etc.
>
> I replied to him, told the outfit we thanked them for their kind consideration . . . bade them good day and returned to my tent, to wait for the snow to disappear.
>
> Soon the beautiful outfit left the camp, without sticking a pick in the ground, cursed the country, the discoverers, and themselves, for coming to the great humbug, which they created themselves.

Henderson's party, the size of which is not known, stayed on. On June 9 he and Horne Miller visited the gulch where their prospector's holes were located but found the snow five feet deep. Apparently the obvious fact that another two or three weeks would elapse before operations could begin led Henderson, Jack Cone, and perhaps James Gourley to return to Bozeman for a spree. And thus ended the first visit to the new mining district for the year 1871.

After his binge, Henderson returned to the diggings, camping on July 11 at Mammoth Hot Springs and loitering there several days. "I found several men who came here for their health and have been here but a few weeks and are all doing well," he entered in his diary on the 13th. "These springs are the ninth wonder of the world. Come one, come all, both great and small. Come and get yourselves cured."

At the Lamar River he discovered further signs of encroaching civilization. "Yellowstone Jack" Baronett, an Englishman of dubious past and unknown fate, had constructed a wooden toll bridge across the Yellowstone just above the mouth of the Lamar. We may assume that Henderson made a dry crossing, continued up the Lamar, paused at Soda Butte, which he described as "one of the finest springs in the world . . . [with] a cone or butte about 40 feet high," and then continued to the diggings. There he "found the boys out of tobacco and very much discouraged and in the act of leaving camp." Bart stayed there about a week, discovering sixteen new lodes, but eight men left for diggings 120 miles eastward with, he commented, "a fair prospect of being set afoot and losing their scalps."

Soon thereafter he discovered eighteen Indians in the vicinity, and so he and the two others left in camp hurried back west, camping at a pretty little body of water west of the East Fork Trail. "This is the most beautiful little lake, and full of the finest trout," he wrote, "hence I gave it the name of Trout lake." The name stuck.

By August 22 he was at Mammoth Hot Springs, where Colonel Barlow and Dr. Ferdinand Vandiveer Hayden were encamped; he then went on to Bottler's, envisioned a toll road from Bozeman to Yellowstone Lake, did odd jobs until May 1872, when the gold bug led him again to the Clarks Fork mines. On May 19 he "called the camp together for the purpose of making laws to govern the mines. The same," he wrote, "to be known as the 'New World District.' "

Again he strayed, working on the toll road some, seeing the first wagon use it through Yankee Jim Canyon (October 7, 1872), went to Bozeman, got religion, then added, "nabbed by police, which busted me up in the Church business." In May 1873 he caught gold fever all over again, and headed for the New World District, killing two bears and "chased by a third," joined a stampede of fifty-four men and two squaws, and pushed on through with them to the Clarks Fork. On June 13, 1873, he and his companions laid out Galena City (now Cooke City), and his diary ends on Sunday, June 14, 1873: "Clear and warm. Raised house. Several lodes discovered. Dog fight in town."[34]

Henderson's beloved New World mining district — whose lone settlement, Cooke City, lies in the valley of Soda Butte Creek in the southern part of the diggings — refused to die. An area extending ten miles north and south and five miles east and west, it lies "on the southwest flank of the Beartooth–Snowy Mountain anticline." Illegally settled — since until 1882 it was on the Crow Indian Reservation — it has continued to survive through nearly a century of mining and tourism, housing about seventy-five souls in winter and a couple of hundred in the summer. But at certain flush times, the population has grown to as many as 2,000 in the summer.[35]

The existence of gold-, silver-, and lead-bearing ores in the Cooke City region has never been disputed, but the problems of transportation preclude vigorous mining operations to this day. One solution was to construct smelters in the district, but coal had to be brought in over the mountains from Red Lodge, and after a time the state prohibited the cutting and burning of timber for the making of charcoal. Even though the district was actually on the Crow Reservation, the miners swarmed over the region. In 1875 a "furnace of the Mexican type"— a small, rustic smelter — was built, and some lead was smelted. How much we will never know, because the records were destroyed by the Nez Perces in 1877, who also stole the lead they found, probably to make into shot.

The Republic Mine, perhaps the most important operation in the early years, was bonded over in 1870 by its principle owner, George Huston, to Jay Cooke, financier of the Northern Pacific, and the name of the settlement was changed from Galena to Cooke City in his honor. The name remained even after Cooke's financial reverses forced forfeiture on his bond after he had put up an initial $5,000.

On April 13, 1882, the district was cut off from the Crow Indian Reservation and opened for settlement. At about this same time, four-horse teams began making their way into the district from Bozeman, and sanguine mining entrepreneurs developed their claims with vigor. In 1884, one Reuben Rickard was hired as general superintendent of the operations upon the recommendation of Clarence King (of Diamond Hoax fame), and by 1886 he had a smelter successfully running the complex silver and lead ores the area produced. But the problem of getting the stuff to market remained, and this gave birth to the idea of running a railroad up from Gardiner to the Lamar–Yellowstone junction, up the Lamar Valley, and up the Soda Butte Creek Canyon to Cooke City and the mines.

When this railroad promotion failed, the smelter closed and Rickard resigned, though other mines — the Morning Star, the Bunker Hill, the Black Warrior — still operated and used the "Mexican furnace." Then in 1888 gold ore was found in the Daisy and the Homestake claims on Henderson Mountain; later a small stamp mill was built, and in 1893 a cyanide mill was constructed on the "Alice F" property. Although probably $104,000 in metals was produced in 1886 alone, it was clear from the earliest stages of mining that cheap transportation was Cooke's only hope of salvation. The cost of $20 per ton — for drayage from Cooke to Gardiner alone — precluded profitable mining of all but the highest grade ores, and most of the mining district's ores were not up to that level.[36]

Hopes die hard, especially in the minds of treasure hunters, and Cooke City boosters talked up the railroad well into the twentieth century. The miners also posed a problem to park officials, for in the line of business, they had to enter the park at Gardiner, advance up to Yancey's in Pleasant Valley, cross Jack Baronett's bridge, go up the Lamar, and then travel up Soda Butte Creek until finally they left the park and found themselves, almost immediately, in Cooke City.

The miners knew about Yellowstone, but gold and silver were their great loves, and aesthetic or scientific marvels never entered their thoughts. Now the Yellowstone remained for others to discover. They were men with vivid imaginations who had some sense of obligation to society and to future generations. To them belongs some of the credit for the final impetus that created Yellowstone National Park.

7

Two Yankee Quakers and a Dane

It is remarkable that Yellowstone ever became a national park. For the population of the areas that bordered it on the north and west was wild, mercenary, and unmanageable without the aid of vigilantes.

If their contemporaries are to be believed, Montana miners were worse than most. The big strikes took place during wartime, and the drifters came like a plague of locusts, "some of the worst elements of both warring sections of the country," wrote one of the better citizens, Cornelius Hedges (important later in Yellowstone history), "deserters from both camps, seeking a cover in the wilderness beyond the reach of the civil or military arm of government, where they could shoot off their mouths or guns with comparative immunity. . . . and to render the situation still worse almost the entire population was gathered in a few camps where the sentiment of the majority represented the whole." The only circulating currency was gold dust, and "there was no Sunday as distinguished from other days except by increased gambling and dissipation."[1]

The miners came to know the mountains, and they told yarns about what they had seen — but for all their hidden virtues, they strike us as a callous, mercenary lot. As Joaquin Miller said, their only talk was of gold. "It seems as if it might be no later than the sixth day in this new world," said Miller, "and the woman is not yet made."[2]

Although a few miners — such as Walter De Lacy — did appreciate Yellowstone, most of those who grasped its true value were men of other callings who possessed an intellectual curiosity about the place. John Colter, little as we know about him, was certainly such a curious man, and so were Jim Bridger, Osborne Russell, Warren Ferris, and the unknown companions of these trappers. Captain Raynolds and his scientist, Dr. Ferdinand Vandiveer Hayden, were certainly curious about the country that so impressed Old Gabe. Captain John Mullan, who supervised the construction of the Fort Walla Walla–Fort Benton Road, 1858–62, had known of the hot springs since the winter of 1853. In that year, as a participant in the Pacific Railroad surveys, he had wintered in the Bitter Root Valley of western Montana. "Upon investigating the peculiarities of the country," he wrote, "I learned from the Indians, and afterwards confirmed by my own explorations, the fact of the existence of an infinite number of hot springs at the headwaters of the Missouri, Columbia and Yellowstone rivers, and that hot geysers . . . existed at the head of the Yellowstone. . . . "[3]

Among those with less mercenary callings was a Jesuit, Francis Xavier Kuppens. Like the renowned Father de Smet, whose proselytizing probably led Father Kuppens to take vows, he was a Belgian, educated at the Jesuit college in his native town of Turnhout. In 1857 he entered the Florissant (Missouri) novitiate of the Society of Jesus, and was ordained at Boston in 1863, at the age of twenty-five. In November 1864 he arrived at the St. Peter's Mission, close to present-day Great Falls, Montana, and there he began his work with the Blackfeet. These nomadic people were as wild as the north country in which they lived; to convert such a people was a challenging assignment indeed.

But young Father Kuppens had been well trained and, like de Smet, he was physically well endowed for the task. His commanding presence helped him gain the respect of tribesmen and whites alike. Tall and muscular, he could also swim and was an expert horseman.[4]

He put these abilities to good use, for he would be no rocking-chair priest, sitting in the warm mission rectory waiting for the heathen to come seeking conversion. He came to them, living with the nomadic people during their travels. He mastered their language and conversed with them, though one suspects that he listened more than he spoke — listened to their tales on evenings when the north wind beat at the skin tepee and smoke from the buffalo-chip fire made the eyes water and burn. Reminiscing more than thirty years later, Father Kuppens still remembered a significant amount, but he wrote down too little to satisfy our curiosity.

He placed his Yellowstone visit in "about the year 1865–66," but it probably took place a year or two earlier. "A great part of that winter and spring," he reminisced, "I spent with the Pigeon Indians [Piegans, a branch of the Blackfeet] roaming from place to place south of Fort Benton, and on the Judith river." It was during this time that he first heard of Yellowstone. "Many an evening in the tent of Baptiste Champagne or Chief Big Lake," he recalled, "the conversation, what there was of it, turned on the beauties of the wonder-spot." His curiosity was whetted, and the desire grew to see for himself "this enchanted if not enchanting land." When spring arrived, his opportunity came. "I persuaded a few young men to show me the wonderland, of which they had talked so much," he continued. "Thus I got my first sight of the Yellowstone [and] you may be sure that before leaving I saw the chief attractions. . . . I was very much impressed with the wild grandeur of the scenery, and on my return gave an account of it to Fathers Ravalli and Imoda, then stationed at the old Mission of St. Peters."[5]

Meanwhile, a stampede of miners to imaginary gold fields along the Sun River in the winter of 1865, followed by a hot dry summer which brought on crop failure for the third year in succession, led the Jesuits to plan the abandonment of the site of St. Peter's and build a new mission a few miles away along the Mullan Road near Bird Tail Rock.[6] It was at this site that a party of VIPs from Helena found Father Kuppens and his helpers living in a large tepee, in November 1865.[7]

Who were these Very Important Persons? What is the significance of their experiences?

Their leader, Thomas Francis Meagher, was an impetuous Irish revolutionary who had escaped from exile in Tasmania, prospered for a time in the States as an orator, served on the Union side in the Civil War, and then headed west to try again for a fame that somehow eluded him. By 1865 he was the controversial acting governor of Montana Territory — a well-educated son of the Emerald Isle, determined to be Montana's first great statesman.[8]

Accompanying him were several other men, of whom one, Cornelius Hedges, would be prominent in the history of the park.

Meagher had invited them to ride with him to Fort Benton, where he was to persuade the Blackfeet to give up a portion of their huge reservation. It was late October and the lingering Indian summer promised the travelers good times. "We were well-mounted and equipped. . . . We expected a splendid and enjoyable excursion," Hedges later wrote. After a first exhilarating day, the weather turned sharply colder toward evening and a storm began to brew. The next morning it began to snow, but the men pushed on, striking directly toward the new mission, where they could get protection from the storm. Conditions grew worse; only their guide kept them from getting lost in a white wilderness, and the dismal day was, wrote Hedges, "very different from our anticipations." They reached the new site of St. Peter's, which Hedges called St. John's Catholic Mission (the name did not stick), and there they huddled in the tepee, along with Father Kuppens, other priests, and their assistants, until smoke from the fire drove them outside. There they rolled up in their blankets and tried to sleep. The next morning, led by Father Kuppens, they pushed on through a foot of snow into the blinding storm, bidding adieu "to the [other] good fathers who were poorly supplied for such a stormy time, let alone entertaining so considerable a party of unexpected visitors."[9]

They received a warm reception at St. Peter's, and there spent two comfortable days, "feasting on the fat of the land and reserved stores rarely opened." Governor Meagher was the life of the party, "a charming conversationalist with a wonderful store of experiences, garnered from travel in all quarters of the globe, and in addition, he was a royal son of the true church." They left when the storm abated, "with benedictions from the good fathers."[10]

At this stage the specifics of the story lie buried with the participants, but the conclusions are sound. Both Hedges and Father Kuppens wrote of their experiences some thirty years after the events, so neither may be depended upon absolutely. Father Kuppens, who with age appears to have become very hazy on dates, places his meeting with the Meagher party in the spring of 1867 rather than the autumn of 1865. (Hedges and Meagher agree on this.) He does describe a blizzard, however, and says that they were compelled to stay a few days at the mission.[11]

For our purposes these differences are trivial. The substantive part of Father Kuppens's reminiscences are what interest us:

On that occasion I spoke to him [Meagher] about the wonders of the Yellowstone. His interest was greatly aroused by my recital and perhaps even more so by that of a certain Mr. Viell — an old Canadian married to a Blackfoot squaw — who during a lull in the storm had come over to see the distinguished visitors. When he was questioned about the Yellowstone he described everything [in] a most graphic manner. None of the visitors had ever heard of the wonderful place. Gen. Meagher said if things were as described the government ought to reserve the territory for a *national park*. All the visitors agreed that efforts should be made to explore the region and that a report of it should be sent to the government.[12] (Italics mine.)

There is sufficient reason to believe that Father Kuppens did indeed meet with Governor Meagher and Cornelius Hedges, and that Meagher did plan to explore Yellowstone. Indian troubles prevented an expedition in 1866, but by the early summer of 1867 conditions appeared sufficiently peaceful for the move. The *Montana Post* (Virginia City) carried an announcement of the proposed expedition and suggested that those interested contact Judge Samuel T. Hauser or Truman C. Everts for further details.[13]

But on July 1, 1867, Meagher fell from a steamboat tied up at Fort Benton and drowned. The expedition collapsed, except that Dr. James Dunlevy, surgeon for the Territorial Volunteers, appears to have led a party up to the Mud Volcano, according to a descriptive news item in the *Montana Post,* August 24, 1867. In 1868 there was only talk of an expedition, and in 1869 the ambitious plans fell through when an Indian scare swept the Gallatin Valley.

By that time most knowledgeable Montanans knew that the Upper Yellowstone held wonders, best known of which were the lake and falls. "The source of the Yellowstone is a clear, deep beautiful lake, far up among the clouds," wrote an eastern artist who published a picture book about Montana in 1868. "Near the lake the river makes a tremendous leap down a perpendicular wall of rock forming one of the highest and most magnificent waterfalls in America."[14]

Meanwhile other changes were taking place in Montana: men with agrarian backgrounds were turning their eyes from the mountains to Montana's plains and valleys. Such men scanned the terrain and envisioned not mines, but farmhouses and barns, pastures and corrals, fields of wheat and hay. Even as mining expanded, the valleys of Montana began to fill with farms and ranches. When the buffalo disappeared, they were replaced with cattle and sheep; fences, roads, and irrigation ditches appeared. In 1868 plows for breaking virgin sod were selling for $125 to $150 gold, common plows for $80, hoes for $8, and axes for $9 gold. Already the Gallatin Valley was filled with great hay ranches, and livestock were being driven there from the mining districts for the winter. In the newspapers advertisements for farm implements appeared next to assay-office notices, feed store ads next to such articles as "News from the Mines," which in turn might appear next to articles on "Agricultural Prospects," or beside a headline warning of a "Sioux Invasion of Lower Gallatin Valley." Montana was indeed the land of opportunity, and the farmer, the cattleman, and the merchant were already vying with the miner in importance.

By 1869 many a Jason had abandoned his search for the golden fleece. The riches men had hoped to find in Montana were not forthcoming. For most people — older but wiser — a steady job meant three square meals a day, a roof overhead, and a little money for clothing. Instant wealth was a dream, a nearly abandoned hope.

Three men who had almost given up the search for wealth were thrown together in the late 1860s. They were hired by the same employer, the Boulder Ditch Company, which furnished water to the placers at Diamond City, a ludicrously named boomtown at the head of Confederate Gulch, about midway between Helena and White Sulphur Springs. The three men were no longer young in 1869. Two of them, Charles W. Cook and David E. Folsom, were thirty, and the third, William Peterson, was thirty-eight. They were still searching for the big chance, however, and one of them, Charles Cook, who was in charge of the Ditch Company operation, was endowed with an unusual strain of curiosity. His closest friend in the Ditch Company was David E. Folsom. Both men were Yankees and Quakers. Cook was from Unity, Maine, and Folsom

from Epping, New Hampshire; they had been schoolmates together in Quaker institutions, and were lifelong friends.[15]

Twenty-five-year-old Charles Cook had headed for Montana
in 1863, but upon arriving at Omaha, had discovered that he
would have to make his way to Montana via Denver. He purchased
a team and wagon and drove to Denver, arriving just about the
time it was nearly washed away by a flood that came roaring
down Cherry Creek. (Shortly thereafter the bodies of the Hungate
family, mutilated by Indians, were brought into the city. This
caused panic among the citizenry, and, months later, was partly
responsible for the Chivington massacre.) Cook left Denver after
a few days, however, taking a job on a freight train bound for
Virginia City. His job was herding 125 head of cattle. The train
was led by seasoned frontiersmen, and in forty days they covered
500 miles across alkali wastes and swollen streams.[16]

Between Rock Springs and Fort Bridger they had an Indian
scare. Cook's party was surrounded by "one hundred fifty to two
hundred renegades." "Some were naked and had their chests daubed
with red, yellow, and black; some would have one-half painted
red and the other yellow, and with their faces painted, giving [some]
a grotesque, some a terrifying appearance," Cook reminisced. The
crisis lasted most of a day and a night. By evening fears had
begun to lessen, even though the Indians, who had feasted on one
of the party's cows, built a big fire and indulged in a dance cele-
brating the fresh scalp they had taken that morning, just before
meeting Cook's party.[17]

"I was tired," Cook remembered, "and [as] I spread my
blankets and prepared to lie down some of the boys said, 'Why
you aren't going to lie down, are you?' 'Well,' I remarked, 'they
can scalp me just as well lying down as standing up; anyway, I
am not going to sit up to see it done.'" The next day they
joined up with a troop of soldiers and were safe.[18]

Cook worked at Virginia City for a time, then at Helena,
and finally took employment at Diamond City, to the southeast,
where he met his old friend, David Folsom. The two must have
had many a story to tell one another.

Folsom had arrived in Montana before Cook. He had hired
out as a hunter with the so-called Fisk party of 130 persons that
had come west from St. Paul in 1862, the year of the Sioux up-

rising in Minnesota. The "Second Assistant and Commissary" with the party was Nathaniel Pitt Langford, who would later make his strong pitch for immortality on the grounds — implied if not flatly stated — that *he* was the most important individual in the creation of the Yellowstone National Park. Folsom and Langford undoubtedly had a passing acquaintance from this time on.[19]

In Virginia City Folsom had made something of a name for himself when, in a poolhall altercation, he had knocked his adversary cold by hitting him on the forehead with a billiard ball. His prostrated tormentor, it developed, was the notorious outlaw George Ives, and Folsom used Quaker wisdom (although he had not exerted Quaker patience nor practiced Quaker nonviolence) by getting out of town — fast! By 1869 he was working with his old friend Charley Cook at the Ditch Company.

The third man was a Dane named William Peterson. He had been a seaman for a decade before he headed for the Idaho mines from San Francisco in 1861. But fortune never smiled on him, and in 1865 he went to work for the Ditch Company. Thus Cook knew him well by 1869, and Folsom he knew as a brother. It is these three men of Montana's "New Breed," none of them young or really successful as success was measured in the territory (though later Cook and Folsom would become prominent sheepranchers around White Sulphur Springs, and Peterson would be a respected citizen of Salmon Falls, Idaho), who figure in the next episode of the Yellowstone story.

Rumors spread rapidly, and somehow Charley Cook knew that some of Montana's Very Important Men had planned to make an exploration into the upper Yellowstone country, first in the summer of 1867 and then in 1868, and he knew that the plans had failed to materialize. In 1868 he had even made an effort to organize his own party for such an exploration, but the season had been late — it was mid-September — and he had abandoned the project for another year.[20]

As early as June 1869, rumors of an expedition to be led by some very prominent men were again rife throughout the territory. Cook and his two friends applied and were accepted. Cook felt highly complimented to be invited along. By July, however, the news spread that a number of the more notable members had excused themselves on the pretense of "pressing business engagements"; then a change in orders canceled out the military contingent they had expected to furnish them protection from Fort Ellis, and with barely a dozen persons left, the whole trip was canceled. Cook returned home. "If I could get one man to go with me," he exclaimed, "I'd go anyway." And Bill Peterson said, "Well, Charley, I can go as far as you can."

"Well, I can go as far as both of ye's," countered David Folsom. And so they went.

They had five horses — three to ride, two for the packs — and the usual campers' gear for a six-week outing. This included fishing tackle, a pick and a pan, repeating rifles, Colt six-shooters (probably Army 44s), sheath knives, and a double-barreled shotgun "for smaller game." They also had a good field glass, a pocket compass, a thermometer, and a dog named Flora. They carried a copy of De Lacy's map of Montana that included part of Yellowstone.

September 6. Time: sunset. Place: Crow Creek 30 miles from Diamond City. Scene: a haystack in the foreground and five horses helping themselves to their supper, a campfire in the rear with all the paraphernalia of a camper's outfit scattered around promiscuously, three unpretentious looking individuals also scattered around promiscuously. The long-talked-of-expedition to the Yellowstone is off at last but shorn of the prestige attached to the names of a score of the brightest luminaries in the social firmament of Montana, as it was first announced. It has assumed proportions of utter insignificance, and of no importance to anybody in the world except the three actors themselves. Our leave-taking from friends who had assembled to see us start this morning was impressive in the highest degree and rather cheering withal. "Goodby, boys, look out for your hair," "If you get back at all you will come on foot," "If you get into a scrap remember I warned you," "It is the next thing to suicide," etc. etc., were the parting salutations that greeted our ears as we put spurs to our horses and left home and friends behind.

They crossed the Missouri on a "water-logged ferry-boat" at Three Forks (then called Gallatin City), the pipe dream of some town speculator's hope. Since it was laid out ostentatiously on paper in 1863 it had progressed to the sum total of "two 'she-bangs' which fulfill[ed] all requirements of the place by dispensing bacon, coffee, tea, sugar, and calico in limited quantities and forty-rod liquor in unlimited quantities." They continued across the Gallatin Valley, with its "wide fields thickly studded with golden shocks." Soon they entered the town of Bozeman, which they found a thriving community, buzzing with the good news that the Northern Pacific surveyors had decided to run their railroad over Bozeman Pass.

They purchased additional supplies, appointed Billy Peterson as "supercargo and general factotum" (he had had previous experience with packhorses), Charley Cook as captain "to serve during good behavior," his position identified by his possession of the field glasses, and David Folsom as the geographer, since he "had once carried a surveyor's chain two days." They passed by Fort Ellis, two or three miles east of Bozeman. "We think whoever located the post displayed strategic talent of a high order," Folsom commented, "for no Indian would have the temerity to attack it so near the settlements and besides being close to Bozeman it is very convenient for the poor soldiers to exchange their greenbacks for whiskey and all the other little luxuries so necessary to their happiness." They pitched camp four miles beyond the fort, at the foot of the Gallatin Range.

When they resumed their trek, they entered the Yellowstone country almost immediately; they left it (by way of Virginia City to the west) over three weeks later. They appear to have spent just about twenty-one days within the present park boundaries. In general, they followed the Yellowstone River to about a mile east of the mouth of the Gardner. Then they climbed to the top of the ridge that is now called Mount Everts. They headed southeast over Blacktail Deer Plateau, forded the Yellowstone above the mouth of Tower Falls, advanced up the Lamar Valley, turned south onto the Mirror Plateau, then west to the Grand Canyon of the Yellowstone, crossed the river near the Mud Volcano, recrossed the river and advanced up to the outlet of the lake, explored the northeast shore, then advanced up the west side to the Thumb, then crossed over to Shoshone Lake, then went northwest to the Firehole River, observed the thermal activity at the Middle and Lower Geyser basins (but not the Upper Basin — they did not see Old Faithful), and then advanced west to Virginia City. This simplified itinerary may help the reader follow a somewhat more detailed narration of their exploration.

When they broke camp just outside Bozeman, they headed southeast up the East Fork of the Gallatin, crossed the Gallatin–Yellowstone water divide, and followed Trail Creek down to where it joins the Yellowstone. Now they were in Paradise Valley, that beautiful space between the First Canyon just above Livingston and the Second Canyon, also known as Yankee Jim Canyon, nearly twenty-five miles up the river. The whole area bore marks of settlement. There were mines on the east side, at and around the hamlet of Emigrant, but our three adventurers did not go there. They missed the trail that led to a ford and on to the mines, so they continued up the west side. In due time they came upon a ranch, but the cabin was unchinked, the wheat field unfenced, and a stack of antelope and elk hides testified to the rancher's preoccupation with hunting. Although no one was about, Cook, Folsom, and Peterson assumed that the homestead belonged to "Pike County people" — a derogatory phrase signifying shiftless frontiersmen from southern Missouri and Arkansas. But they were wrong; this was the residence of the Bottler brothers, who had been there but a few months after having sold a ranch in the Gallatin Valley, and had not yet had the time to improve their new homestead.[21]

They camped in a cold rain some three miles south of the ranch, but Folsom caught "four splendid fellows whose aggregate weight could not be less than ten pounds," so at least they dined on trout that cold evening. Two days later, with no incidents save their meeting with the old Sheep Eater crone,[22] the trio were camped on Mount Evarts.

"Our road today has been a rough one," Folsom wrote in his diary, "and we are beginning to experience a little of the romance of traveling over an unfrequented country, where the everchanging panorama of mountain scenery is different from anything we have ever seen before. . . . At one point we noticed a slate formation [which] passed through a hill which in wearing away had left two smooth unbroken walls . . . about 60 feet apart and . . . parallel to each other, as a line from the bottom to the top of the hill" — a perfect description of the Devil's Slide, on Cinnabar Mountain, a few miles north of the present park boundaries. The country was also a hunter's paradise. "We saw the tracks of elk, deer, and sheep in great abundance and for several miles were scarcely out of sight of antelope . . . , " he noted.

The next day was the day of their big Indian scare. Shortly after striking camp they spied a lone Indian who was driving a herd of horses toward a clump of willows from which a column of smoke was rising. The Indian had quite obviously seen them, and was hurrying to inform his people. "We halted on the spot and called a council of war," wrote Folsom. "We over hauled our packs, tightened the cinches of our saddles, put new caps upon our revolvers, filled our bullet pouches with cartridges for our rifles, and putting on a bold front started forward, making a slight defection to the left in order to shun them if possible."

Soon two of the red men came dashing up and, to the relief of Cook, Folsom, and Peterson, turned out to be harmless Tukarikas — Sheep Eaters. They soon learned that the old crone they had seen the day before had tried to inform them of this Indian encampment. Compliments were exchanged in limited language and pantomime. Cook, who was known as something of a ladies' man, asked if there were any squaws in the wickiups; Peterson, with a speculative turn of mind, wanted to do some swapping; and Folsom, who prided himself as a hunter, inquired about game and asked whether they had been lucky in hunting. "We did not visit their camp and one of them accompanied us four or five miles begging for ammunition and matches," Folsom said.

Thus began the Cook–Folsom–Peterson tour of Yellowstone. They saw an impressively large number of Yellowstone's wonders through sheer coincidence.

They worked southward, keeping on the plateau two or three miles west of the third canyon (the Black Canyon) of the Yellowstone. Even this was beautiful country: "a high rolling table-land, diversified by sparkling lakes, picturesque rocks and beautiful groves of timber." Then they descended from the plateau and struck a well-worn Indian path, the Bannock Trail. Peterson, in his brief reminiscence, says that they fell in with a band of wild horses which crossed the Yellowstone south of the mouth of the Lamar, forded that river to the north side, and disappeared to the northeast. The explorers, on the other hand, followed the Indian trail southeastward. It wound through the Blacktail Deer Plateau, somewhat west of the present Mammoth–Tower Falls highway, crossed Tower Creek and continued south over Antelope Creek, over a ridge, and then down to one of the few fordable places on the Yellowstone River.

Somewhere in the general vicinity of Tower Falls they camped. For a day they explored the region. They viewed Overhanging Cliff from about the site of the present Calcite Springs overlook, and they were fascinated by the brown basaltic hexagonal columns, and by the formation known today as Cleopatra's Needle. Then they worked their way down the bluff to a "chalky looking bank from which steam and smoke were rising" — Calcite Springs, close to the so-called Bannock Ford. Here were numerous sulphur springs, making an unpleasant stench, but if one could ignore the odor, great beauty could be seen. "All the crevices were lined with beautiful crystals of sulphur, as delicate as frost-work," wrote Folsom, adding that somehow — perhaps by a volcanic eruption — a bar had been created, protruding far out into the stream. "While we were standing by, several gallons of black liquid ran down and hardened upon the rocks. We broke some of this off and brought it away, and it proved to be sulphur pure enough to burn readily when ignited." Folsom picked his way gingerly along the steaming crevices lest the ground should give way, "but the Captain [Cook] with the most reckless abandon had to sniff the vapor from every crevice and test the temperature of every spring." Sure enough, Captain Charley fell through the top of "a crevice fifteen inches wide and several feet in depth"; only a headlong tumble away from it into a mass of ashes saved him. They lowered the thermometer by a string into the hole, and the temperature shot up immediately to 194°. The captain was bothered not a whit. He continued choosing specimens and burdening his subordinate with enough "sulphur, carbonate of lime, pumice stone, basalt and cinders" to load a mule. However, said Folsom, "as I had an aversion to carrying more than I can lift, the most of them are lying there yet."[23]

The lengthening shadows of evening warned them to leave, and they reclimbed the bluff and emerged at the head of the canyon. "Here," recorded Folsom, "a stream of considerable size that arises in the mountains away to the west, goes dashing along the bed of a deep ravine over a succession of cascades which increase in height and beauty, and culminate in a perpendicular fall of 138 feet, thence flowing between vertical walls which taper off towards the river. . . . The sides around the falls were covered with lichens which, being constantly wet with spray, gave the wall the appearance of being painted green of the deepest hue." They had seen Tower Falls.[24]

Thus far their exploration had been geographically logical, but an explanation is in order for their having crossed the river and gone up the Lamar, then south onto the Mirror Plateau, then west to the falls. "Before leaving our camp on the Yellowstone River just above the outlet of Tower Creek, near Tower Fall, we carefully considered our course," Cook reminisced more than fifty years later.

"We saw that the Yellowstone river flowed from a deep canyon, and on account of the difficulty we had in getting around Tower Creek, we considered it best to cross over and follow what seemed to be an almost parallel branch of the Yellowstone river." Cook was referring to the Lamar, which was not parallel to the Yellowstone, but at the time they did not know this. When they became aware of their error, they headed back for the Yellowstone.[25]

On September 16 they broke camp, forded the river as the Indians — and perhaps John Colter — had done, and followed the trail east for nine miles along the northern fringe of Specimen Ridge, until it reached the Lamar. They worked upstream until timber surrounded them, and pitched camp. Here their isolation from all the rest of mankind, and the presence all about them of thousands of living things of a lesser order, penetrated their souls; they felt poignantly lonely. Surrounded by a black forest of spruce and pine, with a star-studded sky above them, at first they heard only the sigh of the wind whispering through the branches, and then came the noises of prowling beasts. "The wolf scents us afar," wrote Folsom, "and the mournful cadence of his howl adds to our sense of solitude; the roar of the mountain lion awakens the sleeping echoes of the adjacent cliffs and we hear the elk whistling in every direction. . . . Even the horses seem filled with a feeling of dread, stop grazing and raise their heads to listen and then hover around our campfire as if their safety lay in our companionship. We pile up the logs and build a fire that shall last all night. . . ."

It stormed that night, and the next day they advanced a mere six miles over ridges and hills south to a better camping place where there were wood, water, grass, and a place beneath spruce trees for their "blanket tent," with spruce boughs piled to protect them on the windward side. By noon it was snowing again, and the horses suffered so that the men had to picket them to keep them from running away. All the next day the storm continued, and they remained in camp while a half-foot of snow fell all about them. But the following day was clear, and the Absarokas to the east of them "glistened like burnished silver in the sunlight."[26]

Their vantage point was from the divide separating one of the northeast-flowing tributaries of the Lamar (probably Flint Creek) from those streams flowing westward to the Yellowstone. Actually they were on the east side of a vast area of woods, lakes, marshes, and thermal phenomena, a wild paradise known as the Mirror Plateau. Their aim was to head west toward the Yellowstone, not retracing their steps but instead advancing in the direction of the falls. They could travel only by guess and by God, for the view that spread out before them, northwest to southwest, hid surface features: "the dark, green foliage deepened in hue as it receded till it terminated at the horizon in a boundless black forest," as the diarist described it. To the south, however, rising in the crisp after-storm air, they could see "dense clouds of steam rising above the tree tops." So they headed for the falls (that is, in the direction where they thought the falls should be), by way of the hot springs.

They plunged into the wood and made the acquaintance of the Yellowstone's hellish jackstraw pine forests. They progressed barely a mile an hour. The going was a little better in the afternoon. One stream they crossed turned out to taste bitter, "like a mixture of alum, vinegar, and water." They camped two miles farther on after a hard eight-mile advance.

The next day the trio saw their first hot-spring basin. In all probability it was the one that had sent up the steam cloud they had observed the previous morning. This was undoubtedly the Basin Group on Shallow Creek, even today accessible only by trail. They had arrived at a shallow ravine "from which steam rose in a hundred columns and united in a cloud so dense as to obscure the sun," recorded the diarist.

In some places it spurted from the rocks in jets not larger than a pipe-stem; in others it curls gracefully up from the surface of boiling pools from five to fifteen feet in diameter. In some springs the water was clear and transparent; others contained so much sulphur that they looked like pots of boiling yellow paint. One of the largest was as black as ink. Near this was a fissure in the rocks several rods long and two feet across in the widest place at the surface, but enlarging as it descended. We could not see down to any great depth on account of the steam, but the ground echoed beneath our tread with a hollow sound, and we could hear the waters surging below, sending up a dull resonant roar like the break of the ocean surf into a cave. At these springs but little water was discharged at the surface, it seeming to pass off by some subterranean passage. About half a mile down the ravine the springs broke out again. . . .

One of these thermal phenomena was a collection of mud springs of different colors which all discharged downhill into a 10′-by-30′ vat where their union created a greenish-yellow compound of the consistency, the diarist said, of white lead or hasty pudding. This they christened the Chemical Works; today it is called Joseph's Coat Springs. Three miles farther on, by the side of a substantial creek twenty feet wide, they struck still more hot springs. It was here, on Broad Creek, that they would have witnessed the activity of the Whistling Geyser: "Near the bank of the creek, through an aperture four inches in diameter, a column of steam rushed with a deafening roar, with such force that it maintained its size for forty feet in the air, then spread out and rolled away in a great cloud toward the heavens." All around were beds of alum and saltpeter; a small pond about 300 yards by 150 yards contained all it could hold in solution, and the mud along the shores was white with the same substance.

On September 21, they had a pleasant ride of eighteen miles to the Grand Canyon of the Yellowstone. Cook reached it first, but even after his companions caught up with him, no one spoke for several minutes, so awe-inspiring was the view. "It is pretty, beautiful, picturesque, magnificent, grand, sublime, awful, terrible," wrote Folsom.[27]

Because grass was lacking there, they worked on up to a more favorable place about a half-mile above the Upper Falls and camped there; this would be slightly above the present Chittenden Memorial Bridge. The next day they explored. To measure the falls they used a ball of twine to which a rock was tied for a weight; they let the string out from a forked pole so that it would clear projections along the edge of the crevasse. They estimated the depth of the canyon on the basis of the time it took for a stone to drop to the canyon floor. These were crude methods but better than none, and they testify to the intelligence, curiosity, and thoroughness of the trio. As Cook's brother-in-law later said, "Only men of education and long experience in the West could correctly estimate distances, sizes, and depth as this party did in 1869."[28]

Early on the morning of September 23 they broke camp and advanced up the east bank of the Yellowstone. The river became placid and the terrain opened out. Myriads of ducks and geese were about; Cook shot two of them. Some eight miles above the falls they crossed over to the west side. As they worked upstream, the sounds of thermal activity grew louder. "Dull explosions could be heard half a mile away, sounding like the discharge of a blast underground," and the source soon came into view. There was a large cave running back into the hillside "from which mud had discharged in such quantities as to form a heavy embankment twenty feet higher than the floor of the cave which prevented the mud from flowing off. . . . The cave seemed nearly filled with mud, and the steam rushed out with such volume and force as to lift the whole mass up against the roof and dash it out into the open space in front, and then, as the cloud of steam lifted, we could see the mud settling back in turbid waves into the cavern again," Folsom recorded in his diary. Three hundred yards away was a spring, its entrance into the hillside a perfect arch seven feet high by five feet wide, discharging pure water. Camp was pitched a half-mile away, "and yet," says the diary, "we can distinctly hear every explosion and almost imagine we can feel the ground tremble beneath our feet. . . ." They had seen the Mud Volcano and the Dragon's Mouth Spring.[29]

The next morning, September 24, the trio forded the river again to the east side, and advanced on up the eight miles to the lake. They surveyed it visually in sufficient detail to grasp its general outline, noted the forest cover on all sides and the three islands; they also noted the trout in the lake, and the thousands of wild ducks, geese, pelicans, and swans that fed in its shallow places. They worked around to the eastern extremity, then returned and crossed to the west side of the outlet below the present site of Fishing Bridge. Provisions were getting low, and perhaps they were beginning to hanker for a little more civilization. They decided to go up the west side of the lake to the head (actually they only went to the

West Thumb), then search for the headwaters of the Madison River and follow it downstream until evidence of placer activities, and eventually the "civilization" of Virginia City, would come into view.

As they approached the Thumb, they examined the thermal phenomena from the Potts Hot Spring Basin on up to the Thumb Basin, which, unfortunately, few people bother to examine today. They examined several hundred springs, from tiny fountains to pools seventy-five feet in diameter and very deep. The water had a "pale violet tinge, and was very clear," so that they could see fifty or sixty feet below the surface. "In some of these, vast openings led off to the side, and as the slanting rays of the sun lit up these dark caverns," the diarist described, "we could see the rocks hanging from the roofs. . . . Some of the springs would lower ten feet or so while another would rise and overflow, sending a torrent of hot water sweeping down to the lake. At the same time, one near at hand would send up a sparkling jet of water ten or twelve feet high, which would fall back into its basin, and would then perhaps instantly stop boiling and finally settle into the earth or suddenly rise and discharge its waters in every direction over the rim; while another, as if wishing to attract our wondering gaze, would throw up a cone six feet high, with a loud roar." They also noted the cones in the lake, giving out hot water to the icy sea surrounding them — the origin of the "Fishing Cone" so commonly mentioned in the first half-century of the park's history — and they witnessed the mud pots, which are still active at the Thumb. Fifty-three years later, Cook declared that the thermal phenomena around the Thumb were far less active than they had been at the time of his first visit.

Two days later they left, first taking a final look at the Yellowstone Lake, where it lay nestled amid the forests, "its crystal waves dancing and sparkling in the sunlight as if laughing for joy for their wild freedom." With a hint of clairvoyance, the diarists added: "It is a scene of transcendent beauty which has been viewed by but few white men, and we felt glad to have looked upon it before its primeval solitude should be broken by the crowds of pleasure seekers which at no distant day will throng its shores."

On the 29th they headed west, hoping to meet the Madison. "I do not remember where we camped the evening of the 29th," Cook wrote in 1922, "but distinctly remember arriving at a lake deeply set in the mountains sometime in the early afternoon. . . ."

One of the packhorses slipped and rolled to the water's edge. The body of water was Shoshone Lake, about twelve miles southwest-by-west of the Thumb. Then they turned north and on October 1, after a tiring and disagreeable climb to the Snake–Madison divide, came down into a small valley about six miles across. It proved to be the south fork of the Madison — the Firehole River — but they had heard stories of a "Burnt Hole" and a "Death Valley," and they concluded, wrongly, that this must be it.[30]

They had followed the ridge, or "Dike," as they called it, down into the Lower Geyser Basin, from which great clouds of steam arose. What later bore the name of the Great Fountain Geyser was in the early stages of eruption, and, taking advantage of a strong breeze that blew the steam away, they approached the edge of the geyser hole from upwind:

At that moment the escaping steam was causing the water to boil up in a fountain five or six feet high: It stopped in an instant, and commenced settling down — twenty, thirty, forty feet — until we concluded that the bottom had fallen out, but the next instant, without any warning it came rushing up and shot into the air at least eighty feet, causing us to stampede for higher ground.

When they were safe, they turned around and gazed upon it, with the "setting sun shining into the spray and steam drifting toward the mountains [giving] it the appearance of burnished gold. . . . We could not contain our enthusiasm," Cook reminisced, "with one accord we all took off our hats and yelled with all our might." The geyser spouted for a few minutes more and then settled down for the remainder of the time they were there.

They traveled up the Firehole five miles to what is today called the Midway Geyser Basin, and there found such gigantic springs along the riverbank that the waters turned the stream "blood warm a quarter of a mile below . . . and," the diarists add, "one of the springs was 250 feet in diameter, and gave every indication of spouting powerfully at times." This was the great Excelsior Geyser, which blew itself out in 1888 and is now a giant, bubbling hot spring.

They had arrived in the valley on October 1, and they left it on the 3d. It is to be noted that they did not advance beyond the Midway Geyser Basin and so did not see Old Faithful or the thermal

phenomena of the Upper Basin at all. Without telling us much about
their trip down the Madison or even mentioning the junction of the
Firehole and the Gibbon which creates the Madison, the diarists
merely state that by the 4th they were in the "broad valley of the
lower Madison. . . ." The next day they recognized familiar landmarks, and they arrived at home at Diamond City on October 11,
thirty-six days after their departure.

A statement made by Cook during the Golden Anniversary of
the Park (1922) places their last camp on the Firehole River, just
above Madison Junction. Cook also said that they felt the settlers
should be kept out and the country "kept for the public some way,"
and that later Folsom made the "definite statement to General
Washburn that he hoped to see the Government step in and prevent
private settlement."[31]

The Cook–Folsom–Peterson expedition did not result in the
immediate dissemination of knowledge of the valley of the Upper
Yellowstone, nor in the creation of the park. The three men were
well aware of their humble status in the territory, and they did little
to advertise their achievements. The heavily edited article about
their expedition that appeared in the *Western Monthly Magazine*
for July 1870 was read by very few people, and most of the copies
were destroyed in the great Chicago fire.[32]

Nevertheless Charles Cook, David Folsom, and William Peterson
deserve respectful mention. They conducted a successful exploration
in a day when unforeseen events were even more likely than they
are today to destroy the best laid plans. A scratch could bring on
fatal blood poisoning, a frightened horse could throw its rider into
a clump of stones that could crack bones or break a neck, a loaded
rifle could discharge accidentally, Indians could drive off stock, or the
stock could stray, become lame, or slip, fall, and have to be destroyed.
In such a free society as existed in Montana Territory, a group of
men could form quickly and dissolve with equal rapidity, occasionally
with a little gunfire for accompaniment.

None of these things happened to Cook, Folsom, and Peterson.
As with Lewis and Clark nearly sixty-five years before, these men
seemed to accept a division of tasks while sharing a mutual desire to
succeed in the undertaking. Moreover, they possessed something
else in abundance: an acute, highly sensitive intellectual curiosity,
and sufficient will to satisfy it. They went out of their way to see

hot springs, they climbed down and examined the deposits on the floor of the Yellowstone below Tower Falls, they went to great trouble to measure the depth of the Grand Canyon of the Yellowstone and the height of the falls, and they possessed sufficient aesthetic sensitivity to scan the lake as they were leaving it, waxing poetic about its beauty, and prophesying about its future. They carried a prospector's pick and pan with them, but if they ever paused to try the gravel of a promising stream for gold, they never mentioned it in their diaries. And it is likely that they lamented Yellowstone's probable fate and did wish that it could somehow be reserved for the public at large. No doubt about it, Cook, Folsom, and Peterson deserve more credit than they have received.

But they did receive some. Their exploits were heralded in the sparsely settled territory of Montana by word of mouth, and some of the prominent Montanans — such as Nathaniel P. Langford, Sam T. Hauser, and General Henry D. Washburn — were perhaps chagrined that they had not pushed through their exploration and grew doubly determined to accomplish it the next year. "Langford remarked to me in a jocular way," Cook remembered in 1922, "that they were going up to see that country we lied so much about."[33]

8

The Washburn-Langford-Doane
Expedition and the First
Hayden Expedition

The chain of circumstances leading from the Cook–Folsom–Peterson expedition of 1869 to the Washburn–Langford–Doane exploration of 1870 is clearly defined. The story is traced in the early maps of Montana and the changes that were made in them. And it concerns David E. Folsom.

Shortly after his return from Yellowstone, Folsom went to work for the surveyor-general of Montana, General Henry D. Washburn. The office assistant was Walter W. De Lacy, who had been through the southwest corner of Yellowstone in 1863.

De Lacy had a natural interest in that fascinating area, and if his expedition had not been made up of such wild, uncontrollable men — remember that he called them the "Forty Thieves" — he would have spent more time there than he did. In 1864 he was commissioned by the territorial legislature to make a map of Montana. He completed it, "one of the more famous western maps," in 1865.[1]

The part of Yellowstone that he actually traversed is shown fairly correctly. There is an unnamed lake above Jackson Lake which should have been named De Lacy since he discovered it and correctly affiliated it with the Snake River system, rather than with the Madison system, which Hayden and others insisted on doing. But Hayden named it Lake Shoshone, and the name stuck. De Lacy also has an approximately correct position for the Firehole region, which he labeled "Hot Spring Valley," and he was aware of Captain Raynolds's journey (though he misspelled the captain's name), and of the position of Henry's Lake. To the east, where he had never been, De Lacy was totally off, placing the Yellowstone Lake too far east with the Wind River Mountains *west* of the lake.[2]

164

What was more logical then for De Lacy to begin asking Folsom, and Cook too, when he saw him, for information on the terra incognita known as Upper Yellowstone? In 1870 a revised De Lacy map of Montana was published, which embodied all the intelligence De Lacy could cull from Cook and Folsom, including a tracing of their route. "The map," explained Cook's son-in-law, "indicates more accurately than can all the historical writings of the early days the actual knowledge that the outside world had of the Yellowstone Park region prior to the exploration of the Washburn Expedition in 1870." And he adds that General Washburn took one of these maps with him, "arranged to fold so as to be carried," on his exploration trip to the Yellowstone region in 1870, "and also a copy of the diary of Mr. Cook and Mr. Folsom." And there is evidence that Washburn followed some of their advice concerning the route. The linkage between Cook–Folsom–Peterson, 1869, and Washburn–Langford–Doane, 1870, is now complete.[3]

In 1870 the Union Pacific was a year old, Grant was in the second year of his presidency, and the post-Civil War boom — which has been called the Great Barbecue — was under way. A generation born in the late 1830s and early 1840s, having spent the beginning of its manhood on the Civil War, was trying to make up for lost time, grasping for the big chance. Even those who had not fought in the war found themselves caught up in the spirit of the time, which was intensified by the infusion of Civil War veterans, loose money, and a conscious awareness of a West that was undespoiled, rich in resources, and available for the taking. Men of that generation wanted everything at once — wealth, prestige, political power, the honor of their contemporaries and of posterity.

Most of them did not succeed. Cook, Folsom, and Peterson remained middle class. But remember Cook's delight at being "invited" — "accepted" would be a better word — to accompany the ruling lions of Montana on an expedition to the Yellowstone? Then those illustrious dignitaries dropped out for one reason or another, and the three solid middle-class citizens in a sober, methodical, common-sense way took a journey into the Upper Yellowstone. This must have piqued Montana's Very Important Men, for the next year they explored the Yellowstone and made of it a big, well-publicized operation.

Who were these social lions? They were led by General Henry D. Washburn, Nathaniel P. Langford, and Lieutenant Gustavus C. Doane, 2d U.S. Cavalry. Other Montana notables were Walter Trumball, Truman C. Everts, Jacob Smith, Cornelius Hedges, Samuel T. Hauser, Warren C. Gillette, and Benjamin Stickney — ten men in all. Not all of them were VIPs but all were at least sufficiently prominent to be accepted as fringe members of the "establishment." This applies to Lieutenant Doane too: a more ambitious, constantly frustrated army officer has seldom been seen. Most of these men were proud of their prominence in business, law, and politics, and some of them desired a great deal more fame than they commanded — or deserved. There was one other bond between them: most of the ten men were Masons in good standing, and the Masons are of considerable historical importance in territorial Montana.

General Henry D. Washburn was thirty-eight years old at the time, a native of Ohio who had become a surveyor in western Indiana. He trained in the law, entered the Civil War, and received the breveted rank of major general. He then served two terms in Congress, 1866–69, but did not run for reelection in 1868. Instead he accepted an appointment as surveyor-general of Montana, which post he held until his death in Indiana, January 26, 1871. Although a newcomer to Montana, he appears to have commanded respect, or at least authority.[4]

Of Lieutenant Gustavus C. Doane we shall also hear a good deal more. Born in Galesburg, Illinois, in 1840, he was educated at the University of the Pacific at Santa Clara, California, and fought in the Civil War. He saw service along the Mississippi, acquired a wife, and subsequently served on the Indian frontier. In 1869 he was stationed with the Second Cavalry at Fort Ellis, just east of Bozeman. In 1878 his southern wife divorced him at Virginia City on grounds of "desertion, abandonment, and extreme cruelty." He then made a locally propitious marriage to the daughter of Dr. Hunter, owner of Hunter's Hot Springs, down the valley below Livingston. A tall, muscular, dark-haired man in 1870, Doane would spend the remainder of his life searching vainly for glory. At one time he worked desperately to be appointed superintendent of Yellowstone National Park, but to no avail.[5]

Cornelius Hedges lived a long and useful life in Montana, being a leader of the Montana bar and an advocate of quality education.

He was born in Westfield, Massachusetts, in 1831, so he was thirty-nine years old in 1870. He was a graduate of Yale and had a law degree from Harvard; he later practiced in Iowa and went to Montana in 1864. He would be the Mason delegated by his brethren to perform the Masonic formalities at the laying of the cornerstone of the Roosevelt Memorial Arch at the North Entrance to the park in 1903.[6]

Samuel T. Hauser, who appears from the diaries to have been very irascible and as insensate to beauty as a buffalo, was a civil engineer and president of the First National Bank of Helena; President Cleveland appointed him governor of the territory in 1885. Warren Gillette and Benjamin Stickney were merchants, and Gillette had interests in Diamond City, so he certainly knew of Cook and Folsom. Walter Trumbull was an assistant assessor of internal revenue and the son of Senator Lyman Trumbull of Illinois. A man named Jake Smith enlisted at the last moment. Smith was at various times a butcher, a tanner, a stockbroker, and a millionaire, and he was an inveterate gambler.

Then there was Truman C. Everts, the assessor of internal revenue for Montana. Because he lost his way in Yellowstone and thus achieved a certain kind of notoriety, Everts deserves a little more attention. He was a native of Vermont, had once lived in Jackson County, Michigan, and then in Kentucky. He had joined the Union forces and when a Colonel Norris (who was later to be second superintendent of the park) first met him he was a sanitary commission agent. Subsequently Everts went to Montana, where he was appointed assessor of the territory. In 1870 he and Colonel Norris had traveled down to Fort Ellis together, Norris to head on into Yellowstone country.[7]

In 1870, Hauser was thirty-seven, Gillette was thirty-eight, Stickney was thirty-two, Trumbull was twenty-four, Everts was fifty-four, Langford thirty-nine, and Smith forty. That so many of these men had had connections with the internal revenue department is interesting, in view of the fact that the treasury farmed out the offices and levied a certain sum to be paid to the federal government; what was left over went to the tax collector. This system, which dates back to the Roman Empire at least, served to enrich these Montanans, especially Langford and Hauser, the latter using such moneys to launch his bank. Some rather dark rumors are still floating around in Montana about some of their maneuvers.

Indeed it was an unlikely roster of explorers: politicians, tax gatherers, merchants, lawyers, career officers, surveyors, bankers, gamblers. Yet something attracted them to the expedition. Possibly they succumbed to an ardent sales pitch, which would certainly have been delivered by N. P. Langford, or perhaps they simply wanted the chance to take a junket away from the humdrum duties of home and business. Some may have had an eye out for business possibilities. And perhaps the hint of danger and adventure and the opportunity to participate in something with possible historical significance caused them to give up the comforts of home and duties of business and join the exploration.

The expedition, which lasted from August 17 to September 27, Helena to Yellowstone and back — forty-two days or six weeks — originated with these Helena men. Hedges knew the two New Englanders Folsom and Cook and believed their story,[8] and Langford knew Folsom. All the men knew each other, either through business or as friends; they were fellow Masons. It is impossible, under these circumstances, to pinpoint the prime mover.

Incentives to get moving kept hounding the group in those first nine months of 1870. That lover of the West, Philetus W. Norris, came into town from an abortive Yellowstone trip with Frederick Bottler, and pleaded with Washburn, Everts, and Hauser to get under way, but, discouraged by their procrastination, he left town. And General Sheridan breezed into Helena for a couple of days in June and years later, in his *Memoirs,* mentioned his interest in Yellowstone at that time.[9]

The man who would most especially have liked mankind to give him credit for being the prime mover was Nathaniel P. Langford. On his own authority he took the credit for contacting Major General Winfield S. Hancock in St. Paul, in the spring of 1870, and outlining the operation with a request for a military escort; Sam Hauser, also in St. Paul at the time, backed him up. The escort was assured with certain reservations — and when conflict with the Crow Indians arose that summer, those reservations were applied. Also, of the twenty or so members who had applied to go along, half of them found it convenient to back out. Then James Stuart, the Indian fighter, was invited along, but ultimately he too was unable to go. Finally General Washburn telegraphed Hancock for help and secured an escort consisting of Lieutenant Doane and an imposing troop of five enlisted soldiers. They, along with two packers, two black cooks, and the ten men left on the roster, became the personnel of the Washburn–Langford–Doane expedition into upper Yellowstone.[10]

The expedition started from General Washburn's office on Rodney Street in Helena, with estimated time of departure 9:00 A.M., Wednesday, August 17, 1870. Actually it did not get under way until midafternoon; Benjamin Stickney was "tight" — according to Sam Hauser's skimpy diary — and "several of the party," according to a news item in the *Helena Herald*, "were 'under the weather' and tarried in the gay Metropolis until 'night drew her sable curtain down,' when they started in search of the expedition."[11]

Very Important Men could not be bothered with such trivialities as recalcitrant mules, however, and when three packs came off in the first 300 yards the men merely bade adieu to the packers, and rode on out of town. They spent the night at the home of a rancher named Greenish, where they enjoyed a card game while a strong, cold wind howled outside. Already some of the men were facing the unpleasant fact that they were, in truth, dudes, soft from sitting at rolltop desks and unwise in what they had brought along, or what they had failed to bring along, or even in bringing *themselves* along. "Didn't sleep at all," Hedges entered succinctly in his diary, "dogs bothered."

The next day they pushed a few miles on down the road to another ranch, Vanletburg's, where it began snowing. This was sufficient excuse to stay over a day. "It was so cold and so stormy, and some of the party so sore [we] concluded to lay over yesterday," Gillette commented, and Hedges noted that the pack train, under the control of experienced packers, had passed them by. The men whiled away the hours playing cards and the following day galloped into Bozeman with great éclat, whether they really felt like it or not. There they put up at the Guy House, the best hotel in Bozeman.

Their arrival made quite a stir in the little town. That evening they were invited to the home of a Mr. Rich, coowner of Willson and Rich, a leading commercial establishment. "All had white collars but self, much embarrassed," Hedges noted. "There were nine pretty rough looking men to come into the presence of three fine ladies," Gillette added, but apparently the ladies did not mind. They fed the men well, and after dinner they all went into the parlor, where Mrs. Wilson sang for them. Back at the Guy House they met with officers from Fort Ellis, including Lieutenant Doane. "Late in the evening a black man by the name of Lewis and an assessor by the name of Isaacs played on the banjo and guitar together," wrote Gillette. "Slept with Trumbull on a very hard bed, with expectations of bugs, etc. Trumbull, a miserable bedfellow."

On Sunday, August 21, they breakfasted at the hotel. There was much commotion, everyone running around, saying good-byes, "everyone kind, with many good wishes." With a bon voyage gift of a box of cigars, the party rode down to Fort Ellis, and there enjoyed their first camp meal. The army furnished them with a large Sibley tent "which came very acceptable, as the sun was shining hotly."[12] There they played cards, and Jake Smith lost as usual. They packed their goods well, for tomorrow they would be on the trail. "They were furnished with a saddle a piece, and nine pack animals for the whole outfit; they were provided with one aneroid barometer and one thermometer, and several pocket compasses," Lieutenant Doane noted, and he could have added that they carried long-range repeating rifles and needle guns, some of which were borrowed from the army. By agreement they would leave camp each morning by 8:00 A.M. and make camp at 3:00 P.M., thus eliminating the need of a lunch stop.

The first day on the trail, August 22, they crossed Bozeman Pass to Trail Creek, about fifteen miles from Fort Ellis; the second day's journey took them to Bottler's ranch, this in spite of the setback caused when the cavalry horses and mules broke away from the herders and made a beeline home to Fort Ellis. The weather was cool, the scenery superb, with snow on the mountaintops. Some antelope were seen, and a few Crow Indians thirty miles from their reservation made their presence known. In the evening of this second day it began to rain, and at midnight, when Gillette took his turn at guard duty, rain began to fall in torrents, even coming into the tents. But the good farm food, with plenty of milk and butter, fresh corn, and luscious wild serviceberries, made the camp tolerable — that, and for Hedges, the addition of a horn of whiskey, then to bed "and soon was warm at least." Not until noon of the next day did the leaders decamp, and even when the stragglers left at 2:00 P.M., poor Everts had to remain behind with a fever.

The third day brought them twelve miles farther up the Yellowstone, to the base of the Second (Yankee Jim) Canyon, where they camped "on one of the loveliest spots in Montana," with the snow-capped peaks glittering in the setting sun. And they ate well that night. "Our mess table was here supplied with antelope, hare, ducks, and grouse killed during the day with fish caught *ad libitum* in the afternoon," wrote Doane in his official report.

When camp was broken the next morning they followed a rough trail high above the river, through sagebrush and scrub, past the Devil's Slide (which Langford says they named), and came down to the junction of the Gardner with the Yellowstone. During the day they saw unmistakable Indian signs such as the marks of travois poles. They also passed many a prospect hole and remnants of miners' camps; they found some petrified wood, but no fossils. Not far from where they were camped at the mouth of the Gardner was Bear Gulch, "an almost inaccessible mining district," not being worked at that time. Everts rejoined the party there. Hedges was still exhausted, and that night he smoked the last of his box of cigars, took some whiskey, and felt better. "We had a nice bed in river sand," he wrote, "the dashing waters and winds in cedar tops made music, the stars shown brilliant." Lieutenant Doane did not share Everts's naive point of view. "This is our first poor camping place, grass being very scarce, and the slopes of the range covered entirely with sage brush," he said. "From this camp was seen the smoke of fires on the mountains in front, while Indian signs became more numerous and distinct."

The fifth day, August 26, they crossed the boundaries of the future park. They forded the Gardner and kept on the south side of the Yellowstone, but the canyon proved impassable, just as it had to Cook, Folsom, and Peterson, so they turned south after about two miles and emerged upon the same "immense, rolling plateau extending as far as the eye could reach," dotted with ponds, streams, lakes, and groves of pine and aspen, a paradise for elk, deer, antelope, and the beasts that prey on them. It is cleft by Yellowstone's third canyon, the Black Canyon. "Standing on the brink of the chasm the heavy roaring of the imprisoned river comes to the ear only in a sort of hollow, hungry growl, scarcely audible from the depths, and strongly suggestive of demons in torment below," wrote Doane. Appearances were deceptive; the water looked like oil, lofty pines like shrubs. Fish hawks glided about high above the water "and yet a thousand

feet below the spectator"; in clefts in the rocks below, bald eagles
had their eyries, from which they swooped to rob the ospreys of their
trout. Doane described it as "grand, gloomy, and terrible, an empire
of shadows and turmoil." Today this spectacular canyon is seldom
noticed because of the Grand Canyon of the Yellowstone upstream.

The going was rough that day. Packs came loose, trails led
nowhere, and steep hills had to be surmounted. To Lieutenant Doane
this was all part of the job, but it was so tiring and irritating to the
rest that not a single one of them, not even Langford, who was consciously writing for publication, made any mention of the forbidding,
gloomy beauty of the Third Canyon. Instead they all noticed the
difficulties. The great plateau had recently been afire — they sur-
mised the Indians were responsible, although it could have been
set by lightning — and the woods were still ablaze in every
direction, with some moist places left untouched.

Doane worked on ahead, spending the night beyond the regular
pitched camp, which was only five or six miles beyond the previous
one. As the explorers of the previous year had done, he followed
the Indian trail through a deep canyon to the south and into the
valley where the Lamar meets the Yellowstone, which would later
be known as Peaceful Valley, or Yancey's. He kept to this Bannock
Trail, passed a cluster of fifteen deserted Crow wickiups, crossed
"Warm Spring Creek" (shortly thereafter to be named Tower Creek),
and then went into camp. When the rest of the party came into
this camp on the 27th, tired, crotchety, sore, and hungry, they all
acquiesced in Everts's name for it: Camp Comfort. Hedges caught
four big trout, and the hunters (two nameless men who had joined
them for a time) came in with a deer, which they roasted over a
fire, so they ate well. Even the insensitive Sam Hauser noted the
beauty of the place: "Didn't move camp Cenery too beautiful."

From Overhanging Cliff, Hedges scanned the Yellowstone and
gazed down upon Tower Falls — so named, say their diaries, because
of the basaltic columns — and the Tower Creek Canyon, which
Washburn described as looking "like some old castle with its turrets
dismantled but still standing."[13]

They were delighted with the falls, and all of them tried to
estimate its height. Langford figured it at 105 feet, Hauser said 115,
and Gillette insisted it was 113.[14] "I thank God for creating such
scenery and again for permitting my eyes to behold it," Hedges wrote

in his diary, noting that upon his return to camp he found most of the boys playing cards. Lieutenant Doane, suffering excruciating pain from an infected thumb which had been growing worse ever since he left Fort Ellis, nevertheless waxed poetic over the sight. "Nothing," he wrote, "can be more chastely beautiful than this lovely cascade, hidden away in the dim light of overshadowing rocks and woods, its very voice hushed to a low murmur, unheard at the distance of a few hundred yards. Once seen, it passes to the list of most pleasant memories."

Doane's thumb, though lanced with a dull knife, failed to respond, and the lieutenant "passed the night walking in front of the camp fire, with a wet bandage around [his] arm to keep down the pain." Quite possibly he talked with the men about the route to be followed the next day. Washburn and Langford had been advised by Cook and Folsom to seek a short cut from Tower Falls to the Yellowstone Canyon,[15] and some reconnoitering that afternoon by Washburn led them to believe they could head southwest and come to the Grand Canyon of the Yellowstone and the falls.

"Mon. 29. — quite cool this morning. Last night the water froze in the camp. We were up early and broke camp. It takes a long time and is tedious business. All the party went together today." The information in Hedges's diary is supplemented by that in Gillette's: "Took trail in southerly direction right up the mountain." They struck a ridge, from which they could see the Grand Canyon of the Yellowstone, and at one place "a column of steam, rising from the dense woods at a height of several hundred feet, became distinctly visible." Trumbull, Langford, Hauser, Stickney, and Gillette climbed the mountain to their right, named it Mount Washburn, and estimated its height at 10,579 feet (Gillette), or 10,700 feet (Hauser), or 9,800 feet (Langford), or 9,966 feet (Doane — though he did not climb it.)[16]

From the summit of Mount Washburn, as thousands who have taken the rickety Park Company buses up there can appreciate, the explorers were able to obtain a good perspective on the lay of the land. Washburn perhaps described the view southward most succinctly: "The country before us was a vast basin. Far away in the distance, but plainly seen, was the Yellowstone Lake." Gillette's diary adds, "flowing to the north came the Yellowstone River from the lake with silvery brightness, and on either side [of] the river dense black forests of spruce and pine seemed to hold it like a stolid army from the approach of man. Below us and apparently about 10 miles distant was the canyon."

They descended the mountainside a couple of miles and pitched camp at the head of a small stream. Hedges, Washburn, and Doane found a group of remarkable mineral springs — "Hell Broth Springs," Hedges named them, although today they are known as the Washburn Hot Springs. They then followed the creek downstream about three miles, where they came to "a dense growth of small timber on the brink of the Grand Canyon," where the small stream had cut out its own channel before plunging into the Yellowstone. Then they retraced their route to camp. Game abounded in the vicinity: Doane met two buck elk face to face, Jake Smith started up a small bear, and animal tracks were all over. Smith also nearly burned up the expedition with a dried pine tree he fired that got out of control.

On August 30 they trekked around Mount Washburn to a ravine and followed it down to the floor of the Grand Canyon of the Yellowstone, where they pitched camp. They were below a chasm-grotto which they named the "Devil's Den," today known as Crystal Falls, located between the Upper and Lower falls of the Yellowstone — and now seen by few people. Lieutenant Doane, desperate to be a participant in the discovery of these wonders, galloped from spring to spring so he could moisten the wrapping he kept on his hand. "Following this canyon kept me away from water so long that the pain became unsupportable," he recalled. "I abandoned my horse, and have no distinct recollection of how I got to the water's edge, but presently found myself with my arm up to the elbow in the Yellowstone a few yards below the foot of a graceful cascade. In a few minutes, the pain becoming allayed, I proceeded to explore the locality."

All the diarists described the canyon and the falls. Hedges said that he "staid two hours in one spot and drank in inspiration," and even Sam Hauser wrote that the Upper Falls were "probably the prettiest in the world." Jake Smith soon announced that he had seen everything and was ready to move on. (Langford did not like Smith, who, he said, could "burn more and gather less wood than any man he ever camped with." The ill feelings were reciprocal: Smith called Langford "the Yellowstone sharp.") Hauser and

Stickney then scrambled down to the river below the Lower Falls for a drink of water, "the first men that ever reached [the] bottom of [the] canyon below [the] falls." They stayed for over a day and scattered in all directions, exploring. Langford estimated the height of the Upper Falls at 115 feet, of the Lower Falls 320 feet (*Haynes Guide* says they are 109 and 320 feet, respectively). Poor Lieutenant Doane continued to suffer: "Langford and Washburn up all night with him," Hedges recorded.

On September 1, they struck out first west, then south at the bend of the river. They were intrigued at the inky blackness of the bed and banks of a creek which they accurately named Alum, and they worked on upstream to a thermal area which they named Crater Hills (both of these names are still used). There being no good grass, they advanced another three miles to a place surrounded by thermal activity but providing better grass, and there they camped. They were two or three miles above the Mud Volcano, or Geyser, which had attracted so much attention from the Cook–Folsom party. It was still hyperactive; the surrounding trees were covered with its deposits, as was the grass for 200 feet around it. Lieutenant Doane estimated that to produce such effects the mud must have been thrown perpendicularly at least 300 feet. "Occasionally," he wrote, "an explosion was heard like the bursting of heavy guns behind an embankment, and causing the earth to tremble for a mile around." They remained at this camp an extra day.

They had encamped almost at the site of what was later called the Nez Perce Ford. As Washburn described it, "a narrow bench of rock rose up from the bottom, stretching from bank to bank." On the bench the water was only about three feet deep, although in traversing the river deeper water would probably be encountered. Here they crossed to the east side of the river. Then they floundered through timber and thermal phenomena for about ten miles until they reached the lake, where they encamped in a grove on the shore. Had the suffering Lieutenant Doane noticed Langford, riding along with an open penknife in his hand, whetting the blade on the pommel as he rode along? For nine days and nights the lieutenant had been without sleep or rest, even when hanging his ailing arm in a bucket of the coldest water. He wanted to be chloroformed, but Langford hesitated to use the stuff even though he had some with him. On the evening of September 3, they stretched the willing lieutenant out, Hedges held his arm in place, and *then* they informed him that they did not want to use the chloroform! Before the sick man could do much protesting, Langford had plunged the sharpened blade to the tip into the festering thumb and cut to the bone. "An explosion ensued," wrote Doane, "followed by immediate relief." They applied a poultice of bread and water to his hand and by 8:00 P.M. he was asleep. Late the next morning he was still sound asleep, and they stayed over a day because of him.

Doane estimated the altitude of the lake at 7,714.6 feet (*Haynes Guide* fixes it at 7,733); he was intrigued by the black obsidian particles that dotted the beaches and made them sparkle. There was no marine life except trout, which were numerous. "Two men could catch them faster than half a dozen could clean and get them ready for the frying pan," said Doane, adding that many were wormy, and in poor condition for want of food.

Walter Trumbull appears to have been the first person to compare the contours of the lake with the form of the human hand. "Its shape resembles a broad hand of an honest German," he began, "who has had his forefinger and the two adjoining shot off at the second joint, while fighting for glory and Emperor William."

On September 5, the fifteenth day of Doane's journal out from Fort Ellis, they left their camp on the northern shore to go around the east side of the lake, only Jake Smith and Sam Hauser voting against the move. By evening of the 6th they had passed the Brimstone Basin and were camped a little way from the extreme end of the southeast arm of the lake. Hedges complained that they had had nothing but salt meat all that day and that the camp was the poorest they had yet experienced. Langford and he slept between two logs.

They were in the Thorofare area, where the Upper Yellowstone flows into the lake from its source at the base of Yount's Peak. Only Lieutenant Doane appreciated the wildness of the area, describing the swamp valley as being about four miles across and grown up with willows. It was a haven for waterfowl. "The ground was trodden by thousands of elk and sheep, bear tracks and beaver trails were also numerous, and occasionally was seen the footstep of a California lion. . . . During the night we were several times disturbed by the dismal screaming of California lions, and in the morning found their huge tracks close around camp."[17]

The expedition was now entering the most difficult part of the journey. There were no trails save game trails that led nowhere; many large trees had fallen, some close to shore with branches jutting into the lake, and of course these had to be crossed. At one point they camped on a headwater stream of the Snake River, but they did not realize this for another day or two, believing instead that their stream flowed into the lake.

On September 7 — which Doane considered the seventeenth day out of Fort Ellis — he and Langford climbed the highest peak of the mountains immediately to their east. Upon returning, they intended to pick up the trail of the party, which had moved on. And they did accomplish this, crossing the Yellowstone where it was 100 feet wide and a yard deep; then they advanced west through a beautiful open forest, across a grassy valley, passing two little gems of lakes at the foot of high ridges on the west side. Then, as it was getting dark, they discovered that they had lost the trail and were following a herd of elk instead. So they struck for the shore, but were again misled by following a band of elk. They then built a fire, looked for tracks, found the right ones, and arrived in camp at 10 P.M.

The next day Everts and Hedges set out to climb a mountain, get the lay of the land, and possibly determine how best to extricate the party from the primeval mass of fallen timber, jagged rocks, and swamps in which they were struggling. Later, upon returning, the party split for awhile, following two different routes, and for a short, agonizing time Hedges thought he had lost them. "Had neither ammunition or matches. Couldn't find Benj. [Stickney] started to go back to Lake shore and came providentially upon train in camp." And then he added, "some disputing and wrangling over the days failure."

On the nineteenth day, September 9, they advanced west easily for three or four miles, crossing a south-running creek which Doane knew to flow into a heart-shaped lake. Then they turned north. As Hedges recorded in his diary, they "had an awful time floundering through timber, packs off, torn open, men swearing." His steed rolled down hill, did several somersalts, and finally came to a stop between two trees. Fortunately the animal was unhurt. "Everybody," Hedges added, "finding fault and having all sorts of opinions where we were." Under such conditions, they pitched camp early at the first level grassy place they found. All but Everts were accounted for.

The hours slipped by. Packers went back up the trail for a horse that was jammed between two trees, but they saw no sign of Everts. Private Williamson worked his way north to try and find the lake, but returned without seeing Everts, and reported the route impossible. A good pine-knot fire was blazing, and Hauser, Gillette, and Smith played poker deep into the night. Still there was no sign of Everts. The firing of signal-guns and the maintaining of watch fires did no good. Everts did have matches with him, Gillette remembered, but he had no coat or blanket nor a lariat for his horse. He had a gun and some ammunition, but he was notoriously nearsighted.

Everts disappeared on the 9th. On the 10th the party struck out for the northwest, men even climbing trees to help chart their course, and they finally struck the long, slender arm (almost certainly the Flat Mountain Arm) of the lake. Hauser and Langford tramped all the way back to where they had camped on the 7th, and Gillette went off for a full day searching for Everts, but to no avail. They chopped blazes on the trees, even set the woods on fire, but Everts never appeared.

They finally established a semipermanent camp on the south side of the Thumb and there remained through the 15th. On the night of the 11th it began snowing and continued all the next day, until the snow was 15 to 18 inches deep. Fortunately the temperature did not fall too low. It snowed still more on the 14th and 15th. "Poor Everts," lamented Gillette. "I fear he has perished. . . . How I pity him, hungry, wet and cold. I wonder if he killed his mare. I would do it, and dry the meat, so I could pack enough on my back to carry me to the settlements. . . . I fear he is still wandering in the mountains bewildered."

Not all the members were bothered that much. When it stormed, several of them huddled in the tent around a prospector's gold pan raised on a platform, where they kept a small fire blazing. There they played cards: whist, casino, and seven-up. And Jake Smith even found time to construct a boat, which Hedges rowed on the lake. (When they were first at the lake, more than a week before, they had made a raft, but a storm had wrecked it.)

"Twenty-fifth day. — September 15. — The snow-storm abated,

clouds hung overhead in heavy masses, an oppressive dampness pervaded the atmosphere, the snow melted away rapidly under the influence of a warm wind from the west," Doane entered in his journal. He had found a few abandoned wickiups but no other signs of Indians. Save for the mountain lions with a taste for horseflesh, the southern side of Yellowstone seemed perfectly safe.

The next day, September 15, General Washburn ordered the expedition to pack and head west for the Firehole. "I asked him if he deemed further search [for Everts] useless," said Gillette. Washburn took a vote on a resolution put forth by Jake Smith to move on, and only Gillette voted no. They advanced about five miles to some hot springs on the west side (West Thumb Geyser Basin or Potts Hot Springs; Hedges said that the place where they left the lake was one of the stage stations, as of 1904), and from there, the next day, Gillette offered to return and make further search for Everts if one of the party would go with him. "Hauser remarked that, that was a pretty good bluff, as I knew that no one would be willing to stay back from the train," Gillette noted in his diary. But Doane agreed to let Moore and Williamson accompany him, Hedges lent him some boots, his own having deteriorated, and so Gillette and the soldiers backtracked at about the time the main party headed west. (One reason for Gillette's concern was that he had courted Bessie, Everts's daughter.)

Later that day, in a dense growth south of the lake, Gillette met a man in the woods. "He said he was of a party of four who came up Snake River and were camped near our Snow Camp [the camp prior to the Hot Springs Camp]. From his illy repressed nervous manner took him for a man who was fleeing justice." Still later, in a more open part of the woods, Gillette's group "found the trail of the party, plainly discernible in the snow, and made by eighteen or twenty horses, all or nearly unshod. . . . It was evident from the appearance of the trail, that there were more than four men, as the evenness and uniformity of the trail through the snow plainly evidenced the fact that it was made by horses under the saddle and not by loose or packed animals; there being but comparatively few tracks outside of the trail, in the snow." The horse thieves were following the frontier underworld's "skull and crossbones" trail from one side of the mountains to the other with their stolen mounts.[18]

Gillette and the two soldiers never did find Everts. Caches and provisions left behind at camps for his use were found undisturbed. By the 21st, with provisions getting low, they headed back to the lake and then followed the tracks of the main party out through the Madison River. "How he must have suffered at the . . . reflection that he may be within ten or fifteen miles of us," Gillette wrote that day. Less than a week later, on the 27th, they struck a wagon road leading to Virginia City. They arrived at Virginia City with about fifteen pounds of elk left, the remains of an elk heifer killed by one of the soldiers on the 18th.

As for the main party, Washburn and his men headed west by northwest after leaving Gillette, plunging through woods and snow with "much doubt as to where we are and where we should go," wrote Hedges. On the 18th he woke with cold water seeping into his bed — they had slept on a cold, raw, cheerless, hillside, and it was raining again. "Prospect gloomy enough. Felt double disgust. Feet wet, clothes wet. . . . Sat in the rain under tree moodily meditating." The expedition members must have looked especially dismal that morning, like mongrels caught in the rain. Langford, who possessed dry clothes and (if his diary can be believed) was in high spirits and the best of health, even confessed that they "presented a sorry appearance. . . . It is a matter of surprise to me," he added, "that I am the only member of our party who has a rubber coat, or a pair of oil-tanned waterproof boots, or who has brought with him any medicines, tools, screws, etc.; and, except for myself, there is but one member of our party . . . who had the foresight to bring with him a flask of whiskey."

But things improved. In two hours they struck the Firehole River, followed it down past Kepler Cascades (not then named), and when the terrain leveled out again, they found themselves "once more in the dominions of the Fire King." They camped about noon in the Upper Geyser Basin and marveled at what they saw. They christened one of the geysers "Old Faithful" and called others the "Castle," the "Giant," the "Grotto," "Fantail," the "Giantess," and the "Beehive." The next day they rode slowly down to the junction of the Firehole with the river that would eventually be named the Gibbon, noticing the thermal phenomena on the way, and on the 19th they camped at the Madison Junction. On the 20th they were twenty-seven miles farther down the Madison, but this night they were careful, for the district had a bad reputation as a rendezvous for horse thieves and highwaymen, "its dense forests, moderate climate, enormous range, and abundance of game rendering it a pleasant and secure retreat for lawless men." On the 21st they went twenty-six miles, and on the 22d they found numerous prospect holes and reached Farley's, "the frontier *rancho,* on the Madison river," fourteen miles or so above Virginia City.

On the 23d, some ten miles below Virginia City, Lieutenant Doane left the party, reaching Fort Ellis the next day. Sam Hauser galloped up the main street of Helena, "the very impersonation of a prepossessing and gallant cavalier," on the 26th. Hedges, Jake Smith, and Langford reached Helena on the 27th, and probably the remaining members did too.

The dudes from Helena were back. A hot bath, a shave, a haircut, clean clothes, a wife's home-cooked food, the warmth of a kitchen, and the comfort of a bed with springs and mattress did wonders for the veterans of the Washburn–Langford–Doane expedition. Except for what we can infer from their diaries, no permanent animosities seem to have resulted from their trip. This is remarkable, as most of the men were not outdoorsmen, and sore muscles and physical discomfort certainly made them touchy. Even though they lived in the West, they were business or professional men who seldom did more than ride a horse out of the city limits to look over some land they owned — and then they were more likely to ride in a buggy. Granted that the place and the times made them a little tougher than their modern counterparts who go soft fifty weeks a year in an office and then go deer-hunting for two weeks at 10,000-foot altitudes in the crisp October air and die of heart attacks — the one group was still ancestor to the other.

Cornelius Hedges was a fine man in every way, sensitive to beauty and with a feeling for his fellow men, but he was no outdoorsman, and he had felt nauseated, ill, and forlorn during much of the expedition. Truman C. Everts not only was no outdoorsman, he appears to have been singularly lacking in common sense. Jake Smith was a wheeler-dealer, totally insensate to true beauty and devoid of feelings for the wilderness, making of the trip one long, continuous card party. General Washburn had only been in Montana a few months when the expedition took place; he caught a bad cold and died back in Indiana, January 26, 1871 — one suspects he may have been consumptive and have come to Montana for his health.

Sam Hauser, who was later governor of Montana Territory, was another wheeler-dealer, though he knew his way about the West — he had been with the Stuart party in 1863, and a bullet had penetrated his left breast-pocket, bored through a thick memorandum book, and ended flattened against a rib. Hauser had little sensitivity, did not want to go around the lake, and was at best sarcastic to other members of the party — to Gillette, for example. About young Trumbull we know little, though we do credit him with a good report of the expedition which was published in the *Overland Monthly*. Benjamin Stickney, like Trumbull, was rarely mentioned in the diaries, save as a companion for small projects such as climbing a mountain. He became a rancher.

This leaves Langford, Gillette, and Doane. Langford was an ambitious man difficult to appraise, but he appears to have possessed the outdoorsman's knowledge of the woods and to have been sensitive to beauty. Gillette possessed true pioneer lore; we have read his sensible statement that if he were lost he would have killed his mare, dried the meat, and with it have had sustenance to last him to the settlements. He was also concerned enough about Everts to head back into the morass of fallen timber, swamps, and nearly impenetrable terrain from which they had just emerged, to make one last attempt to find the lost man. Lieutenant Doane was definitely the explorer, the adventurer endowed with a sense of destiny.

While they appear to have accepted General Washburn as their leader, it is quite apparent that each man went his own way much of the time. When the going got rough, as on the south side of the lake, they fussed and wrangled, and some went one way, some another. It is surprising that they stayed together as well as they did, that some — Hauser and Smith, for example — did not turn around and go home. When we read between the lines and understand the grumbling, cursing, and just plain obstinacy and cantankerousness of men under trying conditions, the success of the expedition, with the loss of only one man and that only temporarily, becomes simply miraculous. If they had staged an occasional shoot-out over a card game or a dispute about the correct route, we would not be surprised.

But like soldiers returning victorious from terrible battle, the Washburn–Langford–Doane boys had succeeded. They had seen wonderland, and it far exceeded their greatest imaginings. The sufferings of the expedition were forgotten in the adulation they received at home. A few gulps of forty-rod whiskey with the drinks on the house or paid for by the editor of the local newspaper made all experiences take on a rosy hue. It had been a great expedition.

It was also remarkably well publicized. The *Helena Daily Herald* had manifested interest from the inception of the project. It printed all intelligence, accurate and otherwise, during the span of the expedition, and it ran both Washburn's and Langford's narrations of the trip as soon as they were available, prior to October 1. Hedges's articles appeared two weeks later.[19]

Before another year was out, Trumbull would have published a two-part narration in the *Overland Monthly* and Langford a single article in *Scribner's Monthly* (with hideous sketches of Yellowstone wonders by Thomas Moran, who must have blushed at his faulty imagination when he saw the realities a few months later). Lieutenant Doan's *Report* was also published in 1871. Two of the articles, Doane's and Langford's, were accompanied by maps, the latter almost certainly a copy, with slight changes, of the former.[20] In a very short while the newspaper articles were lifted, in whole or in part, and published from coast to coast.[21]

Part of the continuing publicity was a result of the lost man, nearsighted Truman C. Everts. Langford told the press that he must have been captured by Indians, and Gillette and the local editors speculated that he had been done away with by horse thieves.[22] All was sorrow and mourning for the poor man. The local paper reported on October 6 that Judge Lawrence, a prominent Helena citizen, had offered a reward of $600 for Everts's recovery, and George A. Pritchett and Jack Baronett, two men familiar with the country, had outfitted themselves, talked with Sam Hauser, who drew them a map, and headed for the Crow Agency. There they planned to enlist two or three Indian trackers, go to the lake, and begin the search.[23] Meanwhile Cornelius Hedges had written to the paper an account of Everts's good judgment as a woodsman, how he had climbed a high mountain with him the day before he was lost, and how that mountain should be named in honor of that "noble, self-reliant spirit, destined . . . to be quenched by a dismal fate in the wooded wilderness near its base."[24]

Just what *had* happened to Everts? In his well-known article, "Thirty-seven Days of Peril,"[25] he simply stated that the party was floundering through the woods, that under those circumstances each man made his own way, and that it was while thus employed, with the idea that he had found a route, that he strayed out of sight and hearing of his comrades.

This was the same day on which Hedges wrote, " . . . had an awful time floundering through timber, packs off, torn open, men swearing . . . everybody finding fault and all sorts of opinions where we were." In 1885, fifteen years after the event, Jack Baronett, who found Everts, added some more information during an interview, and although he was not there when Everts was lost, we can assume that he talked with most of the members of the expedition before he went in search of the man. "There was some discussion as to the route they should take," he said. "At the close of the conversation, Everts, who was a man of strong prejudices, shouldered his gun and other equipment and started forth alone in the direction he had urged the party to follow. He evidently expected that the party would divide and a portion of them follow him. In this he was mistaken, for the balance of the party remained together and went off in another direction, supposing that Everts would join them when he found they did not follow him."[26]

If Everts was headstrong and started off with a vengeance in the direction he believed correct, then it is understandable why all the shooting of rifles, making of signal fires, and actual searching failed to find him. He was simply too far away to be seen, or found. Certainly he *was* lost, and the only source we have for what happened to him from September 9 until his rescue in mid-October is his own narration. Whether it is truth or fiction or half of each, it is a good yarn. Everts says that his horse ran away from him, carrying with her his blankets, pistols, fishing tackle, and matches — everything save a couple of knives, a small opera glass, and the clothes on his body. In a storm he was frostbitten. While sleeping at some hot springs he fell through the crust and severely burned his hip, a cougar chased him into a tree one night, his brush shelter caught fire and burned his left hand, his spectacles were broken, and, when he was rescued, he was on the brink of death.[27]

Jack Baronett found him making his way along the ridge between Tower Creek and Blacktail Deer Creek, which indicates that Everts had somehow made his way around the lake and along the south side of Mount Washburn to Tower Creek, had crossed Tower

Creek, and was on his way down the Yellowstone toward the Gardner River. When found, he was about six miles from the mountain that bears his name, and a miserable sight he was. Baronett remembered the occasion well. There was an icy sleet falling, barely making the ground white, when the mountaineer noticed that his dog had found some kind of trail. Looking more closely, Baronett saw that something had been dragging itself along the ground. Thinking it was a bear wounded by a hunter, he followed the trail for a mile or so, until his dog began to growl, and, he added, "looking across a small canyon to the mountain side beyond, I saw a black object upon the ground." He was sure it was the bear. "My first impulse was to shoot him from where I stood," he added, but the creature was moving so slowly that Baronett crossed over to where it was. "When I got near to it I found it was not a bear, and for my life I could not tell what it was. . . . I went up close to the object; it was making a low groaning noise, crawling upon its knees and elbows, and trying to drag itself up the mountain." Suddenly it occurred to Baronett that this miserable thing was the object of his search, although it did not answer to the name Everts. Baronett reached down and picked up the miserable person with one hand. "He was nothing but a shadow," he said. "His flesh was all gone; the bones protruded through the skin on the balls of his feet and thighs. His fingers looked like bird's claws."[28]

The stories that appeared in the local press after Everts's rescue are amusing. One was that he had subsisted all thirty-seven days on one snowbird, two small minnows, and the wing of a bird which he found and mashed between two stones and with which he made some broth in a yeast-powder can he had found — that, and thistle roots, kept him going all that time.[29] Another item stated that he weighed less than eighty pounds, that one arm was paralyzed and that "he does not admit of the idea that he was deprived of a sound mind, but at the same time fancied that he had plenty of company; thought his right leg was one man, his left leg another, his arms two others, and his stomach a fifth; thought they were good fellows and was sorry he could not give them all they wanted to eat. . . . [He] chased a toad for two days, but without catching it."[30] Later he was quoted as pleading with his friends not to believe stories that he was deranged, for, he said, he "only suffered from exhaustion."[31]

In his own narration, Everts says that Baronett brought him to the cabin of an old miner, and there, finally safe, he vomited everything they give him to eat. The miner responded by bringing in a sack of fat from a bear he had recently shot, warmed it on the stove until it was liquid, and gave Everts a pint of the clear fluid to drink. This started the lost man's internal machinery functioning normally, and he made a rapid recovery.

Everts's rescue was an item of considerable interest in the press throughout the country, and it impressed Yellowstone's mysteries upon the American mind. Besides the varying stories of Everts's rescue, a few other unpleasant rumors made their way into print. It was stated that Everts was convinced that his "comrades did not make much search for him" although he had been "disabused of that opinion."[32] A few years later a writer told of some "conflicts with Mr. Everts' statement as regards to his horse." A year later, according to this source, some of Hayden's packers found, near where Mr. Everts was lost, "a brush wickiup and the remains of a camp fire that had apparently been used for ten or twelve days. Around this were the partly burnt ribs and other bones of a horse, and it is believed that here he killed his horse, and lay, waiting for a rescue party, until he had eaten it."[33]

But whatever the true story, Everts was able to attend a banquet in his honor at the Kan-Kan, a Helena restaurant, on Saturday afternoon, November 12, 1870. It was given "as a token of appreciation . . . and as a mark of our heartfelt joy at your miraculous and wonderful escape. . . . " All the VIPs attended but Lieutenant Doane, who was on duty at Fort Ellis. The bill of fare was surprisingly cosmopolitan for Helena in 1870, before a railroad had come closer than 500 miles (Corinne, Utah) to disturb her wilderness peace. They had oyster soup, raw and roasted oysters, mountain trout, leg of mutton with capers, tongue, egg sauce, spring chicken, *vol a vout (vol-au-vent?)*, breaded veal and mushrooms, breast of lamb with green peas, sweetbreads, oyster patties, sweet potatoes, green corn, tomatoes, asparagus, string beans, and desserts of fruitcake, poundcake, strawberries in cream, coffee, champagne, and imperial wine.

There were toasts and speeches, and to the toast, "Our Respected Guest, the Hon. Truman C. Everts," that gentleman rose from his seat at the head of the table, "and supported by his walking stick, in a tremulous voice, briefly responded" — whether he needed the support of the cane from weakness or from an excess of feasting we are not informed.[34]

All may have been sweetness and light there, but Jack Baronett was having trouble collecting his reward. "His friends refused to pay me because I found him alive, they saying that it was his place to pay the bills," said Baronett in 1885. "He [Everts] would not pay me because he said that if I had left him alone he would have found his own way out."[35]

The story is that some time later, when Everts was living in New York City, Jack Baronett dropped in to see him. Everts received him so coldly that, as the trapper explained, "he wished he had let the sun-of-a-gun roam!"[36]

And, in a manner of speaking, Mr. Everts did roam. He recovered quite remarkably, marrying a second time in 1880 or 1881, when he was sixty-six and his bride fourteen years of age. A decade later a son was born to them, who is still alive and well, with children and grandchildren. As for Truman Everts, Sr., he finally gave in to the grim reaper, who had quite a wait — from October 1870, when he thought he had a victim, until 1901, when Everts, aged eighty-seven, finally died. His widow lived until 1949.[37]

Nearly sixteen months were to elapse between the Everts banquet of November 1870 and the creation of the Yellowstone National Park on March 1, 1872. The issue of the *Helena Daily Herald* that detailed the banquet also carried an excerpt from "Our Washington Letter," in which the news of Everts's rescue was described as sending "a thrill of sympathetic joy through the whole community." General Washburn's reports were mentioned with the additional intelligence that the discoveries "are likely and almost certain to lead to an early and thorough exploration of those mysterious regions, under the patronage of the General Government and the Smithsonian Institution."[38]

Those sixteen months were a period of beehivelike activity in the United States. The prosperity brought on partly by the great industrial advance in the North after the Civil War, partly by the Franco–Prussian War, which insured high prices for agricultural commodities, and partly by the early success of the new wave of western expansion, fostered three times as many new moneymaking schemes as had been envisioned less than two years earlier. For years it had been assumed that the nation could afford only one transcontinental railroad, but now, barely a year and a half after the pounding of the golden spike (May 10, 1869), ideas for half a dozen such roads were in the air. One of the projects was for a Northern Pacific Railroad, to run from Duluth to Puget Sound. Its originators were a group of Vermont financiers, but in due time it passed into the control of the great financial wizard of the Civil War, Jay Cooke. Cooke tackled his projects from all angles; he made use of public relations men before the term "public relations" had been coined. He even hired lecturers to advertise the glories of the golden lands through which the great Northern Pacific would travel.[39]

One of those lecturers was Nathaniel P. Langford. Just when that Montana gentleman began speaking for a fee is not certain. But on November 18, 1870, he gave a lecture before the Helena Library Association, and he appears to have delivered the same speech in Virginia City a little later. His hometown paper announced that "Hon. N. P. Langford was to lecture in the States during the winter, on the wonders of the Yellowstone country." In January 1871, he took employment with the Northern Pacific Railroad to go on speaking tours, lecturing on the Yellowstone.[40]

During those winter months of 1870–71 Langford, Hauser, Hedges, and Washburn all headed east, though not together. Washburn died in Indiana in January, Hauser and Hedges apparently transacted personal business, and Langford lectured. He had no competition, and he was truly in his element standing at the rostrum before a capacity audience. He spoke at Lincoln Hall in Washington, D. C., on January 19, 1871, with Speaker of the House James G. Blaine presiding; a few evenings later he spoke at Cooper Union in New York City, describing Yellowstone with reasonable accuracy save for exaggerated imagery. By May he was in Philadelphia giving a private lecture at the home of Jay Cooke.[41]

At this point a geologist, Dr. Ferdinand Vandiveer Hayden, enters the story. Of humble origin, this ambitious man carved his niche in the history of American geology by sheer will and intelligence. He explored parts of Dakota as early as 1853; in 1867 he obtained his own survey to study the geology of Nebraska, and by 1871, when he was forty-one years old, he was in charge of the United States Geological and Geographical Survey of the Territories, a governmental endeavor of his own making. It was growing in size each year, as governmental enterprises do; nevertheless, in those days far more than in our own, a scientist in the federal government had to wage a biennial fight not simply for funds, but for the very existence of his enterprise. The rising interest in Yellowstone, then, was a godsend to Hayden, who needed money to continue his work the next year.[42]

One of his champions in Congress at this time was James G. Blaine, Speaker of the House and for many years one of the most powerful men in the Congress. Another of Hayden's friends was Henry L. Dawes, at that time a representative from Massachusetts, and chairman of the powerful Committee on Appropriations. So when Hayden proposed that his survey investigate Yellowstone scientifically and requested increased funds, they were forthcoming — $40,000 to be expended "under direction of the Secretary of the Interior."[43]

This was a large sum of money for the times, especially since the army furnished the survey with mounts and equipment. These were obtained from the quartermaster at Fort D. A. Russell near Cheyenne in Wyoming Territory. They were placed on freight cars and transported to Ogden, Utah Territory, by the Union Pacific at reduced rates. Survey personnel traveled free — a commentary on that railroad's concept of good public relations and its understanding of the possible long-range monetary results of such an expedition.[44]

Hayden's force numbered twenty-one in 1871. It included a mediocre artist named Henry Elliott, the pioneer photographer William Henry Jackson, the well-known landscape artist Thomas Moran, who was aided financially in this endeavor by Jay Cooke, William B. Logan, nephew of powerful Senator Logan of Illinois; and Chester M. Dawes, the son of Henry Dawes, chairman of the Appropriations Committee.[45]

Hayden also had competition from the army, and neither he nor the army was very happy about it. Colonel John W. Barlow and Captain David P. Heap were under orders to conduct a reconnaissance of the Upper Yellowstone at the same time as Hayden's survey was scrambling over the hills and hot spring formations; meanwhile General Sheridan had sent a small escort to accompany Hayden, and at Yellowstone Lake its command was taken over by the experienced Lieutenant Doane.[46]

Both expeditions traveled across South Pass via the Union Pacific, Hayden leaving the train at Ogden and working north to

Virginia City and across to Fort Ellis, a distance of 429 miles, and
Barlow and Heap enjoying the comfort of the Central Pacific railroad car to Corinne, some 30 miles north of Ogden and the northernmost point of the Central Pacific. Hayden's journey to the park
was a geological reconnaissance; it was still June, which was earlier
than his survey usually got into the field, and he took his time. Dr.
Albert C. Peale, a young geologist who was accompanying the survey
this year for the first time, found the life of Virginia City, where
exotic Chinese could be seen in the streets, worth noting in his diary.
The survey came into town on the morning of July 4. American flags
were flying, and he wrote, "we found a parade forming we followed
it up the main street where it was photographed after which we
formed in a double rank and joined as a cavalcade. . . . A brass band
headed the procession each member of which seemed to be trying to
play a different tune."[47]

The survey arrived at Fort Ellis in good condition, but did not
leave for the Upper Yellowstone until July 15. Meanwhile Colonel
Barlow and Captain Heap struggled along, bumping their way up
the road out of Corinne in a stagecoach packed with 800 pounds of
baggage and seven passengers including themselves. All stage rides
were cheerless experiences, Colonel Barlow admitted, "but the Montana route particularly has usually been considered almost unendur-
able. The heat, the dust, the crowded condition of the stage, and
above all the loss of sleep for three or four nights and days, it is
said, reduces the traveler to a state bordering on insanity." Things
went from bad to worse. The stagecoach deteriorated into a "jerkey,
a two-seated covered wagon drawn by a single pair of horses."[48]

Dr. Peale had already heard strange stories about the two army
officers — how they liked to halt two hours for lunch, for instance —
but their appearance at Bottler's on July 18 revealed two men more
ludicrous than even Dr. Peale had imagined. It had been rumored
that Colonel Barlow carried an umbrella, and indeed he did. He
"had his umbrella strapped to his saddle, and Captain Heap was
the most comical looking man," wrote Peale. "He had a buck-skin
suit with fringes and he had a lot of traps stuck about his person.
He is a small man."[49]

Both parties left their wagons at Bottler's and headed up the
Yellowstone with pack trains. At the mouth of the Gardner, however,
they turned south up the river, unlike the Cook–Folsom or Washburn–

Langford–Doane parties. In due time they came to Mammoth Hot Springs, which Hayden called White Mountain Hot Springs and Barlow dubbed Soda Mountain.[50] They also indulged in the kinds of abuses that have made the present formations but a sorry reminder of the splendor they once possessed. The men went splashing about through the pools, testing the water until they found a pool of the most pleasing temperature; in that one they bathed. It never occurred to them that they were destroying the delicacy of nature. "They were even quite luxurious," wrote Barlow, "being lined with a spongy gypsum, soft and pleasant to the touch. I walked over a part of the hill by the faint light of a new moon, which gave to its deep blue pools of steaming water a wild and ghostly appearance." The fauna of the Yellowstone began to suffer too. That night Barlow and Heap feasted on bear cub steak.[51]

Jackson busily went about his photography while Moran sketched, but before long the parties left the area to go up the Yellowstone. Hayden advanced up the west side of the river to Tower Falls while Barlow and Heap crossed Jack Baronett's new bridge, just above the confluence of the Lamar (then called the East Fork) with the Yellowstone. Barlow thus saw something new to comment upon in his report and was able to gather specimens of agate, crystal, and petrified wood from Specimen Ridge.[52]

Duly impressed with Tower Falls, the Hayden party next went around the south side of the mountain, and, after hard labor, both Hayden and Barlow reached the summit of Mt. Washburn, grasped the lay of the land, and headed for Cascade Creek. "Our trail was a tortuous one," wrote Hayden, "[in order] to avoid the fallen timber and dense groves of pine. The country immediately around the Creek looked like a beautiful meadow at this season of the year [July 25] covered with grass and flowers."[53] In due time the trail brought them to the Grand Canyon of the Yellowstone.

Again Jackson and a photographer who was with Barlow and Heap, Thomas J. Hine by name, plus a Bozeman photographer named Crissman and the artist Moran, photographed or sketched the scenery. The wind blew Crissman's equipment over the precipice, but Jackson lent him an extra camera.[54]

The two parties, slightly separated, advanced up the river, examining thermal activity on both banks, to the shores of the lake. Here Hayden's men launched a twelve-foot boat whose frame they had brought with them. They christened it the "Anna," in honor of Representative Dawes's daughter — even in Yellowstone they knew that a little political sagacity might bring dividends. Two of the men made a sketch of the 175-mile shoreline of the lake, placing its islands in approximately the correct positions; they even probed its depths with a lead and line.[55]

Next they established camp at the hot springs on the southwest arm — the Thumb — and on July 31 Hayden headed west for the Firehole with a small party, while Barlow's group headed for the same place by a different route. They met on the divide and continued down what Hayden called the East Fork of the Firehole River but which must have been the Firehole River proper. In the ensuing days Hayden, Barlow, Heap, and Lieutenant Doane (who appeared, sent the escort back to Fort Ellis, but himself remained part of the expedition) would explore the Upper, Middle, and Lower geyser basins.[56] When the parties returned to the Yellowstone Lake, Barlow and Heap tarried behind. Hayden, more impetuous, had glimpsed a lake through the trees and forthwith pronounced it the source of the Madison River. It was Shoshone Lake (the name he gave it later, to the everlasting chagrin of Walter W. De Lacy, who rightfully believed it should have been named for him); furthermore, it is part of the Snake River system, not the Madison. Hayden's error was caused by his failure to realize, in his rapid trip back to the camp on the West Thumb, that he had crossed the Continental Divide not once but twice in the same day (the divide twists like a snake in this area). Barlow and Heap, better trained, did not commit any such error.[57]

Now the West Thumb camp was broken up and Hayden continued counterclockwise around the lake, battling the dense jackstraw forest and climbing some mountains on the east, which he named Mount Doane and Mount Stevenson. On August 20 earthquake shocks gave them a start when they were camped on the southeast arm. When they struck Pelican Creek on the northeast side of the lake, they followed it up to the Yellowstone–East Fork divide, then worked back northwest to Baronett's bridge, where they crossed. From there they made their way to Bottler's, arriving there in the last week of August, and from there the long journey began to the Pacific Railroad via Virginia City and so home.[58]

Barlow and Heap continued their explorations south of the lake. Barlow and his draftsman, a man named Woods, climbed the high reddish peak west of Heart Lake and named it for General Sheridan; Barlow then climbed a peak south of there, and named it Mount Hancock for the commanding general of the Department of Dakota, and on their map they named a mountain after General Humphreys, chief of the Army Corps of Engineers. Although they would have liked to have pushed on up the Thorofare to discover the source of the Yellowstone, time was running out and their animals were in bad condition, so they too turned north, returning to Fort Ellis by September 3.[59]

These two explorations produced five poor maps by Hayden and one by Barlow and Heap which correctly attached Shoshone Lake (they called it Madison Lake) to the Snake River system. The Gibbon River, the Norris Geyser Basin, and the entire area north of the junction of the Firehole and the Gibbon had yet to be explored and mapped.[60] Far more important were the paintings and, especially, William H. Jackson's photographs. Moran's paintings took some time to complete and so do not enter into the immediate story of the creation of Yellowstone National Park. Crissman, the Bozeman photographer who lost his camera over the brink of the Grand Canyon of the Yellowstone, sold his photographs locally but never nationally.[61]

Ferdinand V. Hayden's survey disbanded on October 1, 1871, and on March 1, 1872, just five months later, President Grant signed the Yellowstone Park Bill. Even if the progression from the idea to law is extended back thirty months to a campfire on the evening of September 19, 1870, at the junction of the Firehole and the Gibbon rivers, it was still remarkably swift. Ideas do not normally advance from inspiration to presidential signature in so short a time. Clearly, there is a complex narrative concerning the political and legal manipulations and the individuals who pushed the bill through the Congress. That story is the subject of the next chapter.

9

The Creation of Yellowstone National Park

The long-range story behind the establishment of Yellowstone National Park involves the growth of the American's love for his land for its beauty rather than for its wealth. It was said that a tree left standing on the horizon irritated the pioneer's eyes. A change had to take place before the sons and daughters of that pioneer could look upon the American wilderness as a place of beauty and a source of pride, rather than as something to be civilized and exploited.

The growing love of the land can be traced through our literature beginning perhaps with Colonel William Byrd's *A Journey to the Land of Eden* and including through the years the writings of Hector St. John Crèvecoeur, William Bartram, Philip Freneau, James Fenimore Cooper, Washington Irving, William Cullen Bryant, Ralph Waldo Emerson, and Henry David Thoreau.[1]

As early as 1833 the painter George Catlin suggested that parts of the wilderness *"might* in future be seen (by some great protecting policy of government) preserved in their pristine beauty and wildness, in a magnificent park, where the world could see for ages to come, the native Indian in his classic attire, galloping his wild horses . . . amid the fleeting herds of elks and buffaloes. . . . A *nation's park,* containing man and beast, in all the wild and freshness of their nature's beauty."[2] Similar quotations can be found in the writings of many American literary figures from the 1830s through the 1860s, advocating the creation of "parks" without explaining precisely what was meant by the word.[3]

Meanwhile precedents were being established. In 1832, Congress enacted legislation providing that the Hot Springs in Arkansas Territory, "together with four sections of land including said springs, as near the centre thereof as may be, shall be reserved for the future disposal of the United States, and shall not be entered, located, or appropriated, for any other purposes whatsoever."[4] President John Quincy Adams had some virgin hardwood lands removed from the public domain in northeast Florida, but his successor in the White House, Andrew Jackson, rescinded the order.[5]

Furthermore, city parks were no longer conceived simply as beautifully landscaped cemeteries. In 1856 New York City purchased the land for Central Park. Frederick Law Olmsted was appointed superintendent and remained there until May 1863, when a strain of serendipity led him to accept a position as director of mining on John Charles Frémont's vast estate at Mariposa, California. From there he saw the groves of giant sequoias and was able to journey to Yosemite.

It was during this period — the 1850s and the first half of the 1860s — that the world began to learn of the wonderful treasures in California. Photographs and stereoptican slides of the valley and the falls of Yosemite graced many a marble-topped parlor table. Yosemite was already widely known and — what is perhaps more important — Americans looked upon it as a national treasure.

The result was that in 1864 a group of public-spirited Californians, concerned over the increasing number of private claims in their valley, signed their names to a letter to California's Senator John Conness, written by Israel Ward Raymond:

> It will be many years before it is worthwhile for the government to survey these mountains. But I think it important to obtain the proprietorship soon, to prevent occupation and especially to preserve the trees in the valley from destruction and that it may be accepted by the legislature at its present session and laws passed to give the Commissioners power to take control and begin to consider and lay out their plans for the gradual improvement of the properties.[6]

Senator Conness liked the idea, and on March 28, 1864, he entered a bill "authorizing a grant to the State of California of the Yosemite Valley, and of the land embracing the Mariposa Big Tree Grove"; it was passed and became operative on June 30. The embryo of the whole national park idea was embodied in those lines of the act which state " . . . that the said State shall accept this grant upon the express conditions that the premises shall be held for public use, resort, and recreation; shall be unalienable for all times; but leases not exceeding ten years may be granted for portions of said premises. . . ."[7]

Although the word *park* does not appear in the act, and although it gave lands to a state, rather than preserving them for the federal government, the lines quoted above show the acceptance by the United States of the whole national park idea. Furthermore, in terms of its national reception, Yosemite was successful. In 1865 Olmsted met the first eastern tourists there. The most illustrious was Schuyler Colfax, Speaker of the House of Representatives and later Vice-President in Grant's first administration. With him were Samuel Bowles of the Springfield (Massachusetts) *Republican* and Albert Richardson, a correspondent for the *New York Tribune*.

Bowles, writing about the federal action toward Yosemite, said that "the idea is a noble one, and though somewhat obstructed temporarily by the claim of several squatters in the Valley to nearly all its available lands [a problem Yellowstone would subsequently share with Yosemite] we cannot doubt it will in time be fully realized. It is a pity that the other great natural objects of interest and points of attraction for travelers in our counry could not be similarly rescued from subjection to speculating purposes, or destruction by settlement."[8]

Richardson, in writing about Yosemite and the Mariposa groves, described the federal legislation as "setting them apart as pleasure grounds for the people of the United States and their heirs and assigns forever." He called it "wise legislation" which secured the region for all time "to the proper national uses."[9]

Frederick Law Olmsted, in his first report to the California Yosemite Commission, of which he was clearly the chairman, justified the principle of congressional creation of parks. The first reason given was mercenary and practical, the "direct and obvious pecuniary advantage which comes to a commonwealth from the fact that it possesses objects which cannot be taken out of its domain, that are attractive to travelers and the enjoyment of which is open to all." An example was scenic Switzerland, whose inns, as well as the farms, railroads, and carriage routes serving them, had, wrote Olmstead, "contributed directly and indirectly for many years to the larger part of the state revenue and all this without the exportation or abstraction from the country of anything of the slightest value to the people."

The second "class of considerations" was moral and aesthetic. The government had, he wrote, "a political duty of grave importance to which seldom if ever before has proper respect been paid by any government in the world but the grounds of which rest on the same eternal base of equity and benevolence with all other duties of republican government." This duty was "to provide means of protection for all its citizens in the pursuit of happiness against the obstacles, otherwise insurmountable, which the selfishness of individuals or combinations of individuals is liable to interpose to that pursuit." This happiness included the right to the free contemplation "of natural scenes of an impressive character, particularly," he said, "if this contemplation occurs in connection with relief from ordinary cares, [and] changes of air and habits. . . . " In other countries the rich owned the places of beauty, accepting the concept that "the large mass of all human communities should spend their lives in almost constant labor. . . . " Such folly, Olmsted suggested, "has caused the appearance of dullness and weakness and disease of these faculties [of appreciating natural beauty] in the mass of the subjects of kings. And it is against the limitation of the means of such education to the rich that the wise legislation of free governments must be directed. . . . " Thus had a wise Congress legislated to protect Yosemite for all the people, to help them in the pursuit of happiness, to aid them in their mental well-being, and to insure wealth from the inns and other facilities which would serve the visitors.[10]

Clearly a precedent had been established with Yosemite. The legislation had been on the books for eight years in 1872, and the whole idea had had time to gain acceptance in the American mind. It had met with wide approval. Thus, when the newspapers carried "intelligence from the West" of the wonders of the Yellowstone, the populace, once it was convinced of the credibility of these wonders, was quite prepared to acquiesce in the creation of a *national* park — *national* because Yellowstone was surrounded by federally administered territories, whereas Yosemite was within the boundaries of a state.

This, then, is the historical background for the creation of a great national park. Now let us examine the legislative history of Yellowstone National Park.

If President Grant had followed modern protocol and invited the key proponents of significant legislation to be present when it was signed into law, a most interesting group of men would have been present when he scrawled his signature to the "Act to Set Apart a Certain Tract of Land Near the Head-waters of the Yellowstone River as a Public Park." They would have shoved and pushed and jockeyed for position, and it is a good bet that Nathaniel P. Langford and Ferdinand V. Hayden would have come close to fisticuffs over which one was to stand at the front, in the center. Others in the group would have been Cornelius Hedges, Representative Henry L. Dawes, Territorial Delegate William Clagett, General Philip H. Sheridan, and William Henry Jackson. Quite possibly David Folsom and the painter Thomas Moran would also have been present.

Meanwhile, down under the portico, several shrewd characters (as Beadle's dime novels called such fellows) would have been strolling back and forth, smoking expensive havanas, and exchanging compliments. Among them would have been the railroad financier Jay Cooke; A. R. Nettleton, Cooke's publicity man; W. Milner Roberts, another of Cooke's aides; and possibly Senator Samuel Pomeroy of Kansas and William Darrah "Pig Iron" Kelley, a representative from Pennsylvania.

Each of these men could have claimed — and most did claim — credit for the success of the proposal. Several of them vowed that they had originated it, and the controversy engendered resentment among them. "Since the passage of this bill there have been so many men who have claimed the exclusive credit for its passage," wrote William Clagett in 1894, "that I have lived for twenty years suffering from a chronic feeling of disgust whenever the subject was mentioned." Following this broadside, Clagett look the credit for himself. "So far as my personal knowledge goes, the first idea of making it a public park occurred to myself," he wrote in 1894 (though we must acknowledge what he said in the remainder of the sentence: "but from information received from Langford and others, it has always been my opinion that Hedges, Langford, and myself formed the same idea about the same time. . . ").[11]

Clagett claims to have written the park bill, but the facts do not seem to agree with his memory. The Honorable William Clagett had sat for barely two weeks in Congress when he introduced the bill in the House on December 18, 1871. Clagett was clearly involved in pushing the bill through, however, and deserves credit for his work.[12]

Representative (later Senator) Henry L. Dawes willingly took credit for writing the bill, and in the balance the evidence grants him the honor. In later years he would say as much, and so would Senator George Graham Vest of Missouri, who became the park's watchdog in the Senate. In 1892 Dawes categorically stated, "I have taken an interest in this park from the day of its creation. I had the honor to write the bill which created it." He had made similar statements before.[13]

Dawes's experienced hand is very evident in the successful passage of the bill through both houses of Congress. He had administered the oath of office to Speaker James A. Garfield and certainly knew another congressional veteran (in an era in which nearly every succeeding Congress contained a majority of new members), one William Darrah Kelley, a fellow Republican from Pennsylvania. All three of these men — Dawes, Garfield, and Kelley — were interested in the West and had supported Hayden. Dawes's son had spent the season of 1871 with Hayden in the field, and "Anna," the boat launched on Yellowstone Lake, was named in honor of Dawes's daughter. The senator does not, however, deserve credit for the idea of the park or even for the crystallization of the plan to create the park. Dawes never made any such claims; indeed, the credit belongs elsewhere.

The man who introduced the bill in the Senate was in fact a typical Gilded Age politician, Senator Samuel C. Pomeroy of Kansas. Since he was chairman of the Committee on Public Lands, it was logical for him to perform this service. Also, he had informed Langford that he wanted the honor.[14] The senator was a Radical Republican, the model (and everyone knew it) for Senator Dilworthy, the fictional politician in Mark Twain and Charles Dudley Warner's *The Gilded Age*. Pomeroy was "large and portly, though not tall — a pleasant spoken man, a popular man with the people."[15] He was a supporter of Hayden's, and later in the year he introduced a resolution in the Senate calling for the printing of Hayden's 1871 *Report*.[16]

As it happened, the man who most desired to be affiliated with the national park never claimed credit for originating the idea. But once the vision was born — regardless of its parentage — he claimed to have masterminded the scheme through, and in his published works, he always created the impression that but for him, there would be no Yellowstone. As he informed his readers, he was so well known as the "Man of the Park" that friends, capitalizing on his initials, frequently addressed letters to him as National Park Langford.[17]

What was the validity of his claim? It will be remembered that when the Washburn–Langford–Doane expedition ended, Langford immediately began lecturing on Yellowstone, first in Montana and then in Washington, D.C., New York City, Philadelphia, and Minneapolis. Langford states that he ended each lecture by saying that "this new field of wonders should be at once withdrawn from occupancy, and set apart as a National Park for the enjoyment of the American people for all time." Unfortunately, none of the press reports of his speeches include this statement, even though reporters were most verbose and thorough in those days.[18]

In May and June 1871 Langford published his Yellowstone experiences in *Scribner's Monthly,* but again there was no inkling of a suggestion for a national park; neither did Trumbull hint at such an idea in his work for the *Overland Monthly* published in the May and June 1871 issues.

However, there can be no question of Langford's interest, and in the autumn of 1871 and the winter of 1872 his presence in Washington and activity in promoting the legislation cannot be denied. He was also with Hayden in the park in 1872, and he was, after all, the first superintendent, 1872–77. None of this makes Langford any more than an active participant in the movement — though his activities certainly deserve credit. But in his zeal to be remembered in history, he apparently overdid his case and confused truth with wishful thinking, as in his statements purportedly made in speeches just prior to the passage of the act.

The other individual who wanted primary credit for the national park idea was Dr. Ferdinand V. Hayden of the Geological Survey. He is quoted as having originally been against the bill, but in the autumn of 1871 he changed his mind and pushed for its passage.[19] Unfortunately for his claims, his *Fifth Annual Report,* the one detailing the 1871 expedition, did not appear until April 1872, after the park bill had been signed. However, the February 1872 *Scribner's Monthly* ran an article of his on Yellowstone in which he did say: "Why will not Congress at once pass a law setting it apart as a great public park for all time to come, as has been done with that not more remarkable wonder, the Yosemite Valley?" He also published an article in the *American Journal of Science and Arts* in that same month, mentioning the park bill, hoping for its successful passage, and warning of the danger of squatters "taking possession of the springs and destroying the beautiful decorations. . . . "[20]

Although Hayden was indeed an advocate of the bill, the evidence shows that his interest arose in the autumn of 1871, along with Langford's. When congressmen requested information from Secretary of the Interior Columbus Delano, he ordered Hayden to prepare a statement for them, which Hayden did; later he filled in the boundary statistics of the bill. There is no question of his interest, nor of his activity on behalf of the bill, nor of his liberal use of Jackson's photographs and Moran's sketches to help convince congressmen of the beauties of Yellowstone. But how accurate was the geologist's statement to the secretary of the interior that "so far as I know, I originated the idea of the park, prepared the maps designating the boundaries, and in connection with Hon. W. H. Clagett . . . wrote the law as it now stands. . . . It is now acknowledged all over the civilized world that the existence of the National Park by law, is due solely to my exertions during the sessions of 1871 and 1872."[21] Or his statement five years later: "So far as is known, the idea of setting apart a large tract about the sources of the Yellowstone River as a National Park originated with the writer."[22] How accurate is Senator Pomeroy's statement on the floor of the Senate on January 22, 1872, upon his introduction of the bill: "This bill is drawn on the recommendation of that gentleman to consecrate for public uses this country for a public park."[23]

The sad thing is that Hayden did work very hard for the passage of the bill, but he then destroyed his image by adding to his credit things he never did. The idea of a national park was not his brainchild, and Langford, Hauser, Everts, Hedges, and Trumbull were in the East at the same time, for the most part in Washington, conducting lobbying activities to help the passage of the bill. Hayden's ambition to appear favorably and prominently in the record of history harmed his image.

Another of those interested in the bill would have been David Folsom. He was never very verbose about it, but Langford says that upon the return of the Washburn expedition, General Washburn informed him (Langford) "that on the eve of the departure of our expedition from Helena, David E. Folsom had suggested to him the desirability of creating a park at the grand canyon and falls of the Yellowstone."[24]

The army got into the picture, of course, in the person of General Sheridan. By coincidence, the general was present in Helena for two days in May 1870, when Langford, Washburn, et. al. were making their plans for the expedition. But Langford and Hauser are said only to have seen General Hancock while they were in St. Paul that spring; there is no mention of General Sheridan. We must assume that Sheridan was not approached by the gentlemen from Helena; we cannot assume, however, that he did not correspond with Hancock and approve of the use of Lieutenant Doane and a small contingent to accompany the expedition.

From the time of that trip on, however, General Sheridan did manifest a sincere, strong interest in the park. He states in his memoirs that on the stage from Corinne to Helena an old mountaineer named Atkinson had told him in glowing generalities, but vague specifics, about the geyser basins of Yellowstone. He further states that he devoted his time in Helena (cut short because of the outbreak of the Franco-Prussian War) "to arranging for an exploration of what are now known as the Upper and Lower Geyser Basins in Yellowstone Park."[25]

All available evidence fails to show that Sheridan participated in the Yellowstone business until June 1871, more than a year later, when he ordered the commanding officer at Fort Ellis to furnish supplies to Captain Barlow. But when Sheridan's brother reissued the general's memoirs in 1902, his family pride ran away with him, and he wrote: "While he was not alone in this undertaking, it was largely through Sheridan's personal efforts that Congress created the Yellowstone National Park. . . . "[26]

Sheridan had absolutely nothing to do with the creation of the park, so far as we can tell, but he did support it and use his office to protect it until his death. It is unfortunate that he, and later his brother, should have thrown dust in posterity's eyes by making claims about the general's part in the park's creation that simply were not true.

Then who *was* responsible for the idea?

At this point, to make the story clear and in order to be fair to every claimant concerned, the narrative must be divided into two parts. Part I concerns the members of the Washburn expedition as well as some other men, and it makes clear that there was an idea in the air. It had not yet jelled, but in the minds of several men was the semiconscious feeling that something in the way of governmental action should be done to preserve the valley of the Upper Yellowstone and the geyser basins. But it was just talk. It did not receive the solid group effort necessary to push a measure through Congress. The phrase "national park" was not used, or if it was used, it was not dwelt upon. Neither specific boundaries nor methods of policing such an area were discussed. But it is significant that there was a general opinion in the air that some kind of a reservation protected by the government should be created.

In the hypothetical circle of men around President Grant's desk there is only one man left whom we have not mentioned. He is a Yankee educated at Yale and Harvard, a respected lawyer in Montana Territory. He is the Honorable Cornelius Hedges.

Two incidents trace the lineage of the park idea to him. The first, never mentioned by Hedges, was his 1864 trip to the Blackfoot Indian Reservation (see Part II, chapter 4). He went along with Acting Governor Thomas Francis Meagher, it will be remembered, in the late autumn of that year. A blizzard struck, and for three days the party lived at St. Peter's Mission, exchanging stories and enjoying their enforced leisure while the blizzard raged outside. It was at this time that Father Francis X. Kuppens described the Yellowstone wonders that he had seen with the Piegan Indians. Governor Meagher's reaction, wrote Father Kuppens many years later, was that "if things were as described the government ought to reserve the territory for a national park. All the visitors agreed that efforts should be made to explore the region and that a report of it should be sent to the government."[27]

Meagher died the following June, but Hedges remained very much alive and very active in Montana. As we have seen, the rumors of the Yellowstone wonders prompted expedition plans in 1867, 1868, and 1869 and finally culminated in the Washburn–Langford–Doane expedition of 1870. Hedges, who was a member of the party, kept a diary in which the first hint of making Yellowstone a national park appears, though Hedges did not use the phrase "national park."

Hedges wrote several descriptive letters to the *Helena Daily Herald*. In his letter of November 9, 1870, on the subject of Yellowstone Lake, he explained (1) that it was in the northwest corner of

Wyoming and (2) that it was cut off from Wyoming Territory by "impassable and eternally snow-clad" mountains. "Hence," he said, "the propriety that the Territorial lines be so readjusted that Montana should embrace all that lake region west of the Wind River Range, a matter in which we hope our citizens will soon move to accomplish, *as well as to secure its future appropriation to public use"* (italics mine).

This statement reflected Hedges's nascent concept of a public reservation controlled by the Territory of Montana. His idea was remarkably similar to the Yosemite experiment which had been so favorably received by the public and of which Hedges, as an active, educated citizen, was certainly aware. It also reflects a growing concern among public-spirited Montanans over the rush to stake out land claims at strategic points in Yellowstone. By the winter of 1870 Jack Baronett had his bridge across the Yellowstone, and well-founded rumors told of plans for claims under the Homestead Act at Boiling River (where waters from the Mammoth Hot Springs enter the Gardner), at the geysers, and at the lake. Several of these would become realities in 1871.[28]

So far in our search for the originator of the Yellowstone Park idea, we have a direct line from Governor Meagher (who was a well-informed man and certainly knew about Yosemite) to Cornelius Hedges, who was present during the long days in the St. Peter's Mission. And this constitutes the only direct historical link to substantiate the so-called campfire legend, first enunciated in 1904 — thirty-four years after the events — when both Langford and Hedges published their diaries. Here is how the legend appears in the first edition (1905) of Langford's *Diary of the Washburn Expedition,* under the date of September 20:

> Last night, and also this morning in camp, the entire party had a rather unusual discussion. The proposition was made by some member that we utilize the result of our exploration by taking up quarter sections of land at the most prominent points of interest, and a general discussion followed. . . .
>
> Mr. Hedges then said that he did not approve of any of these plans — that there ought to be no private ownership of any portion of that region, but that the whole of it ought to be set apart as a great National Park, and that each one of us

might make an effort to have this accomplished. His suggestion met with an instant and favorable response from all — except one — of the members of the party, and each hour since the matter was first broached, our enthusiasm has increased. It has been the main theme of our conversation today as we journeyed. I lay awake half last-night thinking about it: — and if my wakefulness deprived my bed-fellow (Hedges) of any sleep, he has only himself and his disturbing National Park Proposition to answer for it.[29]

Hedges also kept a journal during the expedition, and it is strange that he had nothing to say in it about any national park plan; the only similarity to Langford's account is Hedges's complaint that he had not slept well. "Didn't sleep well last night," his entry for September 20 begins, " — got to thinking of home and business, seems as if we were almost there — started out at 9½ [o'clock]. . . . " However, in an introductory footnote to the published *Journal* he added one very brief concluding paragraph: "It was at the first camp after leaving the lower Geyser basin when all were speculating which point in the region we had been through, would become most notable that I first suggested the uniting of all our efforts to get it made a National Park, little dreaming that such a thing were possible. Cornelius Hedges, August, 1904."[30]

Except for his suggestion in his article of November 9, 1870, Hedges never mentioned the park idea in print until the publication of his diary in 1904. Langford, for all his talk and all his writing, never mentioned it as far as we can prove until he published *his* diary in 1904. Walter Trumbull made no mention of the discussion in his article in the *Overland Monthly*, General Washburn said nothing about it in his article in the *Helena Daily Herald,* and Lieutenant Doane made no mention of it in his *Report.* Yet in 1904 it was presented as the most exciting event of the expedition after leaving the geysers. The campfire legend has grown over the years. Langford saw to it that a plaque was erected at the site; the National Park Service in later years added to the myth by presenting a pageant there about the whole affair; today a small structure at the site commemorates the story. Whether the story is true or not, the national park idea was a wonderful thought. Regardless of who was responsible, the commemoration at Madison Junction reminds a callous public of what can be achieved by men of good will.

In any event, not one person had mentioned a national park in speeches, articles, or news items until the middle of October 1871. Then the clan gathered in Washington. Langford arrived in mid-November. Hayden, Hauser, Clagett, Trumbull, Dawes, and Sheridan were probably in the city, and Jackson was preparing photographs at the survey offices. Things began to move. On December 18 the bill was introduced in the House as H.R. 764 by Clagett; it was introduced in the Senate on the same day as S. 392 by Senator Pomeroy of Kansas. It passed the Senate on January 30, 1872, and the Senate bill was the one adopted later by the House, 115 ayes, 65 nays, and 60 abstaining, on February 27. No speech was delivered against the bill, and Grant signed it on March 1. For a new bill embodying a new subject — segregation of lands in northwest Wyoming Territory — to pass through a slow-moving Congress on its first try, and in less than three months, was nothing short of miraculous.[31]

It is here that Part I of the story of the establishment of the park fails to answer our questions. A few of Montana's leading citizens, some army officers, and a scientist or two led by F. V. Hayden had all been in the upper Yellowstone country. They were disorganized, but it is clear that they all shared an as yet unjelled idea: the country they had traversed should be set aside, somehow, as a national park. By coincidence, a number of them were in Washington, D. C. in the autumn of 1871. But it is clear that these men, either alone or in concert, could not have brought the bill to passage. Someone had to give them a concrete idea and then channel their activities; someone with power in Congress had to smooth the way for the bill.

This brings us to Part II, which involves a different group of men. And there is a link between the two groups. It is contained in a letter in Dr. Hayden's Geological Survey files in the custody of the National Archives. On October 27, 1871, Hayden received a letter from A. R. Nettleton of the firm of Jay Cooke and Company and the Northern Pacific Railroad. The pertinent part of the letter read as follows:

> Judge Kelley has made a suggestion which strikes me as being an excellent one, *viz*. Let Congress pass a bill reserving

the Great Geyser Basin as a public park forever — just as it has reserved that far inferior wonder the Yosemite Valley and the big trees. If you approve this, would such a recommendation be appropriate in your official report?[32]

While Hayden's exact relationship with the Northern Pacific promoters is not clear, there are letters from Nettleton to Hayden which indicate that there was a sharing of interests between Hayden and the Northern Pacific officials. A letter from Nettleton to Hayden dated June 16, 1871, for example, indicates that Moran received funds from *Scribner's* and "our own Cooke" in order to make the Yellowstone trip. Thus Moran was not in Hayden's employ, but partially in Cooke's.[33]

Nettleton was Jay Cooke's publicity man, and who was Judge Kelley? He was William Darrah Kelley — "Pig Iron" Kelley — Republican congressman from Pennsylvania who served in Congress for nearly thirty years, for twenty of which he was a member of the Committee on Ways and Means. In business, he was deeply involved with Jay Cooke in the Northern Pacific, had a great interest in the Northwest, and even did some lecturing on behalf of the national park.[34]

Two other fragments, culled by Mr. Robert Budd, substantiate the Northern Pacific link. The first is a letter from Jay Cooke to his aide, W. Milner Roberts, dated October 30, 1871. It seems to indicate the interest of the Northern Pacific officials, implying that, months before, they may have given the army, and Hayden, too, the idea of making a government investigation of the Yellowstone:

> We are delighted to hear such good accounts of the Yellowstone expedition from both ends. Gen. Hancock and Gen. Sheridan have both telegraphed that the report will be a splendid one from the expedition at this end.
>
> It is proposed by Mr. Hayden in his report to Congress that the Geyser region around Yellowstone Lake shall be set apart by government as park, similar to that of the Great Trees & other reservations in California. Would this conflict with our land grant, or interfere with us in any way? Please give me your views on this subject. It is important to do something speedily, or squatters and claimants will go in there, and we can probably deal much better with the government in any improve-

ments we may desire to make for the benefit of our pleasure travel than with individuals.[35]

And, on November 21, 1871, from Helena, Montana, W. Milner Roberts telegraphed Jay Cooke as follows:

Your October thirtieth and November sixth rec'd. Geysers outside our grant advise Congressional delegation be in East probably before middle December.

W. Milner Roberts[36]

All of this adds up to pretty strong evidence of Northern Pacific interest in the creation of a park. In fact, the evidence, though fragmentary, is sufficient to credit the inspiration for the creation of the Yellowstone National Park to officials of the Northern Pacific Railroad.

There were others in Congress who had more than a cursory interest in Yellowstone. Schuyler Colfax was the vice-president of the United States and president pro tem of the Senate. He had visited Yosemite and was favorable to the concept of national parks. James A. Garfield, a powerful man in the House, was a supporter of Hayden's survey and had a peak named after him. He was interested in the West and would journey to Montana later in the season to make a treaty with the Flathead Indians.[37] Truly, everything was in favor of the creation of Yellowstone National Park: powerful men in Congress, the backing of financial tycoon Jay Cooke and the whole Northern Pacific enterprise, and the Montanans' vision of a golden future when the railroad reached their territory.

And so Langford, Hayden, and Clagett became ardent advocates of the bill. Jackson prepared a collection of his photographs, which was discreetly placed for viewing by members of the Senate. Some of Moran's watercolor sketches were judiciously distributed. The bill was, so to speak, well oiled, and it slid through with a minimum of trouble. And naturally, since the suggestion had been made by Kelley and then by Nettleton, it hit a most receptive audience. A national park? Of course! There is nothing so powerful as an idea whose time has come. All of a sudden a group of men who wielded considerable political power favored the national park bill.[38]

The Yellowstone Park Act, often called the Enabling Act, was, says Louis C. Cramton, who was an attorney for the Department of the Interior, "a remarkably well-drawn piece of legislation," considering that it was pioneering a new field. Most of the first paragraph of the act specified the park boundaries, which are closely similar to those of the present park. The details of that part were suggested by Hayden.

It is what follows that is significant. (1) It specifies its purpose: that it "is hereby reserved and withdrawn from settlement, occupancy, or sale under the laws of the United States, and dedicated and set apart as a public park and pleasuring ground for the benefit and enjoyment of the people. . . . " This is a restatement and reemphasis of the Yosemite Act of 1864, and it is basic to the whole concept of national parks.

(2) It provides for "the preservation, from injury or spoliation, of all timber, mineral deposits, natural curiosities, or wonders within said park, and their retention in their natural condition"; and "against the wanton destruction of the fish and game . . . and against their capture or destruction for the purpose of merchandise or profit."

The act also gave exclusive jurisdiction to the secretary of the interior, provided for leases, and stated that the revenues therefrom "should be expended under his direction in the management of the same [park], and the construction of roads and bridle paths therein." Trespassers or squatters after the passage of the act were to be removed.[39]

But there was no provision for appropriations or for enforcement of the act. Those who drew up the bill and voted for it must have decided that those things could be determined in the future.

So in 1872 the Yellowstone National Park was a vague reality somewhere in the wilds of the American continent, created hastily by a busy Congress, and then left to become whatever time and circumstances would make of it.

Its chances for survival in its natural state were not propitious. A rambunctious, expanding, loosely governed nation which emphasized the capitalist system, the Calvinist work ethic, and the settlement of the virgin land was as likely to make short shrift of a 55-by-65-square-mile block of land as a catamount of a helpless fawn. It was a park "for all the people," which implied that it was to be used. But how? And under what rules and regulations? How is nature preserved in the midst of usage?

In the balance, then, there was little hope for a lasting Yellowstone Park. Yet the park has survived. How this happened in the face of hunters, miners, railroaders, motorists, innkeepers, agents of technological development, and millions of souvenir-loving tourists is a complex story unto itself, the subject of a subsequent volume.

Notes

CHAPTER 1

1. " 'A Gigantic Pleasuring Ground': The Yellowstone National Park of the United States," *Nature* 6 (September 12, 1872): 397.

The park today retains nearly the same boundaries with which it began its existence. Accurate surveys have resulted in more precise measurements, and the Hoodoos on the east, as well as some elk pasturage along the northern boundary, have been added. According to the latest and most accurate surveys, Yellowstone embraces 2,221,772.61 acres, or about 3,471.51 square miles, and is about 62 miles long and 54 miles wide. Two hundred thirty-six square miles of the reservation are in southern and western Montana, 36 square miles are in eastern Idaho, and the rest are in extreme northwest Wyoming.

2. William A. Donn, Bertram B. Donn, and Wilbur G. Valentine, "On the Early History of the Earth," *Bulletin of the Geological Society of America* 66, no. 3 (March 1965): 293.

3. Ibid., 287–306. From all of this, and much more, scientists estimate an earth existing at least 4 billion years ago, sufficiently formed as a part of an equally formed solar system to contain "quartz-bearing, sialic material," water sufficient to bring about erosion, and heat sufficient to furnish above-freezing temperatures.

4. Walter Harvey Weed, "Geology of the Southern End of the Snowy Range," in *Geology of the Yellowstone National Park,* ed. Arnold Hague, United States Geological Survey Monograph 32, Part 2 (Washington, D.C.: Government Printing Office, 1899), p. 204. Part 1 was never published.

5. Arthur Bevan, "Summary of the Geology of the Beartooth Mountains, Montana," *The Journal of Geology* 31, no. 6 (September–October 1932):442; W. H. Bucher, W. T. Thom, Jr., and R. T. Chamberlin, "Geologic Problems of the Beartooth-Bighorn Region," *Bulletin of the Geological Society of America* 45 (February 28, 1934): 173; Arie Poldervaart and Robert D. Bentley, "Precambrian and Later Evolution of the Beartooth Mountains, Montana and Wyoming," *Billings Geological Society Guidebook,* Ninth Annual Field Conference; "Beartooth Uplift and Sunlight Basin," ed. D. L. Ziegler (Billings, Montana: n.p., 1958), p. 71.

Incidentally, even this test is not absolute, since Soda Butte Creek, Slough Creek, Hellroaring Creek, and a few other small streams and lakes do arise in the Beartooth and flow westward to the Yellowstone.

As recently as 1932 all the mountain ranges from Livingston, Montana, southeast to thirty or forty miles of Cody, Wyoming, were officially designated as the Absaroka Range. United States Geographical Board, Sixth Report (Washington, D.C.: G.P.O., 1933), p. 79, and the *Columbia-Lippincott Gazetteer of the World* (New York: Columbia University Press and J. B. Lippincott Co., 1952), pp. 6, 179, and 1788, list the Beartooth as merely a northwest spur of the Absarokas. Recent nomenclature, however, with geologists leading the way, has isolated the Beartooth as a specific mountain range. (Letter from the United States Geographical Board, Washington, D.C., to author, dated May 5, 1966.)

 6. Bevan, "Summary of the Geology of the Beartooth Mountains," pp. 445–47.

 7. There exists a Yellowstone–Beartooth–Bighorn Research Association.

 8. Donald F. Eckelman and Arie Poldervaart, "Geologic Evolution of the Beartooth Mountains, Montana and Wyoming, Part 1: 'Archean History of the Quad Creek Area,'" *Bulletin of the Geological Society of America* 68, no. 10 (October 1957): 1226; Bevan, "Summary of the Geology of the Beartooth Mountains," p. 448; Poldervaart and Bentley, "Precambrian and Later Evolution," p. 13; Erling Dorf, "Stratigraphy and Paleontology of a New Devonian Formation at Beartooth Butte, Wyoming," *Journal of Geology* 52, no. 7 (October–November 1934): 723.

 9. Bevan, "Summary of the Geology of the Beartooth Mountains," pp. 459–61.

 10. Ibid.

 11. Nevin M. Fenneman, *Physiography of Western United States* (New York: McGraw-Hill, 1931), p. 158.

 12. Joseph Paxson Iddings, "The Dissected Volcano of Crandall Basin, Wyoming," in Hague, *Geology of the Yellowstone Park,* pp. 215–36.

 13. John David Love, "Geology Along the Southern Margin of the Absaroka Range, Wyoming," Geological Society of America, *Special Papers,* No. 20 (1939): 6.

There are two pronunciations: the local inhabitants pronounce the word *absorke;* outsiders pronounce it in the more logical way, *absuroku.* The word was the name for the Crow Indians, its meaning in Crow language being "anything that flies." See Edwin Thompson Denig, *Of the Crow Nation,* ed. John C. Ewars, Smithsonian Institution, Bureau of American Ethnology, Bulletin 151, Anthropological Papers No. 33 (Washington, D.C.: G.P.O., 1953), p. 20.

 14. Arnold Hague, *Yellowstone National Park Folio, Wyoming,* Folio no. 30 (Washington, D.C.: U.S. Geological Survey, 1896), p. 2. Hague's résumé of park geology in this folio is superb. Until the late 1960s it remained for the most part accurate even though it was published more than seventy years ago. See also Fenneman, pp. 158–59.

 15. *Columbia-Lippincott Gazetteer,* p. 2096. Pronounced *togute.*

 16. Arnold Hague, "Description of the Absaroka Quadrangle," *Absaroka Folio, Crandall and Ishawooa Quadrangles, Wyoming,* Folio no. 52 (Washington, D.C.: U.S. Geological Survey, 1899), pp. 2–6.

 17. Arnold Hague, "Descriptive Geology of Huckleberry Mountain and Big Game Ridge," in *Geology of the Yellowstone National Park,* pp. 190, 200–202.

 18. Joseph Paxson Iddings and Walter Harvey Weed, "Descriptive Geology of the Northern End of the Teton Basin," in Hague, *Geology of the Yellowstone National Park,* pp. 149–64.

 19. *New York Times,* June 25, 1925, p. 8; ibid., May 19, 1927, p. 1; *St. Louis Post-Dispatch,* May 19, 1927; S. F. Stewart Sharpe, "Landslides and Related Phenomena," *Columbia Geomorphic Studies* no. 2 (New York: Columbia University Press, 1938), p. 76. The U.S. Forest Service maintains a tourist center at this site.

20. Fritiof M. Fryxell and Leland Hornberg, "Alpine Mudflows in Grand Teton National Park, Wyoming," *Bulletin of the Geological Society of America* 54 (March 1943): 457–72.

21. William A. Fischer, "Yellowstone's Living Geology: Earthquakes and Mountains." This is a 1959–60 special issue of *Yellowstone Nature Notes* 33 (June 1960). These are mimeographed notes submitted by park personnel and distributed to them.

22. Charles R. Ross and Willis H. Nelson, "Regional Seismicity and Brief History of Montana Earthquakes," *The Hebgen Lake, Montana Earthquake of August 17, 1959,* U.S. Geological Survey Professional Paper 435 "E" (Washington, D.C.: G.P.O., 1964), p. 28. This study consists of twenty short monographs listed by chapters "A" through "T." Different authorities have written them, each authority writing on one aspect of the quake.

The 1770 earthquake is dated by the age of a tree stump "near the top of a scarp. . . ." Ibid., p. 27.

23. United States Coast and Geodedic Survey, "Preliminary Report Hebgen Lake, Montana, Earthquakes" (Washington, D.C.: Department of Commerce, 1959), p. 10.

24. It rated 7.1 on the Richter Scale; by contrast the San Francisco earthquake of April 18, 1906, rated 8.2.

25. Leonard M. Murphy and Rutlage J. Brazee, "Seismological Investigations of the Hebgen Lake Earthquake," U.S.G.S. Professional Paper 435 "C," p. 13; José A. da Costa, "Effect of Hebgen Lake Earthquake on Water Levels in Wells in United States," U.S.G.S. Professional Paper 435 "O," p. 167.

26. Nicholas Helburn, "Southwestern Montana Earthquake and Landslide," *Geographical Review* 1, no. 1 (January 1960): 109–11; Irving J. Witkind, "Reactivated Faults North of Hebgen Lake," U.S.G.S. Professional Paper 435 "H," p. 73; W. Bradley Myers and Warren Hamilton, "Deformation Accompanying the Hebgen Lake Earthquake of August 17, 1959," U.S.G.S. Professional Paper 435 "I," p. 91.

27. Irving J. Witkind, "The Hebgen Lake Earthquake," *Geotimes* 4, no. 3 (October 1959):13.

28. Witkind, Professional Paper 435 "G," pp. 38–40; Helburn, "Southwestern Montana Earthquake," p. 110.

29. Helburn, "Southwestern Montana Earthquake," p. 110.

30. Irving J. Witkind, "Structural Damage in the Hebgen Lake–West Yellowstone Area," U.S.G.S. Professional Paper 435 "B," p. 9.

31. Myers and Hamilton, Professional Paper 435 "I," p. 55.

32. Ibid., pp. 70–75.

33. Coast and Geodedic Survey, p. 3.

34. Witkind, Professional Paper 435 "B," p. 11; Edmund Christopherson, *The Night the Mountain Fell: The Story of the Montana Yellowstone Earthquake* (Missoula, Mont.: Lawton Printing, 1960) contains good photographs of the catastrophe.

35. Jarvis B. Hadley, "Landslides and Related Phenomena Accompanying the Hebgen Lake Earthquake of August 17, 1959," U.S.G.S. Professional Paper 435 "K," pp. 124–26.

36. Ibid., pp. 121–24.

37. United States Forest Service, "Madison River Canyon Earthquake Area" (Missoula, Mont.: U.S. Department of Agriculture, Forest Service, Northern Region, 1961), p. 15; Irving J. Witkind, "Events on the Night of August

17, 1959 — the Human Story," U.S.G.S. Professional Paper 435 "A," pp. 1–3; Hadley, Professional Paper 435 "K," pp. 107–8. Witkind says nineteen were buried and seven others killed, the Forest Service says nineteen plus nine; twenty-eight are commemorated on the plaque. The discrepancy lies in the two individuals whose lives were snuffed out on down the canyon.

38. Hadley, Professional Paper 325 "K," pp. 115–16. Mr. Hadley states the figures of 40 million in the abstract of his article (p. 107) and 37 million on pages 108 and 118. I have chosen to use the conservative estimate of 37 million cubic yards.

39. Ibid. See also United States Army Engineers, "Madison River, Montana Report on Flood Emergency Madison River Slide," 2 vols. (Omaha: U.S. Army Engineer District, Omaha, September 1960).

40. Witkind, Professional Paper 435 "G," p. 37.

41. Two excellent sources of information on the earthquake not previously cited, but available in almost any public library, are Samuel W. Mathews, "The Night the Mountains Moved," *The National Geographic Magazine* 117, no. 3 (March 1960): 329–59; and *Life*, August 31, 1959, pp. 17–25.

42. Fischer, "Yellowstone's Living Geology," pp. 35–37, statistics from pp. 47 and 56; George D. Marler, *The Story of Old Faithful*, rev. ed. (Yellowstone Park, Wyo.: Yellowstone Library and Museum Association, 1961), pp. 25–26.

43. *New York Times*, August 23, 1959, sec. 2, p. 19; ibid., October 7, 1959, sec. 1, p. 44.

44. Joseph Paxson Iddings and Walter Harvey Weed, "Descriptive Geology of the Gallatin Mountains," in Hague, *Geology of the Yellowstone National Park*, pp. 57–59.

45. Hague, *Yellowstone National Park Folio, Wyoming*, p. 2.

46. Richard A. Bartlett, *Great Surveys of the American West* (Norman: University of Oklahoma Press, 1962), p. 70.

47. Walter Harvey Weed, "The Cinnabar and Bozeman Coal Fields of Montana," *Bulletin of the Geological Society of America* 2 (March 18, 1891): 349–64.

48. United States Geological and Geographical Survey (the Hayden Survey), *Fifth Annual Report* (Washington, D.C.: G.P.O., 1872), p. 60; idem, *Sixth Annual Report,* (Washington: G.P.O., 1873), pp. 40–41.

49. Walter Harvey Weed, "The Glaciation of the Yellowstone Valley North of the Park," United States Geological Survey Bulletin 104 (Washington, D.C.: G.P.O., 1893), pp. 1–40; quotations from Archibald Geikie, "The Ancient Glaciers of the Rocky Mountains," *The American Naturalist* 15, no. 1 (January 1881):3.

50. Merrill G. Burlingame, *The Montana Frontier* (Helena, Mont: State Publishing Co., 1942), pp. 83, 91–92.

CHAPTER 2

1. From 1965 until 1971 a systematic investigation of Yellowstone geology was conducted by a team of U.S. Geological Survey specialists. Many of their conclusions make obsolete much earlier geologic investigation. See William R. Keefer, *The Geologic Story of Yellowstone Park*, U.S. Geological Survey Bulletin no. 1437 (Washington, D.C.: G.P.O., 1972), pp. 38–51.

2. Arthur David Howard, "History of the Grand Canyon of the Yellowstone," Geological Society of America, *Special Papers* no. 6 (November 1937) : 6.

3. Arnold Hague, "Origin of the Thermal Waters in the Yellowstone National Park," *Bulletin of the Geological Society of America* 22 (1911) : 108.

4. William Henry Holmes, "Report on the Geology of the Yellowstone National Park," United States Geological and Geographical Survey of the Territories (the Hayden Survey), *Twelfth Annual Report,* 2 vols. (Washington, D.C.: G.P.O., 1883) 1:52–55.

5. Howard, "History of the Grand Canyon of the Yellowstone," pp. 8–9, 85–90. Both Holmes and Howard used the nomenclature *Snowy Mountains* where I have chosen to use the term *Beartooth,* in accordance with recent United States Board of Geographical Names policy.

6. Hiram Martin Chittenden, *The Yellowstone National Park,* ed. Richard A. Bartlett (Norman: University of Oklahoma Press, 1964), pp. 2–5. With regard to John Colter, see below, pp. 97–98.

7. O. T. Jones and R. M. Field, "The Resurrection of the Grand Canyon of the Yellowstone," American Journal of Science, 5th ser. 17, no. 99 (March 1929) : 263.

8. Holmes, "Report on the Geology of Yellowstone," p. 39.

9. Howard, "History of the Grand Canyon of the Yellowstone," pp. 151–53. For drawings of the Yellowstone channels see Clyde Max Bauer, *Yellowstone: Its Underworld* (Albuquerque: University of New Mexico Press, 1948), pp. 64–66, 70.

10. Howard, "History of the Grand Canyon of the Yellowstone," pp. 9–13.

11. For Baronett's part in rescuing Truman C. Everts, see below, pp. 185–87.

12. Burton Holmes, *The Burton Holmes Lectures,* 10 vols. (Battle Creek, Mich.: Little-Preston Co., 1901)6:78.

13. Holmes, "Report on the Geology of Yellowstone," pp. 48–50, including an illuminating drawing facing p. 48.

14. *New York Times,* May 13, 1962, sec. 4, p. 9.

15. Philetus W. Norris, *Report Upon the Yellowstone National Park to the Secretary of the Interior for the Year 1880* (Washington, D.C.: G.P.O., 1881).

16. Henry Gannett, "Geographical Field Work of the Yellowstone Park Division," Hayden Survey, *Twelfth Annual Report,* 2:473.

17. Howard, History of the Grand Canyon of the Yellowstone," pp. 90 ff.; Bauer, *Yellowstone,* pp. 61–66.

18. F. V. Hayden, "Report of F. V. Hayden," United States Geological and Geographical Survey of the Territories, *Fifth Annual Report* (Washington, D.C.: G.P.O., 1872), p. 132.

19. Bauer, *Yellowstone,* p. 78.

20. Haynes Guide, 62d ed. rev. (Bozeman, Mon.: Haynes Studios, 1962), p. 77.

21. F. V. Hayden, "Report of F. V. Hayden, United States Geologist," United States Geological and Geographical Survey of the Territories, *Sixth Annual Report* (Washington, D.C.: G.P.O., 1873), p. 55.

22. Eugene T. Allen and Arthur L. Day, *Hot Springs of the Yellowstone National Park,* Publication no. 466 (Washington: Carnegie Institution of Washington, 1935), p. 11.

23. Ibid., p. 15.

24. Edmund Otis Hovey, "Geyser Region of New Zealand" (Abstract), *Bulletin of the Geological Society of America* 35 (March 30, 1924) : 113.

25. Thomas W. Barth, "Geysers of Iceland," *Transactions of the American*

Geophysical Union 28, no. 6 (December 1947): 882–87; idem, "Geysers in Iceland," *American Journal of Science* 238, no. 6 (June 1940): 381–407; idem, *Volcanic Geology Hot Springs and Geysers of Iceland,* publication no. 587 (Washington: Carnegie Institution of Washington, 1950). This book contains an extensive bibliography on geyser phenomena. See also A. C. Peale, "Thermal Springs," part 2, "Thermal Springs and Geysers," Hayden Survey, *Twelfth Annual Report,* 2:304–54, for an outdated but interesting and concise survey of hot springs areas throughout the world.

26. Allen and Day, *Hot Springs,* pp. 171–74; Barth, *Volcanic Geology,* p. 63.

27. Joseph Paxson Iddings, "The Rhyolites," in Arnold Hague, *Geology of the Yellowstone National Park,* United States Geological Survey Monograph 32 (Washington D.C.: G.P.O., 1899), p. 357.

28. Arthur L. Day, "The Hot Springs Problem," *Bulletin of the Geological Society of America* 50 (1939), part 1, p. 319.

29. Arnold Hague, "Origin of the Thermal Waters of the Yellowstone National Park," *Bulletin of the Geological Society of America* 22 (1911): 108–9.

30. Day, "The Hot Springs Problem," p. 317.

31. Allen and Day, *Hot Springs,* pp. 19–23.

32. Ibid., pp. 33–37.

33. Clarence W. Fenner, "Bore-Hole Investigations in Yellowstone Park," *The Journal of Geology* 44, no. 2, part 2 (February–March 1936): 228–34; Allen and Day, *Hot Springs,* p. 38.

34. Allen and Day, *Hot Springs,* pp. 282–90.

35. Day, "The Hot Springs Problem," p. 322; Allen and Day, *Hot Springs,* p. 38.

36. A. C. Peale, "Thermal Springs," p. 357; Hague, "Origin of the Thermal Waters," 109 ff.; Allen and Day, *Hot Springs,* pp. 43–64; U.S.G.S. Bulletin 1487, pp. 79–82.

37. Hague, "Origin of the Thermal Waters," pp. 109–11.

38. Allen and Day, *Hot Springs,* pp. 43–50, 56.

39. Day, "The Hot Springs Problem," p. 321; Allen and Day, *Hot Springs,* pp. 227, 242–48.

40. Allen and Day, *Hot Springs,* pp. 65, 396–400; Day, "The Hot Springs Problem," p. 324.

41. Allen and Day, *Hot Springs,* pp. 68, 360–92; Day, "The Hot Springs Problem," p. 324.

42. Allen and Day, *Hot Springs,* pp. 72–82; Day, "The Hot Springs Problem," pp. 325–26; 331.

43. Allen and Day, *Hot Springs,* pp. 85–88.

44. Day, "The Hot Springs Problem," pp. 330–32.

45. Allen and Day, *Hot Springs,* pp. 208–9; F. Donald Bloss and Thomas F. W. Barth, "Observations on Some Yellowstone Geysers," *Bulletin of the Geological Society of America* 60 (May 1949): 863; Barth, *Volcanic Geology,* p. 76.

46. *Encyclopedia Americana,* 1957 ed., 5:26; 8:720; *Encyclopedia Britannica,* 1964 ed., 4:412; Allen and Day, *Hot Springs,* p. 209.

47. Allen and Day, *Hot Springs,* pp. 109–210; Barth, *Volcanic Geology,* p. 76.

48. Bloss and Barth, "Observations on Some Yellowstone Geysers," p. 866; in 1925 Allen and Day found the temperature warmer, 89.5°C (*Hot Springs,* p. 433).

49. Thorkell Thorkellson, "Letter in Reply to an Article by J. Joly," *Philo-*

sophical Magazine and Journal of Science, 7th series, 15, no. 28, part 2 (February 1928): 441–43.

50. Barth, *Volcanic Geology,* p. 78.

51. Allen and Day, *Hot Springs,* p. 212; Barth, *Volcanic Geology,* p. 78.

52. Bret Harte, "Plain Language from Truthful James," *The Poetical Works of Bret Harte* (Boston: Houghton Mifflin Co., 1902), p. 129.

53. Allen and Day, *Hot Springs,* p. 200; *Haynes Guide,* p. 97. The story has been told so often that even the exact spring is a matter for discussion.

54. Barth, *Volcanic Geology,* p. 78. For Allen and Day's comments, see pp. 200–207.

55. Day, "The Hot Springs Problem," p. 335.

56. George D. Marler, "Effects of the Hebgen Lake Earthquake of August 17, 1959, on the Hot Springs of the Firehole Geyser Basins, Yellowstone National Park," in *The Hebgen Lake, Montana Earthquake of August 17, 1959,* United States Geological Survey Professional Paper 435 "Q" (Washington, D.C.: G.P.O., 1964), p. 186.

57. Ibid., pp. 195–97.

58. Joseph Paxson Iddings, "Obsidian Cliff, Yellowstone National Park," United States Geological Survey, *Seventh Annual Report* (Washington D.C.: G.P.O., 1883, p. 261.

59. Ibid.

60. Ibid., p. 255.

61. Ibid., pp. 261–62.

CHAPTER 3

1. *Encyclopedia Americana,* 1957 ed., s.v. "lichen." See also W. B. McDougall and Herma A. Baggley, *The Plants of Yellowstone National Park,* Yellowstone Interpretive Series No. 8 (Yellowstone Park, Wyo.: Yellowstone Library and Museum Association, 1965), pp. 1–2.

2. *New York Times,* 13 May 1962, sec. 4, p. 9. The authority quoted is Dr. Erling Dorf of Princeton University.

3. McDougall and Baggley, *Plants of Yellowstone,* p. 2. This excellent book serves as the basis of my treatment of plant life in the park, and unless otherwise cited, all statements on this subject are based upon its authority.

4. Vernon Bailey, *Animal Life of Yellowstone National Park* (Springfield, Ill.: Charles C. Thomas, Publisher, 1930), p. 15.

5. United States Geological and Geographical Survey (the Hayden Survey), *Fifth Annual Report* (Washington, D.C.: G.P.O., 1872), p. 99.

6. Two principal sources of information on the mammals of Yellowstone National Park are Bailey, *Animal Life,* and Harold J. Brodrick, *Wild Animals of Yellowstone National Park,* Yellowstone Interpretive Series No. 1 (Yellowstone Park, Wyo.: Yellowstone Library and Museum Association, 1962). Unless otherwise cited, my statements on mammals are based on these two books.

7. Bailey, *Animal Life,* p. 107.

8. Hayden Survey, *Sixth Annual Report* (Washington, D.C.: G.P.O., 1873), pp. 667–68.

9. Lorus J. and Margery J. Milne, *The Mating Instinct* (Boston: Little, Brown and Co., 1954), pp. 132, 86.

10. Olaus J. Murie, *A Field Guide to Animal Tracks* (Boston: Houghton Mifflin Co., 1954), p. 186; Milne and Milne, *The Mating Instinct,* pp. 131–32.

11. Mari Sandoz, *The Beaver Men: Spearheads of Empire* (New York: Hastings House, 1964), pp. 66–74.

12. Milton Philo Skinner, *Bears in Yellowstone* (Chicago: A. C. McClurg and Co., 1925).

13. Ernest Thompson Seton, *The Biography of a Grizzly* (New York: Grossett & Dunlap, 1900).

14. Brodrick, *Wild Animals,* pp. 17–20; Bailey, *Animal Life,* 153–75; Murie, *Field Guild,* pp. 25–34, quotation from page 31; Farida A. Wiley, ed. *Ernest Thompson Seton's America* (New York: Devin-Adair, 1954), p. 197.

15. J. Frank Dobie, *The Voice of the Coyote* (Boston: Little, Brown and Co., 1948), p. 9.

16. Ibid., pp. 65, 73, 89, 194; Murie, *Field Guide,* pp. 94–99; idem, *Ecology of the Coyote in the Yellowstone,* Fauna Series No. 4 (Washington, D.C.: National Park Service, 1940), p. 188.

17. Milne and Milne, *The Mating Instinct,* p. 87; Victor H. Cahalane, *Mammals of North America* (New York: Macmillan Co., 1947), pp. 88–95.

18. Arthur S. Einarson, *The Pronghorn Antelope and its Management* (Washington, D.C.: Wildlife Management Institute, 1948), pp. 37–39.

19. Ibid., pp. 37, 40–41.

20. Cahalane, *Mammals,* p. 62.

21. Einarson, *Pronghorn Antelope,* pp. 45–57.

22. Cahalane, *Mammals,* p. 40.

23. Olaus J. Murie, *The Elk of North America* (Harrisburg, Pa.: Stackpole Co. and the Wildlife Management Institute, 1951), p. 3.

24. Milne and Milne, *The Mating Instinct,* p. 62.

25. Cahalane, *Mammals,* p. 15.

26. Bailey, *Animal Life,* p. 36.

27. Cahalane, *Mammals,* p. 44.

28. Ibid., p. 77.

29. Ibid.

30. James R. Simon, *Yellowstone Fishes,* Yellowstone Interpretive Series No. 3 (Yellowstone Park, Wyo.: Yellowstone Library and Museum Association, 1962), pp. 12–13, 20–21, 30–31, 45–47.

31. Frederick B. Turner, *Reptiles and Amphibians of Yellowstone National Park,* Yellowstone Interpretive Series No. 5 (Yellowstone Park, Wyo.: Yellowstone Library and Museum Association, 1955), pp. 20–36.

CHAPTER 4

1. Waldo R. Wedel, *Prehistoric Man on the Great Plains* (Norman: University of Oklahoma Press, 1961), pp. 46–50.

2. Frank A. Wierzbinski, "Habitations and Habitation Sites of the Northwestern Plains," *The Trowel and Screen,* Billings (Montana) Archaeological Society, 4, no. 5 (May 1963): 4–10. See also Kenneth Macgowan and Joseph A. Hester,

Jr., *Early Man in the New World* (Garden City: Doubleday & Co., 1962), pp. 20–25.

3. Wedel, *Prehistoric Man,* p. 50; Wierzbinski, "Habitation Sites," p. 4.

4. Richard Foster Flint, *Glacial Geology and the Pleistocene Epoch* (New York: John Wiley & Sons, 1947), p. 535.

5. Ake Hultkrantz, "The Indians in Yellowstone Park," *Annals of Wyoming* 29, no. 2 (October 1957): 125–49. See also Hannah Marie Wormington, *Ancient Man in North America,* 4th ed. rev. (Denver: Colorado Museum of Natural History, Popular Series No. 4, 1957), pp. 251 ff.

6. Wormington, *Ancient Man,* p. 41.

7. Frank H. H. Roberts, "Developments in the Problem of the North American Paleo-Indians," *Essays in Historical Anthropology of North America,* Smithsonian Miscellaneous Collections (Washington, D.C.: Smithsonian Institution, 1940), Vol. C, p. 58.

8. Aubrey L. Haines, "A Preliminary Report on High-Altitude Indian Occupation Sites Near the North Boundary of the Yellowstone National Park," unpublished manuscript, Yellowstone Archives, pp. 1–16. The discovery in 1959 of a Clovis point at the site of the new Gardiner Post Office augments these theories. A Clovis point may be older than, contemporary with, or more recent than a Folsom point. This one is estimated to be ten thousand to fifteen thousand years old. See also Aubrey L. Haines, "History of Yellowstone National Park," Part II, "The Indians in our Past," in *A Manual of General Information on Yellowstone National Park,* compiled by the Division of Interpretation for the use of Ranger-Naturalists (Yellowstone Park, Wyo.: 1963), pp. 84–85; Macgowan and Hester, *Early Man,* p. 153.

9. Wedel, *Prehistoric Man,* pp. 249–50.

10. Ibid., pp. 18–19.

11. Aubrey L. Haines, "Preliminary Report on High-Altitude Sites," p. 12.

12. Carling Malouf, "Preliminary Report, Yellowstone National Park Archaeological Survey, Summer, 1958," (Missoula, Mon.: Montana State University, typescript, 1958), pp. 9–11.

13. Aubrey L. Haines, "Preliminary Report on the Rigler Bluffs Prehistoric Indian Site: 24PA401, Near Corwin Springs, Montana. Coop. Research Project No. 68," (Yellowstone Park: 1962). Corwin Springs is about seven miles north of Gardiner on the Livingston Highway.

14. Malouf, "Preliminary Report," p. 12.

15. Ibid.; "A Short History of Montana Archaeology," *Archaeology in Montana* 3, no. 2 (December 1961): 1–2.

The Montana State University Archaeology Survey issued a report on its investigations which is available only in typescript: Dee C. Taylor, "Preliminary Archaeological Investigations in Yellowstone National Park (Montana State University, 1964). There is also an unpublished M.S. thesis based upon these investigations: John Jacob Hoffman, "A Preliminary Archaeological Survey of Yellowstone National Park" (Montana State University, 1961), 109 pp. I have examined both of these, and they are commendable, but as the narration has progressed none of their statements have seemed necessary to my story. Finally, a popularly written article by Stuart W. Conner, "Prehistoric Man in the Yellowstone Valley," *Montana: The Magazine of Western History* 14, no. 2 (April 1964): 14–21, provides an excellent review for the layman.

16. George Catlin, *North American Indians,* 2 vols. (Edinburgh: John Grant, 1926) 1:16.

17. Virginia Cole Trenholm and Maurice Carley, *The Shoshones: Sentinels of the Rockies* (Norman: University of Oklahoma Press, 1964), pp. vii, 3, 19–21.

18. Of the many books on the Lewis and Clark Expedition, I recommend John Bakeless, *Lewis and Clark: Partners in Discovery* (New York: William Morrow and Co., Apollo Edition, 1947), of which pp. 238–39 deal with Yellowstone, and *The Journals of Lewis and Clark*, ed. John Bakeless (New York: New American Library, 1964), see p. 228ff. An excellent recent book on the subject is Paul Russell Cutright, *Lewis and Clark: Pioneering Naturalists* (Urbana: University of Illinois Press, 1969).

19. Ake Hultkrantz, "The Shoshones in the Rocky Mountain Area," trans. Dr. Arne Magnus, *The Annals of Wyoming* 33, no. 1 (April 1961): 31–35.

20. Trenholm and Carley, *The Shoshones*, pp. 3–4. Such fluidity in tribal nomenclature is the bane of the historian striving for accuracy.

21. Hultkrantz, "The Shoshones," p. 34–35.

22. Osborne Russell, *The Journal of a Trapper*, ed. Aubrey L. Haines (Lincoln: University of Nebraska Press, 1964), p. 26.

23. Hultkrantz, "The Indians in Yellowstone Park," pp. 134–36.

24. Ibid.; William Alonzo Allen, *The Sheep Eaters* (New York: Shakespeare Press, 1913), pp. 48, 74–75. Although of questionable authenticity, Allen's book nevertheless includes accounts of warfare with the Plains Indians and the coming of a smallpox epidemic.

25. Philetus Norris, *Annual Report of the Superintendent of the Yellowstone National Park for 1881* (Washington, D.C.: G.P.O.,1882), p. 38.

26. Charles W. Cook, "Reconstructed Diary of the Cook-Folsom Expedition in 1869 to the Yellowstone Region," *Haynes Bulletin,* January 1923, p. 1. This publication was issued during the early 1920s by the Haynes Studios of Yellowstone Park and St. Paul, Minnesota.

A definitive study of the Cook–Folsom–Peterson Expedition is Charles W. Cook, David E. Folsom, and William Peterson, *The Valley of the Upper Yellowstone: An Exploration of the Headwaters of the Yellowstone River in the Year 1869,* ed. Aubrey L. Haines (Norman: University of Oklahoma Press, 1965.)

27. U.S., Congress, House, Exec. Doc. 285, Captain William A. Jones, *Report Upon the Reconnaissance of Northwestern Wyoming Including Yellowstone National Park Made in the Summer of 1873,* 43d Cong., 1st Sess., pp. 39–41, 55. Pages 54–55 list a number of Indian trails in and about the southern sections of the park. Professor Comstock's report, which accompanies the Jones Report, also mentions Togwotee, p. 175.

28. Lieutenant General Philip H. Sheridan, *Report of Lieutenant General P. H. Sheridan, Dated September 20, 1881, of His Expedition Through the Big Horn Mountains, Yellowstone National Park, Etc.,* (Washington, D.C.: G.P.O., 1882), pp. 11–12.

29. Hultkrantz, "Indians in Yellowstone Park," pp. 134–36. As of 1964 there were about 2,000 Shoshones on the Wind River Reservation. Trenholm and Carley, *The Shoshones,* p. 175.

30. Edwin Thompson Denig, *Five Indian Tribes of the Upper Missouri,* ed. John C. Ewers (Norman: University of Oklahoma Press, 1961), pp. 137–39.

31. Ibid., pp. 139–41. Park officials have told me that on the floor of the Grand Canyon of the Yellowstone there are such bituminous springs which break into flames every so often, occasioning a tiring trip down by the rangers, who snuff

out the fire, only to have it break out again about the time they reach the rim of the canyon.

32. Trenholm and Carley, *The Shoshones*, p. 173. The Crow Reservation is still "Crow Country," south-southeast of Billings, Montana.

33. John C. Ewers, *The Blackfeet: Raiders on the Northwestern Plains* (Norman: University of Oklahoma Press, 1958), pp. 5–7.

34. Bakeless, *Lewis and Clark: Partners in Discovery,* pp. 340–43; Cutright, *Lewis and Clark: Pioneering Naturalists,* pp. 316–23.

35. Henry Marie Brackenridge, *Views of Louisiana: Together with a Journal of a Voyage up the Missouri River in 1811* (Chicago: Quadrangle Books, 1962), pp. 80–92; John Bradbury, *Travels in the Interior of North America in the Years 1809, 1810, 1811,* in Reuben Gold Thwaites, *Early Western Travels* (Cleveland: Arthur H. Clark Co., 1904-7) 5:44–46; Ewers, *The Blackfeet,* pp. 50–53.

36. Brigham D. Madsen, *The Bannock of Idaho* (Caldwell, Idaho: Caxton Printers, 1958), pp. 7, 17.

37. Ibid., pp. 122–213.

38. There is no real mystery over this disappearance. The buffalo were exterminated by overhunting.

39. Madsen, *The Bannock of Idaho,* p. 22. The camas root, so often mentioned but seldom described, resembles the hyacinth. It bears a "pretty blue flower," and its root "resembles an onion in shape and a hickory nut in size." The Indians dug it up in June and July. It could be eaten raw, having a taste described as "pleasant and mucilaginous"; when boiled, it tasted somewhat like a common potato. The principal Indian method of preparing it was by roasting, when the roots became a "dark-brown, homogenous mass, of about the consistency of softened glue, and as sweet as molasses." The roots were then shaped into cakes and slightly dried in the sun, when they became "pliable and tough and look[ed] like plugs of blue navy tobacco." In this way the food could keep for a year or more. See "Food Products of the North American Indians," *Report of the Commissioner of Agriculture for the Year 1870* (Washington, D.C.: G.P.O., 1871), pp. 408–9.

40. Wayne Replogle, *Yellowstone's Bannock Indian Trails* (Yellowstone Park, Wyo.: Yellowstone Library and Museum Association, 1956).

This booklet is no longer for sale because "pot hunters" — amateur archaeologists — followed its directions in search of Indian artifacts, in violation of the Federal Antiquities Act.

41. Madsen, *The Bannock of Idaho,* pp. 21–23, 28, 30.

42. Federal Writer's Project, *Idaho: A Guide in Word and Picture* (New York: Oxford University Press, 1950), pp. 133–34.

43. The two best sources for the descriptions of the Bannock Trails are Replogle, *Yellowstone's Bannock Indian Trails,* and Aubrey L. Haines, "The Bannock Indian Trails of the Yellowstone National Park," *Archaeology in Montana* 4 (no. 1): 1–8. This has also been printed in *Yellowstone Nature Notes.* Unless otherwise noted, these are the two sources used.

44. Ferdinand Vandiveer Hayden, *Twelfth Annual Report* (Washington, D.C.: G.P.O., 1883), part 2, contains a map facing page 490 which traces a number of these trails.

45. Madsen, *The Bannock of Idaho,* p. 189, states that the hunt entailed a journey of 600 miles or more.

46. Ibid., p. 122.

47. Ibid., pp. 133–37; quotation on p. 160.

48. Haines, "Bannock Indian Trails," p. 6; Madsen, *The Bannock of Idaho,* pp. 248–71.

CHAPTER 5

1. Louis Armand de Lom d'Arce, baron de Lahontan, *New Voyages in North America,* ed. Reuben Gold Thwaites, 2 vols. (Chicago: McClurg, 1905), 1: 179–95.

2. Pierre Gaultiere de Varennes, sieur de La Vérendrye, *Journals and Letters of La Vérendrye and His Sons,* ed. Lawrence Johnstone Burpee (Toronto: Champlain Society, 1927), pp. 13–24.

3. Mark Brown, *The Plainsmen of the Yellowstone* (New York: Putnam & Co., 1961), pp. 21–23.

4. Abraham P. Nasatir, ed., *Before Lewis and Clark: Documents Illustrating the History of the Missouri, 1785–1804,* 2 vols. (St. Louis: St. Louis Historical Documents Foundation, 1952) 1:85 ff., 101; Paul Chrisler Phillips, *The Fur Trade,* 2 vols. (Norman: University of Oklahoma Press, 1961) 2: 239–40.

5. Nasatir, 2:498.

6. Donald Jackson, ed., *Letters of the Lewis and Clark Expedition, With Related Documents* (Urbana: University of Illinois Press, 1962), p. v.

7. Reuben Gold Thwaites, ed., *Original Journals of the Lewis and Clark Expedition, With Related Documents,* 7 vols. in 14 and atlas (New York: Dodd, 1904–5) 2:176–77. It is significant that the Biddle edition (the first edition published) did not include Clark's statement, nor in recent times have Bakeless or DeVoto chosen to include it in their abridgements. The phenomenon has been noticed, however, by geologists who have tried to trace a historical pattern of earthquakes in Montana. Clark's description of the sounds, writes one geologist, "tallies closely with that of sounds called brontides, which are registered by authorities as partly at least of seismic origin — possibly the final representatives of a series of aftershocks." See J. T. Pardee, "The Montana Earthquake of June 27, 1925," United States Geological Survey Professional Paper 147 "B" (Washington, D.C.: G.P.O., 1926), p. 23. The strange noises that can be heard over the Yellowstone Lake may also be brontides, which are low muffled sounds heard especially along seacoasts and over lakes and thought to be caused by feeble earth tremors.

8. Jackson, *Letters of the Lewis and Clark Expedition,* p. 234.

9. Ibid., p. 526. Biddle was the editor of the first published edition of the journals. Lewis and Clark were both atrocious spellers; the French word *Rochejaune* gave their ingenuity at spelling free rein, and they made full use of the opportunity.

10. Phillips, *Fur Trade,* 2:235.

11. Clarence Edwin Carter, ed., *The Territorial Papers of the United States,* 26 vols., "The Territory of Louisiana-Missouri, 1803–1806," (Washington, D.C.: G.P.O., 1948) 13:199, 243.

12. Quoted in the *Richmond* (Virginia) *Inquirer,* January 4, 1812. The reference is, of course, to the New Madrid earthquake, the severest shock of which occurred on December 16, 1811. Though almost forgotten, this was one of the

greatest earthquakes in recorded history. See Myron L. Fuller, "The New Madrid Earthquake," United States Geological Survey, Bulletin 494 (Washington, D.C.: G.P.O., 1912.)

As for volcanoes, Lewis and Clark mention them but once. This is in Clark's entry, September 14, 1804, when he says he "walked on Shore with a view to find an old Vulcanoe, Said to be in the neighborhood by Mr. J. McKey of St. Charles. I walked on Shore the whole day without Seeing any appearance of the Vulcanoe. . . . " Thwaites, *Journals of Lewis and Clark,* vol. 1, part 2, p. 147. This would have been somewhere in the vicinity of Brule City, South Dakota — a long way from the Yellowstone. It is interesting to note that "in the country of the Omahas," or somewhat above them on the river, Father De Smet mentioned that in several places "you can see steam and sulphurous flames escaping from the earth," and that he was told by a traveler that "subterranean noises are often heard, resembling those of volcanic districts." See Hiram Martin Chittenden and Alfred Richardson, *Life, Letters and Travels of Father Pierre Jean De Smet, S. J., 1801–1873,* 4 vols. (New York: F. P. Harper, 1905) 1: 181–82.

13. Jackson, *Letters of the Lewis and Clark Expedition,* pp. 118n, 125n., 431n.; Burton Harris, *John Colter: His Years in the Rockies* (New York: Charles Scribner's Sons, 1952), p. 14.

14. Ernest Staples Osgood, *The Field Notes of Captain William Clark, 1803– 1805* (New Haven: Yale University Press, 1964), p. 29. Frasure is also spelled Frazier, Frazure, and Frazer.

15. Thwaites, *Journals of Lewis and Clark,* vol. 2, part 2, pp. 341, 343, 344.

16. Harris, *John Colter,* pp. 54–55.

17. Thomas James, *Three Years Among the Indians and the Mexicans* (originally published Waterloo, Iowa, office of the "War Eagle," 1846; also available on microcard of Wagner-Camp, *The Plains and the Rockies* (Louisville, Ky: Lost Cause Press, 1969), card no. 121, pp. 11, 21 ff. Henry Marie Brackenridge mentions Colter briefly in his *Views of Louisiana: Together with a Journal of a Voyage up the Missouri River, in 1811,* March of America Facsimile Series No. 60 (Ann Arbor: University Microfilms, 1966); and John Bradbury mentions meeting him in his *Travels in the Interior of America in the Years 1809, 1810, and 1811* in Reuben Gold Thwaites, *Early Western Travels,* 25 vols. (Cleveland: Arthur H. Clark Co., 1904–7), vol. 5.

18. This map is reproduced in Carl I. Wheat, *Mapping the Trans-Mississippi West, 1540–1861,* 5 vols. in 6 (San Francisco: Institute of Historical Cartography, 1957–63), vol. 2, facing p. 56. It is also reproduced and discussed in Merrill D. Beale, *The Story of Man in Yellowstone,* rev. ed. (Yellowstone Park, Wyo.: Yellowstone Library and Museum Association, 1960), pp. 46, 48–49, 187, 289–97.

19. Washington Irving, *The Adventures of Captain Bonneville, U.S.A.,* ed. Edgeley W. Todd (Norman: University of Oklahoma Press, 1961), p. 173.

20. Conversation during the summer of 1968 with Mr. Paul Henderson of Bridgeport, Nebraska. Mr. Henderson has spent a half-century as an amateur student of Oregon Trail and Wyoming history, and he is recognized as an authority. He knows the Shoshone country well.

21. Beale, *Man in Yellowstone,* pp. 285–300. Professor Beale's theory is intriguing in the extreme, and no ridicule of his theories is intended.

The Colter controversy goes on and on, and cannot be dealt with in depth here. See Stallo Vinton, *John Colter, Discoverer of Yellowstone Park* (New York:

Edward Eberstadt, 1926) ; Harris, *John Colter;* or Merrill Mattes's excellent summary, "Behind the Legend of Colter's Hell: The Early Exploration of Yellowstone National Park," *Mississippi Valley Historical Review* 36 (1949) : 251–82. William H. Goetzmann in his monumental *Exploration and Empire* (New York: Alfred A. Knopf, 1966), pp. 20–25, suggests that Colter was attempting to make contact with Spanish fur traders from Santa Fe. Finally, a stone with COLTER carved on it was ostensibly found in the Teton Basin (on the west, or Idaho, side of the Tetons) a few years ago, and the Park Service has considered it authentic. It is housed at the museum at Moran, Wyoming. According to Mr. Aubrey Haines, formerly park historian at Yellowstone, there is strong evidence that this stone, along with a couple of others bearing carvings, was probably the work of hoaxers with the Hayden Survey in the 1870s (conversations with Mr. Haines, summer of 1964 and autumn of 1966).

22. I acknowledge my indebtedness to Merrill Mattes, whose essay "Behind the Legend of Colter's Hell" provides a definitive account of Yellowstone exploration down to 1869.

23. Daniel T. Potts, "Early Yellowstone and Western Experiences (Daniel T. Potts Letters)," *Yellowstone Nature Notes* 21, no. 5 (September–October 1947) : 49–56. The Potts letters have appeared most recently in Dale L. Morgan, ed., *The West of William H. Ashley* (Denver: Old West Publishing Co., 1964), pp. 161–62, and notes, pp. 228–29.

24. Ibid. An authority on another trapping party, the Ross brigade of the Hudson's Bay Company, says the trappers "crossed the Boiling Fountains" on April 24, 1824, and assumes these to be Yellowstone geysers, but more recent investigation places the hot springs that Ross saw as those near Jackson, Montana. This is in the Big Hole country, far to the west of the park. See Agnes C. Laut, *The Conquest of the Great Northwest,* 2 vols. (Toronto: Musson Book Co., n.d.) 2: 156–57; Phillips, *Fur Trade,* 2: 444–45.

25. E. S. Topping, *The Chronicles of the Yellowstone* (St. Paul: Pioneer Press, 1888), pp. 14–15.

26. Dale L. Morgan, *Jedediah Smith and the Opening of the West* (Indianapolis: Bobbs-Merrill Co., 1953), pp. 307–8; Frances Fuller Victor, *The River of the West* (Columbus, O.: Long's College Book Shop, 1950), pp. 73–80; Harvey E. Tobie, "Joseph L. Meek," in *The Mountain Men and the Fur Trade of the Far West,* ed. LeRoy Hafen, 10 vols. (Glendale, Calif.: Arthur H. Clark Co., 1965–72) 1:315.

Mattes suggests that Meek may have stumbled upon hot springs on the Mirror Plateau, east of the Yellowstone River within the park. His route could not have taken him to Mammoth, Norris, or the Lower, Middle, or Upper geyser basins, which are all west of the river. ("Behind the Legend of Colter's Hell," p. 267.)

27. Aubrey L. Haines, "Johnson Gardner," in Hafen, *Mountain Men and the Fur Trade,* 2:158–59.

28. J. Cecil Alter, *James Bridger* (Salt Lake City: Shepard Book Co., 1925), pp. 106, 114, 148, 161; Victor, *River of the West,* p. 98.

29. Warren Angus Ferris, *Life in the Rocky Mountains,* ed. Paul Chrisler Phillips (Denver: Old West Publishing Co., 1940).

30. Ibid., pp. 192–93. A sketch of Manuel Álvarez, by Harold H. Dunham, appears in Hafen, *Mountain Men and the Fur Trade,* 1: 181–97. Professor Phillips, who edited the Ferris book, believed that Álvarez may have first visited the park

in 1827, and that he was probably the author of the anonymous article about geysers in *Niles Register,* October 6, 1827. (It had first appeared in the *Philadelphia Gazette and Advertiser,* September 27, 1827.) See his footnote on page 251 of the Ferris book. Unfortunately in this instance Dr. Phillips did not make clear his line of reasoning, nor does he include documentation.

31. Ibid., pp. 257–60.

32. Lyman C. Pederson, Jr., "Warren Angus Ferris," in Hafen, *Mountain Men and the Fur Trade,* 2:154.

33. Osborne Russell, *Journal of a Trapper,* ed. Aubrey L. Haines (Portland, Ore.: Oregon Historical Society, 1955; Lincoln, Neb.: University of Nebraska Press, 1965), pp. 5–6.

34. Gardner's Hole lies southeast of Electric Peak and east of the Gallatin Range. It was named for Johnson Gardner, who may have trapped there in the fall of 1831 or the spring of 1832 (Haines, "Johnson Gardner"). An older authority, Hiram Martin Chittenden, *The American Fur Trade of the Far West,* 3 vols. (New York: F. P. Harper, 1902) 2: 738–39, believed Gardner's Hole was the open land above the North Entrance to the park, but Russell's own description — "This Valley is . . . surrounded except on the North and West by low piney mountains on the West is a high narrow range of Mountains running North and South dividing the waters of the Yellow Stone from those of the Gallatin fork of the Missouri" — is an almost perfect description of the later accepted location.

35. Haines has traced the approximate route of Russell on a map facing page 38 of the *Journal of a Trapper.*

36. Ibid., pp. 41–43, with map facing p. 52.

37. This summary of Russell's journeys covers pp. 43–108 of Russell, *Journal of a Trapper.*

38. Aubrey L. Haines, "Osborne Russell," in Hafen, *Mountain Men and the Fur Trade,* 2:313–16.

39. William Thomas Hamilton, *My Sixty Years on the Plains* (Norman: University of Oklahoma Press, 1964), pp. 68–69; Hiram Martin Chittenden, *The Yellowstone National Park,* ed. Richard A. Bartlett (Norman: University of Oklahoma Press, 1964) p. 45, is the authority for the date 1844, adding that the remains of the corral could still be seen in 1870.

Perhaps it is worth clearing up at this point that there never was a trapper's rendezvous in the Yellowstone National Park. See Hafen, *Mountain Men and the Fur Trade,* 1:176 for a listing of the sites of every one held, 1825–40 inclusive.

40. An excellent analysis of the later fur trade is John E. Sunder, *The Fur Trade of the Upper Missouri, 1840–1865* (Norman: University of Oklahoma Press, 1965).

41. George Frederick Ruxton, *Life in the Far West,* ed. LeRoy Hafen (Norman: University of Oklahoma Press, 1951), pp. 112–17.

42. William Clark Kennerly as told to Elizabeth Russell, *Persimmon Hill: A Narrative of Old St. Louis and the Far West* (Norman: University of Oklahoma Press, 1948), pp. 156–57.

43. It might be added that Mae Reed Porter and Odessa Davenport, *Scotsman in Buckskin: Sir William Drummond Stewart and the Rocky Mountain Fur Trade* (New York: Hastings House, 1963), do not place Stewart and his party even close to the Yellowstone. For these reasons, I discredit the evidence presented in the Kennerly book.

44. Alter, *James Bridger,* is vague on Bridger's peregrinations. He has him in Yellowstone in 1831, but in 1850 he concerns himself with Bridger's troubles with the Mormons. However, there is considerable evidence that Bridger did get to the Yellowstone during these two decades. See pp. 114, 117, and 132. See also William F. Wheeler, "The Late James Gemmell," *Contributions to the Historical Society of Montana,* 10 vols. (Helena, Mon.:Montana Historical Society, 1896) 2: 331; see also Topping, *Chronicles of the Yellowstone,* pp. 16, 62.

45. John William Gunnison, *The Mormons or Latter-Day Saints* (Philadelphia: Lippincott, Grambo, and Co., 1852); Wagner-Camp, *The Plains and the Rockies* (Louisville, Ky.: Lost Cause Press, 1969), microcard no. 213, p. 151.

46. Chittenden, *Yellowstone National Park,* pp. 48–49.

47. Hiram Martin Chittenden and Alfred T. Richardson, *Life, Letters and Travels of Father Pierre Jean De Smet, S.J. 1801–1873,* 4 vols. (New York: F. P. Harper, 1905) 2: 660–61. In vol. 4, p. 1377, he refers again to the Yellowstone, mentioning the Lake Eustis of the Clark map of 1814. See also *Rev. Pierre-Jean De Smet, Western Missions and Missionaries: A series of Letters* (New York: P. J. Kennedy, 1859), pp. 86–88.

48. Mattes, "Behind the Legend of Colter's Hell," pp. 277–78. There is a lengthy discussion of the early maps of the Yellowstone in Wheat, *Mapping the Trans-Mississippi West,* vol. 5, part 2, pp. 288–313.

49. U.S., Congress, Senate, Sen. Doc. 77, W. F. Raynolds, *Report of the Exploration of the Yellowstone and Missouri Rivers, in 1859–1860,* 40th Cong., 1st Sess., p. 77. The Bridger stories are related on page 77.

CHAPTER 6

1. William Trimble, "A Reconsideration of Gold Discoveries in the Northwest," *Mississippi Valley Historical Review* 5 (1918): 70–77. This is in reply to Paul C. Phillips and H. A. Trexler, "Notes on the Discovery of Gold in the Northwest," *Mississippi Valley Historical Review* 4 (1917): 89–97. See also Merrill G. Burlingame, *The Montana Frontier* (Helena, Mon.: Montana State Publishing Co., 1942), pp. 78–100.

2. W. Turrentine Jackson, *Wagon Roads West* (Berkeley: University of California Press, 1952), pp. 257–76; Burlingame, *Montana Frontier,* p. 84.

3. Burlingame, *Montana Frontier,* pp. 262–66, 126, 44. For the Crow Treaty see Charles Joseph Kappler, *Indian Affairs: Laws and Treaties,* 5 vols. (Washington, D.C.: G.P.O., 1903–41), 2:1008–11.

4. Burlingame, *Montana Frontier,* p. 298.

5. Ibid., pp. 151–52.

6. Ninth Census (Washington, D.C.: G.P.O., 1872) 1: xvii, 46, 23, 74, 579–80.

7. E. S. Topping, *The Chronicles of the Yellowstone* (St. Paul: Pioneer Press, 1888), p. 28.

8. William F. Wheeler, "Walter Washington De Lacy," *Contributions to the Historical Society of Montana* (Helena, Mon.: Montana Historical Society, 1896) 2:241–51. Peter R. Brady, who was with De Lacy on the railroad survey along the 32d parallel in 1854, described him as a "splendid draftsman and a scientist of no mean repute." See L. R. Bailey, *The A. B. Gray Report* (Los Angeles: Westernlore Press, 1963), p. 226.

9. Walter W. De Lacy, "A Trip to the South Snake River in 1863," *Contributions to the Historical Society of Montana* (1876) 1: 113. Unless otherwise noted, the narration of the De Lacy trip is from this source, pp. 113–43.

10. John C. Davis, "An Interview with a Man who Visited that Region of Wonders as Far Back as 1863 — Account of the Expedition," *Louisville Courier-Journal,* April 3, 1884. Davis said that they came down into the Upper Geyser Basin, but this does not appear likely in view of De Lacy's narration. Davis is listed by De Lacy as being a member of the party. De Lacy, "Trip to the South Snake River," p. 140.

11. Carl I. Wheat, *Mapping the Trans-Mississippi West, 1540–1861,* 5 vols. in 6 (San Francisco: Institute of Historical Cartography, 1957–63), vol. 5, part 1, pp. 149–53, map reproduced facing page 152.

12. Ibid., vol. 5, part 2, pp. 274–77, map facing p. 276.

13. De Lacy, "Trip to the South Snake River," p. 143.

14. U.S., Congress, House, *The Report of Rossiter W. Raymond on the Mineral Resources of the States and Territories West of the Rocky Mountains,* 40th Cong., 3d Sess., Exec. Doc. No. 54, p. 134.

15. There are a De Lacy Trail, De Lacy Lake, a De Lacy Creek, and a De Lacy Park in the general region north and west of Shoshone Lake, in the vicinity that De Lacy traversed.

16. Topping, *Chronicles of the Yellowstone,* pp. 24–25.

17. Ibid., pp. 28–29.

18. Granville Stuart, *Forty Years on the Frontier as Seen in the Journals and Reminiscences of Granville Stuart,* 2 vols. (Cleveland: Arthur H. Clark Co., 1925) 2: 13–14. According to Stuart, the party left in February and all had returned by July and August.

19. Davis, "Interview with a Man who Visited that Region."

20. Topping, *Chronicles of the Yellowstone,* pp. 44–45. The Nebraska State Historical Society has been unable to locate such a letter, but explains that its newspaper files are spotty for the 1860s. Letter from the society, September 7, 1966.

The horse thieves' trail is a nebulous item of Yellowstone legend that has its basis in fact. Known to desperadoes and those who pursued them as the Skull and Crossbones Trail, it appears to have existed at least from the early sixties, and was used by thieves in transporting stolen horses between the eastern plains and Idaho.

21. Topping, *Chronicles of the Yellowstone,* pp. 48–49, 72–73.

22. "The Yellowstone Diaries of A. Bart Henderson," ed. Aubrey L. Haines, *The Yellowstone Interpreter* 2, nos. 1, 2, and 3 (January–June 1964). The 1867 trip described below is in part 1 (January).

In his introduction Haines says: "The three diaries which will be presented here were originally appended to a more extensive 'Journal of the Yellowstone Expedition of 1866 under Captain Jeff Standifer,' and their essential nature as sources of Yellowstone history appears to have escaped notice. Actually, these fragmentary but carefully written diaries document much of the Park's nearly legendary era of mining exploration." They are housed in the collections of the Wyoming Historical Society. Incidentally, the Standifer expedition, although bearing the name "Yellowstone," did not explore the park area, but did pass through it.

23. I am indebted to Mr. Haines, the Yellowstone Park historian, for the meticulous editing of the Henderson diary. The reader may assume that the link-up

of the diary with present place names is the work of Mr. Haines, and I hereby acknowledge my indebtedness to him. It is a masterful job.

24. This ends part 1 of the Henderson diaries. It was fairly easy to trace Henderson's route because he gave an estimate of distance traveled each day.

25. Topping, *Chronicles of the Yellowstone,* pp. 62–63. According to an item in the *Montana Post,* August 24, 1867, a Dr. Dunlevy of the Montana Volunteers apparently saw some of the Yellowstone also in that year.

26. Henderson Diaries, part 2 (March–April 1964): 20–26; James Gourley, "Narration of Mining Trip into the Yellowstone Country, 1870," typed manuscript, Yellowstone Archives. (Heading reads: "Dated June 8, 1870; obtained March 28, 1929.") My narration of this prospecting expedition is based upon these two sources.

27. This area is no longer shown as a thermal area on the park map. It was probably far more active then than it is today.

28. Topping, *Chronicles of the Yellowstone,* pp. 82–83.

29. "Flying time" refers to the swarms of gnats, deer flies, and other winged insects that plague the animals at certain times of the summer season, driving them to the high ridges where the cool, constant breezes stave off the insects and give some relief.

30. Gourley, "Narration"; Topping, *Chronicles of the Yellowstone,* pp. 76–77. See *New York Times,* May 16, 1870, p. 1, for the death of Stambaugh.

31. Topping, *Chronicles of the Yellowstone,* p. 83.

32. Henderson Diaries, part 3 (May–June 1964): 33–44.

Bottler's ranch figures much in post–Civil War Yellowstone exploration. It was just west and opposite the mouth of Emigrant Creek, on the Yellowstone.

33. This reference is to William T. Hamilton. Hamilton does not record this expedition in his interesting but flimsy autobiography but he does say that in 1869 he "moved to the Yellowstone valley, . . . " so this reference certainly applies to him. W. T. Hamilton, *My Sixty Years on the Plains* (Norman: University of Oklahoma Press, 1960), p. 182.

34. Henderson Diaries, part 3 (May–June 1964): 143.

35. T. S. Lowering, "The New World or Cooke City Mining District, Park County, Montana," United States Geological Survey, Bulletin 811 "A" (Washington, D.C.: G.P.O., 1930), pp. 3, 9, 44.

36. Ibid., pp. 44–48.

Chapter 7

1. Cornelius Hedges, "Early Masonry in Montana," *Rocky Mountain Magazine* 1, no. 1 (September 1900): 13.

2. Joaquin Miller, *An Illustrated History of the State of Montana,* 1 vol. in 2 (Chicago: Lewis Publishing Co., 1894) 1: 180.

3. U.S., Congress, Senate, Exec. Doc. 43, Captain John Mullan, "Report on the Construction of a Military Road from Fort Walla Walla to Fort Benton," 37th Cong. 3d Sess., pp. 2–4, 53. This does not mean that he saw Yellowstone, but he did see springs west of there, and he undoubtedly heard stories of the geysers.

4. Gilbert J. Garraghan, S.J., *The Jesuits of the Middle United States,* 3 vols. (New York: American Press, 1938) 3: 587.

5. Francis Xavier Kuppens, S.J., "On the Origin of the Yellowstone National Park, from a Letter of Father F. X. Kuppens, S. J.," *The Woodstock Letters* 16, no. 3 (1897).

6. Lawrence B. Palladino, S.J., *Indian and White in the Northwest* (Baltimore: J. Murphy, 1894), pp. 178–80; Anne McDonnell, "The Catholic Indian Missions in Montana," in Merrill Burlingame and K. Ross Toole, *A History of Montana,* 3 vols. (New York: Lewis Historical Publishing Co., 1957) 1: 111.

7. Thomas Francis Meagher, "A Journey to Benton," ed. Robert Athearn, *Montana, The Magazine of Western History* 1, no. 4 (October 1951): 46–64.

8. Meagher's tactlessness, alcoholic excess, and enormous ego worked consistently against him. Yet he is a fascinating person. See Robert Athearn, *Thomas Francis Meagher: An Irish Revolutionary in America* (Boulder: University of Colorado Press, 1949).

9. Cornelius Hedges, "An Account of a Trip to Fort Benton in October of 1865 with Acting Governor Thomas F. Meagher to Treat with the Blackfeet Indians," *Rocky Mountain Magazine* 1, no. 3 (November 1900): 155–58.

10. Ibid., pp. 156–58.

11. Hedges and Father Kuppens also differ on the composition of the party. Hedges lists the members as Judge L. E. Munson, Captain George G. Wood, Malcolm Clark, Meagher, and himself; Father Kuppens mentions "a United States judge [that would have been Judge Munson], two United States Marshals — X. Biedler and Miel Homie — and two or three friends." Ibid.; Kuppens, "On the Origin of the Yellowstone National Park."

12. Kuppens, "On the Origin of the Yellowstone National Park."

13. June 24, 1867.

14. Alfred E. Mathews, *Pencil Sketches of Montana* (New York: published by the author, 1868), p. 75.

15. The biographical material on Cook, Folsom, and Peterson comes from the following sources: Lew L. Callaway, *Early Montana Masons* (Billings, Mon.: 1951), pp. 23–33; "A Reminiscence of William Peterson," *Yellowstone Interpreter* 2, no. 5 (September–October 1964): 55–61; Charles W. Cook, "Preliminary Statement to Cook-Folsom Diary," *Haynes Bulletin,* December 1922, pp. 7–8.

16. S. Stillman Berry, "Some Notes on the Early History and Early Explorers of Yellowstone National Park," A Paper Presented to the Fortnightly Club of Redlands, California, January 8, 1959. Mr. Berry based his talk on Cook's own experiences, and in his talk he explained how he acquired Cook's written narrative. I am indebted to Mr. Horace Albright and to Mr. Berry for written permission to quote from this paper.

17. Ibid.

18. Ibid.

19. Nathaniel Pitt Langford, *The Discovery of Yellowstone National Park, 1870,* 2d ed. (St. Paul: J. E. Haynes, 1932).

20. The sources for the narration of the Cook–Folsom–Peterson Expedition are as follows: material covering David Folsom in the Fred Sweetman Papers, Minnesota Historical Society, and used by written permission of the society; "Reconstructed Diary of the Cook-Folsom Expedition in 1869 to the Yellowstone Region," *Haynes Bulletin,* December 1922, January–February 1923; David E. Folsom, "The Valley of the Upper Yellowstone," *Contributions to the Historical Society*

of Montana (Helena, Mon.: Montana Historical Society, 1904) 5: 356–69; William Peterson, "Reminiscences of William A. Peterson," Salmon City (Idaho) Public Library, typescript; Charles W. Cook, David E. Folsom, and William Peterson, *The Valley of the Upper Yellowstone,* ed. Aubrey L. Haines (Norman: University of Oklahoma Press, 1965). The Haynes book is the definitive account of the trip.

Folsom, who had some engineering training, and Cook each kept a diary. Every evening they estimated the distance traversed and recorded it, as well as making mention of natural objects of interest, and contours of the land, even its geology.

Then a Mr. Clark, who knew Folsom, asked for a copy of the diary with details of the expedition. It was winter, the Ditch Company was literally frozen up, and the two friends, Folsom and Cook, worked over both their diaries and prepared a single amplified copy; this is what they sent to Mr. Clark. He eventually sold it to the *Western Monthly Magazine* of Chicago for $18.00. But when the article appeared it had been so changed and cut that the true story of the expedition was only half told. Copies were destroyed by the Chicago fire, and probably only two copies still exist, one at the Montana Historical Society and the other one in the Library of Congress.

The diary which I call the "Folsom Diary" is actually the reconstituted diary of 1922, basically the diary sent to the *Western Monthly,* plus Charles Cook's additions as of 1922. See "Preliminary Statement to the Cook-Folsom Party" in *Haynes Bulletin,* December 1922. For a slightly different version see the letter of David Folsom to Charles K. Kessler, September 19, 1916, the original of which is in the William Andrew Clark Library, University of California at Los Angeles. I have used the photostat in the Fred Sweetman papers at the Minnesota Historical Society.

21. Philip Bottler and his brother Fred were of German descent, but were born in the States. Philip served with the Ninth Iowa until wounded in 1862. In 1865 he crossed the plains to the Gallatin Valley and a year or two later established the homestead in the Upper Yellowstone Valley. In later years he raised sheep successfully, and the Bottler lands are still owned in part by his descendants. See *An Illustrated History of the Yellowstone Valley* (Spokane, Washington: no author, no date), p. 574.

22. See above, p. 84.

23. Haines, *Valley of the Upper Yellowstone,* p. 24 *n*37 makes this statement: It seems quite likely that the strong odor of hydrogen-sulphide which is wafted along the river for a considerable distance accounts for the notation, "Hot Springs Brimstone," shown on William Clark's *Map of the West,* published in 1814. The fact that "Colter's route of 1807" is shown to cross the Yellowstone River near such a feature is strong evidence that John Colter crossed at the Bannock Ford. Indeed, it would have been impossible for a man afoot to cross the river at any point for many miles in either direction (and there only at low water in the fall and winter). This is one of the very strongest points in the affirmative of the debate: Resolved: That John Colter did pass through the area that is now Yellowstone National Park. (See above, pp. 98–100.)

24. Jack Ellis Haynes, *Haynes Guide,* 62d ed. rev. (Bozeman, Mon.: Haynes Studios, 1962), p. 145, lists the height as 132 feet.

25. "Preliminary Statement," pp. 7–8.

26. Folsom's diary calls these mountains the Big Horns and the Wind Rivers, but this was due to the party's use of W. W. De Lacy's *Map of the Territory of Montana,* published in 1865. See Haines, *Valley of the Upper Yellowstone,* p. 28n37.

27. According to Haines, they emerged on the rim of the canyon between Artist and Sublime points, across the canyon almost directly from Inspiration Point. Ibid., n45.

28. Oscar Mueller, "Yellowstone Map Drawn in 1870 Shows Cook and Folsom Route of 1869," *Haynes Bulletin,* March 1924. The drop of the Upper Falls is 109 feet. They estimated it at 115 — not a bad difference considering their crude methods of measurement.

29. A case study in the constant changeability of the Yellowstone thermal phenomena is clearly demonstrated by these two springs. When Cook revisited the area after an absence of fifty-three years, he found the Mud Volcano so inactive as to warrant little attention. The Dragon's Mouth Spring, on the other hand, is far more active today than his description indicates it was in 1869.

30. Haines, *Valley of the Upper Yellowstone,* p. 42n75, traces "Burnt Hole" to Ferris's description of the Valley of the Madison where Hebgen Lake now lies, and "Death Valley" to David B. Weaver's description of the thermal areas he visited in 1867.

31. Charles W. Cook, "Remarks of C. W. Cook, Last Survivor of the Original Explorers of the Yellowstone Park Region, on the Occasion of his Second Visit to the Park in 53 Years, During the Celebration of the Park's Golden Anniversary," in Haines, *Valley of the Upper Yellowstone,* pp. 50–52.

32. See above, n20. David E. Folsom stated to Captain Anderson, the superintendent of the park, in a letter dated April 28, 1894, that he had never been back to the park, "but have been intending to take my family there for some time." As far as I know, he never did. Yellowstone Archives, Letters Received, Box no. 5, item 901.

33. "Preliminary Statement," p. 6.

CHAPTER 8

1. Carl I. Wheat, *Mapping the Trans-Mississippi West, 1540–1861,* 5 vols. in 6 (San Francisco: Institute of Historical Cartography, 1957–63), vol. 5, part 1, pp. 149–53, map reproduced facing page 152.

2. Ibid.; Oscar Mueller, "Explanatory Statement to Map," Case 2, Drawer 5, Montana Historical Society.

3. Mueller, "Explanatory Statement"; Wheat has more to say about De Lacy's later maps, but apparently he had never seen the one mentioned above.

4. *Biographical Directory of the American Congress, 1774–1961* (Washington, D.C.: G.P.O., 1961), p. 1779. Philetus W. Norris, the second superintendent of the park, says that he approached Washburn about a trip to the park in 1870. Norris Papers, Huntington Library, San Marino, California. Because this is a small collection consisting of news clippings, scrapbooks, and some typed material, I have found it impractical to be specific in my references beyond the statement, "Norris Papers."

5. Orrin H. Bonney and Lorraine Bonney, *Battle Drums and Geysers* (Chicago: Sage Books, 1970), pp. 3, 26, 96, Appendix C.

6. Wyllis A. Hedges, "Cornelius Hedges," in *Contributions to the Historical Society of Montana,* 10 vols. (Helena, Mon.: Montana Historical Society, 1876–1940), vol. 8 (1910), pp. 181–96.

7. Norris Papers.

8. Hedges, "Cornelius Hedges," p. 189.

9. Norris Papers. See also Philip H. Sheridan, *Personal Memoirs of Philip H. Sheridan,* 2 vols. (New York: C. L. Webster and Co., 1888) 2: 349–50. Sheridan says: "While journeying between Corinne and Helena I had gained some vague knowledge of these geysers from an old mountaineer named Atkinson, but his information was very indefinite, mostly second hand; and there was such general uncertainty as to the character of this wonderland that I authorized an escort of soldiers to go that season from Fort Ellis with a small party to make such superficial explorations as to justify my sending an engineer officer with a well-equipped expedition there next summer to scientifically examine and report upon the strange country."

10. This leaves us with the question of Sheridan's role, since none of the participants makes any mention of him. See Nathaniel P. Langford, *Discovery of Yellowstone Park,* 2d ed. (St. Paul: 1905), pp. 24–32; idem, "The Wonders of the Yellowstone," *Scribner's Monthly* 2, no. 1 (May 1871): 1–17.

11. Unless otherwise cited, the narration of the Washburn–Langford–Doane Expedition is a synthesis drawn from the following sources: Langford, *Discovery of Yellowstone Park;* Cornelius Hedges, "Journal of Cornelius Hedges," *Contributions to the Historical Society of Montana* (1904) 5:370–94; U.S., Congress, Senate, Exec. Doc. 51, Lieutenant Gustavus C. Doane, *Report of Lieutenant Gustavus C. Doane upon the so-called Yellowstone Expedition of 1870,* 41st Cong., 3d Sess., 1871; Samuel T. Hauser, "Excerpts from the Diary of Samuel T. Hauser (August 17 to September 4, 1870), ed. Aubrey L. Haines, transcribed from a microfilm copy furnished by the Coe Collection at the Yale University Library and used with their written permission; Warren C. Gillette, "Diary of Warren Caleb Gillette in 1870 During the Expedition in Yellowstone Park Region," in custody of the Montana Historical Society; the newspaper articles from the notes of General Washburn, appearing in the *Helena Daily Herald,* September 27, 28, and 29, 1870; and Walter Trumbull, "The Washburn Yellowstone Expedition," *Overland Monthly* 6, nos. 5 and 6 (May–June 1871).

12. A Sibley tent is conical, mounted on a tripod, with a ventilating device at the top. Its developer was Henry Hastings Sibley (1811–1891), a pioneer, first governor of Minnesota, and commander of the troops that quelled the Sioux uprising of 1862.

13. Hauser in fact states in his diary: "I named them 'Tower Falls.'" Langford, however, says the men agreed not to name anything in honor of friends or relatives, that Hauser protested the name suggested by Trumbull — "Minarret Falls" — on the grounds that he had a girl friend in St. Louis named Minnie Rhett. So they chose Hauser's suggestion, "Tower Falls," only to discover much later that Hauser had a sweetheart in St. Louis named Miss Tower. Langford, *Discovery of Yellowstone Park,* p. 81.

14. They were all wrong. According to the *Haynes Guide,* 62d ed. rev. (Bozeman: Haynes Studios, 1962), p. 145, the falls are 132 feet high.

15. Mueller, "Explanatory Statement."

16. According to the *Haynes Guide,* p. 139, the actual height is 10,243 feet. Doane wrote a description (pp. 9–10 of his *Report*) of the view from the summit, certainly implying that he climbed the mountain, but neither Hedges, Gillette, Hauser nor Langford gave him credit for making the climb. With his infected thumb, he can hardly be blamed for not going to the trouble. Nor does Doane ever actually say that he made the ascent.

17. A California lion is another name for the American mountain lion, which is also called a puma, a cougar, and a painter.

18. This quotation is from an article in the *Helena Daily Herald,* October 3, 1870. The article then elaborated that a posse had traced some horse thieves up a branch of the Snake River and actually came upon the Washburn party's camp of September 10, but the horse thieves eluded them. It was speculated that Everts had struck their trail, followed it, and been killed by them.

Indeed, many of the West's criminal elements knew much about the Yellowstone. Cavis Willson of the firm of Willson and Rich at Bozeman quoted some of the "Bear Gulch stampeders," miners who went into Yellowstone in 1867, as having met between the lake and the falls "four men on four splendid American horses, driving thirty-six large mules, in fine condition, all branded 'U.S.' Said individuals wore linen dusters and heavy gold rings on their fingers — traveled southward — understood the country — acted suspiciously, and that's all that's known." *Montana Post,* August 31, 1867, photostat in Yellowstone archives. At least a part of this trace was subsequently known as the Skull and Crossbones Trail.

19. Langford's two articles appeared on September 26 and 29; Washburn's on September 17 and 28, featured on page 1.

20. Wheat, *Mapping the Trans-Mississippi West,* vol. 5, part 2, pp. 293–95.

21. The *New York Times* paraphrased a *Helena Daily Herald* article on October 15, for example.

22. *Helena Daily Herald,* September 26, 1870; October 3, 1870.

23. Ibid., October 6, 1870.

24. Ibid., October 8, 1870. The mountain was not so named. The Mount Everts that runs north and south opposite Mammoth Hot Springs has no direct link with Everts — it is at least six miles from where he was found.

25. Truman C. Everts, "Thirty-Seven Days of Peril," *Scribner's Magazine* 7, no. 1 (November 1871): 1–17; *Contributions to the Historical Society of Montana* (1904) 5: 395–427.

26. Theodore Gerrish, *Life in the World's Wonderland* (n.p.: 1886), pp. 236–40.

27. Everts, "Thirty-Seven Days of Peril."

28. Gerrish, *Life in the World's Wonderland,* pp. 236–40.

29. *Helena Daily Herald,* October 21, 1870.

30. Ibid., October 28, 1870.

31. Ibid.; letter quoted from Everts to Judge Lawrence.

32. *Helena Daily Herald,* October 26, 1870.

33. E. S. Topping, *The Chronicles of the Yellowstone* (St. Paul: Pioneer Press, 1888), pp. 84–85.

34. *Helena Daily Herald,* November 14, 1870.

35. Gerrish, *Life in the World's Wonderland,* p. 240.

36. R. C. Wallace, *A Few Memories of a Long Life* (n.p.: privately printed, 1900), p. 4. Copy in Yellowstone library.

37. Correspondence from Truman C. Everts, Jr., to author, April 11, 1963. We could be doing a grave unkindness to Everts. He wanted the superintendency of the park, at least until he discovered that it carried no pay. Philetus Norris says that Everts was in the park again in 1872, at which time he saw Mammoth Hot Springs and the Petrified Forest (Specimen Ridge), and Norris even gives him the credit for naming Mary's Lake. He hoped to publish a long letter from Everts telling of the 1872 trip, but the letter does not appear in the Norris Papers.

38. *Helena Daily Herald,* November 14, 1870.

39. Ellis Paxson Oberholtzer, *Jay Cooke: Financier of the Civil War,* 2 vols. (Philadelphia: G. W. Jacobs and Co., 1907) 2: 236.

40. *Helena Daily Herald,* November 11, 19, 16, 1870; letter from Mr. Robert R. Budd, who is working on the life of Langford, and has done extensive research, November 22, 1968.

41. Louis C. Cramton, *Early History of Yellowstone National Park and Its Relation to National Park Policy,* U.S. Department of the Interior, National Park Service (Washington D.C.: G.P.O., 1932), pp. 18–19. This is a seminal study and is invaluable for this period of Yellowstone's history. See also *New York Daily Tribune,* January 23, 1871; *New York Times,* January 22, 1871, p. 8.

42. Richard A. Bartlett, *Great Surveys of the American West* (Norman: University of Oklahoma Press, 1962), pp. 3–40. See also W. Turrentine Jackson, "Governmental Exploration of the Upper Yellowstone," *Pacific Historical Review* 11, no. 2 (June 1942): 187–99.

43. 16 *U.S. Statutes at Large,* 503.

44. United States Geological and Geographical Survey of the Territories (the Hayden Survey), *Fifth Annual Report* (Washington, D.C.: G. P.O., 1872).

45. Moran was financed with a loan on his painting, "Children of the Mountain," plus a $500 gift from Jay Cooke. See Thurman Wilkins, *Thomas Moran: Artist of the Mountains* (Norman: University of Oklahoma Press, 1966), p. 59; William H. Jackson, "With Moran in the Yellowstone," in *Thomas Moran: Explorer in Search of Beauty,* ed. Fritiof Fryxell, (East Hampton, N.Y.: East Hampton Free Library, 1958), p. 52.

46. Wilkins, *Thomas Moran,* p. 8; U.S. Congress, Senate, Exec. Doc. 66, J. W. Barlow, *Reconnaissance of the Yellowstone River,* 42d Cong., 2d Sess.

47. Albert C. Peale, M.D., "Diary of Albert C. Peale, M.D.," in custody of Yellowstone Park Library.

48. Barlow, *Reconnaissance of the Yellowstone,* pp. 3–4.

49. Peale, "Diary."

50. Invalids already knew of the springs, as did many miners. See above, pages 139–40; see also William Henry Jackson, *Time Exposure* (New York: G.P. Putnam's Sons, 1940), p. 198.

51. Barlow, *Reconnaissance of the Yellowstone,* p. 10.

52. Ibid.

53. Hayden, *Fifth Annual Report,* p. 82.

54. William Henry Jackson, *Time Exposure,* p. 199.

55. Hayden, *Fifth Annual Report,* pp. 86–97, 131.

56. Barlow, *Reconnaissance of the Yellowstone,* p. 30.

57. W. Turrentine Jackson, "Governmental Exploration," p. 195.

58. Hayden, *Fifth Annual Report,* pp. 137–39; Dr. Albert C. Peale, M.D.,

"Preliminary Report," ibid., pp. 190–96; Barlow, *Reconnaissance of the Yellowstone*, p. 38.

59. Barlow, *Reconnaissance of the Yellowstone*, pp. 37–42.

60. Wheat, *Mapping the Trans-Mississippi West*, vol. 5, part 2, pp. 295–97, 344–46.

61. An advertisement of his in the *Bozeman Avant-Courier* ran as follows: "Magnificently Beautiful All the principal scenes in the Wonderful Yellowstone Country, accurately photographed and handsomely framed, for sale at Crissman's Photograph Gallery Main Street Bozeman."

CHAPTER 9

1. See Hans Huth, "Yosemite: the Story of an Idea," *Sierra Club Bulletin* 33, no. 3 (March 1948): 47–48; Albert Matthews, "The Word Park in the United States," Publications of the Colonial Society of Massachusetts, *Transactions* 8 (April 1904): 373–99; Harold D. Hampton, *How The U.S. Cavalry Saved Our National Parks* (Bloomington: Indiana University Press, 1971), pp. 1–17: Roderick Nash, *Wilderness and the American Mind* (New Haven: Yale University Press, 1967).

2. George Catlin, *Letters and Notes on the Manners, Customs, and Condition of the North American Indians,* 2 vols. (London: Tilt, 1842) 1: 294–95.

In the Catlin papers in the custody of the Library of the National Collection of Fine Arts and the National Portrait Gallery, Washington, D.C., there is an interesting letter from Catlin addressed to "the Editor of the Herald" in which he gives his statement suggesting a park, and then adds, "From the singular above quotation it will be seen that the writer contemplated the preservation of native scenery, to be confined and protected within impassable boundaries, from which the ages to come might see and appreciate what once was the great Far West, and what the destructive and remodeling hands of Civilization have done in turning the barren wilds into furrows and harvests of the plough.

"I hope that as much is still contemplated in the Bill that is now before the Congress, and that the noble scheme be so accomplished, as not to allow posterity to say that we have destroyed the living in those wonderful grounds and preserved but the dead." Although his meaning is a little vague, it is nevertheless quite clear that Catlin was happy at the turn of events and was aware that he had fostered the idea a generation before. There is no date on the letter, nor does he stipulate which newspaper named the *Herald* he was writing to.

3. Huth, "Yosemite," p. 5.

4. 4 *U.S. Statutes at Large*, p. 505.

5. Stewart L. Udall, *The Quiet Crisis* (New York: Holt, Rinehart, and Winston, 1963), p. 74.

6. Huth, "Yosemite," p. 67; Carl Parcher Russell, *One Hundred Years of Yosemite* (Berkeley: University of California Press, 1947), p. 182; quotation from Huth.

7. Matthews, "The Word Park," pp. 383–89; 13 *U.S. Statutes at Large,* p. 325.

8. Samuel Bowles, *Our New West: Records of Travel Between the Missis-*

sippi River and the Pacific Ocean (Hartford, Conn.: Hartford Publishing Co., 1869), pp. 384–85.

9. Albert D. Richardson, *Beyond the Mississippi* (Hartford, Conn.: American Publishing Co., 1867), p. 435.

10. Frederick Law Olmsted, introduction by Laura Wood Roper, "The Yosemite Valley and the Big Trees: A Preliminary Report (1865) by Frederick Law Olmsted," *Landscape Architecture* 43, no. 1 (October 1952): 12–15.

11. Nathaniel P. Langford, *The Discovery of Yellowstone Park* (St. Paul: 1905), p. 41.

12. Louis C. Cramton, *Early History of Yellowstone National Park and Its Relation to National Park Policies,* U.S. Department of the Interior, National Park Service (Washington, D.C.: G.P.O., 1932), pp. 28–31; U.S., Congress, *Congressional Globe,* 42d Cong., 2d Sess. (December 18, 1871): 199.

13. Cramton, *Early History of Yellowstone National Park,* pp. 30–33; U.S. Congress, *Congressional Record,* 47th cong., 2d Sess. (August 2, 1886): 7843; ibid.: 7915; 52d Cong., 1st Sess. (May 10, 1892): 4121.

14. Langford, *Discovery of Yellowstone Park,* p. 40.

15. Mark Twain and Charles Dudley Warner, *The Gilded Age: A Tale of Today* (New York: Trident Press, 1964), p. 142.

16. U.S., Congress, *Congressional Globe,* 42d Cong., 2d Sess. (May 2, 1882): 2985.

17. Langford, *Discovery of Yellowstone Park,* p. 53.

18. Cramton, *Early History of Yellowstone National Park,* p. 19. I have examined the *New York Herald* and the *New York Times* for January 21–24, 1871, and no such statements are reported.

19. Olin D. Wheeler, *Sketches of Wonderland* (St. Paul: Northern Pacific Railroad, 1895), p. 31.

20. *Scribner's Monthly* 3, no. 4 (February 1872):396; *American Journal of Science and Arts* 103, no. 15 (March 1872):176.

21. Hayden to Secretary Schurz, February 21, 1879, in U.S., Congress, House, Exec. Doc. 75, "Letter from the Secretary of the Interior in regard to the Better Protection of the National Park from Injury," 45th Cong., 2d Sess. In terms of the next fifteen years of park history, one paragraph in Hayden's statement is particularly worth noting: "While the bill was pending in Congress the principal objection urged against the park was that annual appropriations would be required for its care and improvement. I was myself compelled to give a distinct pledge that I would not apply for an appropriation for several years at least. Had not Congress been assured that no demands would be made upon them for annual appropriations, it is very doubtful whether the bill would ever have become law."

See also Thurman Wilkins, *Thomas Moran: Artist of the Mountains* (Norman: University of Oklahoma Press, 1966), p. 70.

22. United States Geological and Geographical Survey of the Territories (the Hayden Survey), *Twelfth Annual Report,* 2 vols. (Washington, D.C.: G.P.O., 1883) 2: 17.

23. U.S., Congress, *Congressional Globe,* 42d Cong., 2d Sess. (January 22, 1872): 484.

24. Langford, *Discovery of Yellowstone Park,* p. 38. In his third edition of *The Yellowstone National Park* (St. Paul: Haynes, 1924), Hiram Martin Chittenden says (p. 73): "In the manuscript of his article in the Western Monthly was a reference to the park idea; but the publishers cut out a large part of his paper,

giving only the descriptions of the natural wonders, and his reference was cut out with the rest." (This is also quoted in Cramton, *Early History of Yellowstone National Park,* p. 11.)

25. Philip H. Sheridan, *Personal Memoirs of Philip H. Sheridan,* 2 vols. (New York: C. L. Webster and Co., 1888; New York: D. Appleton & Co., 1902) 2:348–50.

26. Ibid., 1902 edition, p. 122.

27. See above, p. 145.

28. W. Turrentine Jackson, "The Creation of Yellowstone National Park," *Mississippi Valley Historical Review* 19, no. 2 (September 1942): 187–206; letter from Clagett to Langford in Langford, *Discovery of Yellowstone Park,* pp. 38–40.

29. Langford, *Discovery of Yellowstone Park,* 2d ed. (1924), pp. 179–80.

30. Cornelius Hedges, "Journal of Cornelius Hedges," *Contributions to the Historical Society of Montana* (1904) 5: 391, 372n.

31. For the final debate and vote in the House, see U.S., Congress, House, *Congressional Globe,* 42d Cong., 2d Sess. (February 17, 1872): 1243–44. See also Cramton, *Early History of Yellowstone National Park,* pp. 25–27.

32. National Archives, Record Group 57, Hayden Survey, General Letters Received, vol. 3, 1871.

33. Ibid.

34. Ellis Paxson Oberholtzer, *Jay Cooke, Financier of the Civil War,* 2 vols. (Philadelphia: G. W. Jacobs Co., 1907) 2: 236.

35. Jay Cooke Letter Press Books, Volume for Year 1871, pp. 139 ff. Mr. Robert R. Budd, an authority on Cooke, has furnished me a copy, but I have also obtained permission for use from the Pennsylvania Historical Society.

36. Telegrams in Cooke collection, Pennsylvania Historical Society, furnished me by Mr. Budd but used with permission of the society.

37. Oliver Wendell Holmes, ed., "James A. Garfield's Trip to Montana in 1872," *Sources of Northwest History,* no. 21 (Missoula, Mon.: State University of Montana, 1934–35).

38. Even in Montana the idea "was in the air." The Territorial Legislative Council passed a "Joint Memorial," January 12, 1872, requesting that much of the park be separated from Wyoming Territory and ceded to Montana, and that it "be dedicated and devoted to public use, resort, and recreation for all time to come as a great national park, under such care and restrictions as to your honorable bodies may seem best calculated to secure the ends proposed." *Laws of Montana, 1871–72,* 7th Sess., pp. 648–49.

39. 17 *U.S. Statutes at Large,* p. 350.

A Brief Essay on Sources

ARCHIVES AND MANUSCRIPT COLLECTIONS

My principal sources of primary materials were the archives of the Yellowstone National Park, housed in the museum building at Yellowstone National Park, Wyoming (which is also the site of Mammoth Hot Springs), and the Yellowstone Library, which is located in the same structure but in a different room. The two together form the single greatest concentration of information on Yellowstone. Materials include archival records, especially since 1882, manuscripts, newspaper and magazine clippings, photographs, government documents, and a substantial collection of secondary materials.

For *Nature's Yellowstone* the manuscripts proved most valuable, for they included not only original documents but copies of pertinent journals, diaries, newspaper articles, and the like, the originals of which are in the custody of other institutions or individuals. Some were simply presented to the library or archives by descendants of the original owners; more than a few were the direct results of the collecting efforts of the custodians. Of particular importance is the period in which Aubrey L. Haines held the position (since eliminated) of Yellowstone Park historian. His energy in collecting Yellowstoniana will forever be appreciated by researchers in park history. Without the collection housed at the museum a researcher would have to contact so many manuscript depositories and individuals that it would be an almost impossible task.

Some of these manuscripts have been edited and printed. A. Bart Henderson's diaries, for example, were edited by Mr. Haines and printed in *The Yellowstone Interpreter*, a house organ dis-

238

tributed for informational purposes to park personnel. Still another example is Charles W. Cook, David E. Folsom, and William Peterson, *The Valley of the Upper Yellowstone,* ed. Aubrey L. Haines (Norman: University of Oklahoma Press, 1964).

Among other manuscripts in the Yellowstone collection pertinent to this study are James Gourley, "Narration of a Mining Trip Into the Yellowstone Country, 1870"; Albert C. Peale, M.D., "Diary of Albert C. Peale, M.D."; Samuel T. Hauser, "Excerpts from the Diary of Samuel T. Hauser," ed. Aubrey L. Haines from a microfilm copy furnished by the Coe Collection at Yale University; and Warren C. Gillette, "Diary of Warren Caleb Gillette in 1870 During the Expedition in Yellowstone Park Region," the original of which is in the custody of the Montana Historical Society. The Yellowstone collection also includes many newspaper transcripts such as John C. Davis, "An Interview With a Man Who Visited That Region of Wonders as Far Back as 1863 — An Account of the Expedition," *Louisville Courier-Journal,* April 13, 1884.

I also made use of the facilities of the Montana Historical Society, especially for early Montana newspapers; the Minnesota Historical Society; the Western History Collection at the University of Wyoming; the Henry E. Huntington Library and Art Gallery, especially for the Philetus Norris papers; the Newberry Library; and the library of the U.S. Geological Survey, Washington, D.C. In the National Archives I used the records of the Hayden Survey in Record Group 57, Records of the U.S. Geological Survey. Of particular importance among the many institutions with which I corresponded was the Beinecke Library at Yale, the William Andrew Clark Library in Los Angeles, and the Pennsylvania Historical Society. Among many individuals with whom I corresponded, I would single out Mr. Horace Albright, Mr. S. Stillman Berry, Mr. Truman C. Everts, Jr., and Mr. Robert Budd as among the most important.

TOPOGRAPHICAL INFORMATION

The United States Geological Survey is the best source for maps of the Yellowstone area. Their basic geologic atlas of the United States includes a *Yellowstone National Park Folio, Wyoming,* Folio No. 30 (Washington, D.C.: G.P.O., 1896), an *Absaroka Folio, Crandall and Ishawooa Quadrangles, Wyoming,* Folio No. 52 (Washington, D.C.: G.P.O., 1899), and a *Livingston, Montana, Quadrangle,*

Folio No. 1 (Washington, D.C.: G.P.O., 1893). Many of these maps are accompanied by descriptive essays, many of which (such as those on Yellowstone by Arnold Hague) are brilliantly written. More current are the U.S. Geological Survey "15 Minute Series," about thirty maps of which embrace small portions of the Yellowstone region (and as a composite whole make a large topographical map of the area). These are available from the U.S. Geological Survey, Denver, Colorado, and Washington, D.C. However, the layman will probably be happy with the maps sold by the Park Service in Yellowstone.

The best source for studying older maps of the region is Carl I. Wheat, *Mapping the Trans-Mississippi West, 1540-1861*, 5 vols. in 6 (San Francisco: Institute of Historical Cartography, 1957–63). The Montana Historical Society has an excellent collection of regional maps, many including the Yellowstone.

The Mountain Bastions and the Plateau Inside

Still the best source on the geology of Yellowstone is the monumental work of Arnold Hague of the U.S. Geological Survey. His own great work, to which he devoted most of his professional life, lists as authors not only his name but those of several of his colleagues. It is entitled *Geology of the Yellowstone National Park*, U.S.G.S. Monograph no. 32, Part 2 (Hague never completed Part 1) (Washington, D.C.; G.P.O., 1899).

Produced prior to this was the extensive work of the United States Geological and Geographical Survey of the Territories (the Hayden Survey), which published twelve Annual Reports between 1868 and 1883. Of these, the Fifth (Washington, D.C.: 1872), the Sixth (Washington, D.C.: 1873), and the Twelfth (Washington, D.C.: 1883) are devoted to the Yellowstone country. A recounting of Hayden's work is in Richard A. Bartlett, *Great Surveys of the American West* (Norman: University of Oklahoma Press, 1962).

A number of U.S. Geological Survey professional papers and bulletins also bear on Yellowstone and its mountain bastions. The most recent one, based upon as yet unpublished but extensive recent research in Yellowstone, is an attractively written booklet by Dr. William R. Keefer, "The Geologic Story of Yellowstone National Park," U.S.G.S. Bulletin no. 1347 (Washington, D.C.: G.P.O., 1972).

The geology of the Beartooth and the Absarokas is complex and not altogether understood, even by geologists. My descriptions are based upon articles in the *Bulletin of the Geological Society of America, The Journal of Geology,* the *Billings Geological Society Guidebook* (1958), and upon the monograph by David Love, *Geology Along the Southern Margin of the Absaroka Range, Wyoming,* Geological Society of America, Special Papers No. 20 (1939).

Mud slides, and especially the Gros Ventre slide, are discussed in C. F. Stewart Sharpe, *Landslides and Related Phenomena* (New York: Cooper Square Publishers, 1938). The Hebgen Lake earthquake is professionally discussed in *The Hebgen Lake, Montana Earthquake of August 17, 1959,* U.S. Geological Survey Professional Paper No. 435 (Washington, D.C.: G.P.O., 1964). This work consists of twenty short essays by various authorities on the many aspects of that disaster. For anyone interested in the way the Army Engineers coped with the problems posed by the quake, there is a report edited and published by the U.S. Army Engineer District, Omaha, *Madison River, Montana Report on Flood Emergency Madison River Slide,* vol. 1, "Main Report," and vol. 2, "Appendixes," (Omaha: 1960).

Of the many intriguing geologic phenomena in the park there exist many studies. Clyde Max Bauer, *Yellowstone: Its Underworld* (Albuquerque; University of New Mexico Press, 1948, 1962) offers a brief and readable survey. The complexities of the Grand Canyon are set forth in Arthur David Howard, *History of the Grand Canyon of the Yellowstone,* Geological Society of America, Special Papers No. 6 (1957). George D. Marler, *The Story of Old Faithful* (Yellowstone Park, Wyoming: 1953, 1961) is good on that subject. See also Eugene T. Allen and Arthur L. Day, *Hot Springs of the Yellowstone National Park,* Carnegie Institution of Washington, publication no. 46 (Washington, D.C.: 1935).

An inexpensive source of Yellowstone information is, of course, the *Haynes Guide,* published through the years in numerous editions by F. Jay Haynes and then by his son Jack Ellis Haynes at St. Paul, Minnesota or Bozeman, Montana.

THE FLORA AND FAUNA

In general, most zoologists, botanists, ornithologists, icthyologists, and other specialists in the natural sciences do not work for the lay reader. When we consider the importance and the interest in the wildlife and the remaining wild areas of the nation, the paucity of good material on flora and fauna is doubly surprising. A good beginning can be made with some of the volumes published by the Yellowstone Library and Museum Association at Yellowstone Park, Wyoming: Harold J. Brodrick, *Wild Animals of Yellowstone National Park* (1954, 1962), and W. B. McDougall and Herma A. Baggley, *The Plants of Yellowstone National Park* (1956), are typical. A recent book on the buffalo which includes information on the herds in Yellowstone Park is Tom McHugh, *The Time of the Buffalo* (New York: Alfred A. Knopf, 1972).

I also used Vernon Bailey, *Animal Life of Yellowstone Park* (Springfield, Ill.: Charles C. Thomas, Publisher, 1930); Lorus J. and Margery J. Milne, *The Mating Instinct* (Boston: Little, Brown and Co., 1854); Olaus J. Murie, *A Field Guide to Animal Tracks* (Boston: Houghton Mifflin Co., 1954); Mari Sandoz, *The Beaver Men: Spearheads of Empire* (New York: Hastings House, 1964); Milton Philo Skinner, *Bears in Yellowstone* (Chicago: A. C. McClurg and Co., 1925); Ernest Thompson Seton, *The Biography of a Grizzly* (New York: Grossett & Dunlap, 1900); Farida A. Wiley, ed., *Ernest Thompson Seton's America* (New York: Devin-Adair, 1954); J. Frank Dobie, *The Voice of the Coyote* (Boston: Little, Brown and Co., 1948); Olaus J. Murie, *Ecology of the Coyote in the Yellowstone,* Fauna Series No. 4 (Washington, D.C.: National Park Service, 1940); Victor H. Cahalane, *Mammals of North America* (New York: Macmillan Co., 1947); Arthur S. Einarson, *The Pronghorn Antelope and its Management* (Washington, D.C.: Wildlife Management Institute, 1948); James R. Simon, *Yellowstone Fishes,* Yellowstone Interpretive Series No. 3 (Yellowstone Park, Wyo.: Yellowstone Library and Museum Association, 1962); and Frederick B. Turner, *Reptiles and Amphibians of Yellowstone National Park,* Yellowstone Interpretive Series No. 5 (Yellowstone Park, Wyo.: Yellowstone Library and Museum Association, 1955).

THE WANDERERS

A good deal is known about ancient man in North America, but, as in the case of the geology of Yellowstone, new discoveries and improved scientific methods of investigation place the accuracy of much of the earlier material in jeopardy. Waldo R. Wedel, *Prehistoric Man on the Great Plains* (Norman: University of Oklahoma Press, 1961); Kenneth MacGowan and Joseph A. Hester, Jr., *Early Man in the New World* (New York: Doubleday & Co., 1962), and

H. M. Wormington, *Ancient Man in North America* (Denver; Colorado Museum of Natural History, 1957) are all interesting; they reveal a variety of theories about ancient man. For Indians in the Yellowstone area, see Stuart W. Conner, "Prehistoric Man in the Yellowstone Valley," *Montana, The Magazine of Western History* 14, no. 2 (April 1964); and Ake Hultkrantz, "The Indians in Yellowstone Park," *Annals of Wyoming* 29, no. 2 (October 1957).

For the American Indians as we have known them during our nation's history, it can be said that nearly every tribe has had its recent historians. A very large number of these studies have been published by the University of Oklahoma Press; pertinent examples are Virginia Cole Trenholm and Maurine Carley, *The Shoshones: Sentinels of the Rockies* (1964) and John C. Ewers, *The Blackfeet: Raiders of the Northwestern Plains* (1958). George Catlin, *North American Indians*, 2 vols., many editions since 1841, presents an excellent picture of the Plains Indians before they were weakened by the whites. Many of the annual reports of the Bureau of American Ethnology deal with Plains Indians and the Indians of the northwest. For its time, W. A. Allen, *The Sheep Eaters* (New York: Shakespeare Press, 1913) is not bad.

THE FIRST WHITE MEN

There is much good secondary material on the coming of the first white men into the Yellowstone country. Abraham P. Nasatir, ed., *Before Lewis and Clark: Documents Illustrating the History of the Missouri, 1785-1800*, 2 vols. (St. Louis: St. Louis Historical Documents Foundation, 1952) conveys a good overview of the white man's push into the northwest. For good and accurate reading, the best books on Lewis and Clark are John Bakeless, *Lewis and Clark, Partners in Discovery* (New York: Wm. Morrow & Co., Apollo Edition, 1947), Richard Dillon, *Meriwether Lewis: A Biography* (New York: Coward-McCann, 1965), Paul Russell Cutright, *Lewis and Clark, Pioneering Naturalists* (Urbana: University of Illinois Press, 1969), and Charles G. Clarke, *The Men of the Lewis and Clark Expedition* (Glendale, Calif.: Arthur H. Clark Co., 1970).

Though the two comprehensive histories of the fur trade are now somewhat outdated, they are still worth mentioning: Hiram Martin Chittenden, *The American Fur Trade of the Far West*, 2 vols., rev. ed. (New York: Harper, 1935) and Paul Chrisler Phillips, *The Fur*

Trade, 2 vols. (Norman: University of Oklahoma Press, 1961). More recent studies include Dale L. Morgan, *Jedediah Smith and the Opening of the West* (Indianapolis: Bobbs-Merrill Co., 1953) and Dale Morgan, ed., *The West of William H. Ashley* (Denver: Old West Publishing Co., 1964). The intriguing John Colter is the subject of two books: Stallo Vinton, *John Colter, Discoverer of Yellowstone Park* (New York: Edward Eberstadt, 1926), and Burton Harris, *John Colter, His Years in the Rockies* (New York: Charles Scribner's Sons, 1952). Unless more material is found (which is most unlikely), these two books tell virtually all that is known of John Colter. Merrill D. Beale, *The Story of Man in Yellowstone* (Caldwell, Idaho: 1949; also Yellowstone Park, Wyoming: 1956 and 1960), has material on Colter and other trappers in the region. So does Hiram Martin Chittenden, *The Yellowstone National Park,* ed. Richard A. Bartlett (Norman: University of Oklahoma Press, 1964). Of special importance is Merrill Mattes, "Behind the Legend of Colter's Hell: the Early Exploration of Yellowstone National Park," *Mississippi Valley Historical Review* 36 (September 1949).

There are many biographies of individual fur trappers or traders. One of the best is Osborne Russell, *Journal of a Trapper,* ed. Aubrey L. Haines (Portland: Oregon Historical Society, 1955; reprinted Lincoln: University of Nebraska Press, 1965). J. Cecil Alter, *James Bridger* (Salt Lake City: Shepard Book Co., 1925), remains the best book about Old Gabe. William H. Goetzmann, *Exploration and Empire* (New York: Alfred A. Knopf, 1966) is encyclopedic about far western exploration, including the role of the fur traders. Finally, LeRoy Hafen, ed., *The Mountain Men and the Fur Trade of the Far West,* 10 volumes (Glendale, Calif.: Arthur H. Clark Co., 1965–72) contains both an admirable essay on the fur trade and excellent biographies of hundreds of known traders.

THE PROSPECTORS

To understand the role of the miners in Yellowstone's history, one must know something of the history of western mining as well as of mining in Montana. For western mining the best source is Rodman Wilson Paul, *Mining Frontiers of the Far West, 1848–1880* (New York: Holt, Rinehart & Winston, 1963); see also U.S., Congress, House, *The Report of Rossiter W. Raymond on the Mineral*

Resources of the States and Territories West of the Rocky Mountains, 40th Cong., 3d Sess., Exec. Doc. 54, 1869. For Montana see Merrill Burlingame, *The Montana Frontier* (Helena: 1942). Walter W. De Lacy, "A Trip to the South Snake River in 1863," *Contributions to the Historical Society of Montana,* vol. 1 (Helena, 1876; reprinted Boston, J. C. Canner & Co., 1966) is excellent on that man's adventures. Aubrey L. Haines, ed., "The Yellowstone Diaries of A. Bart Henderson," *The Yellowstone Interpreter* 2, nos. 1, 2, and 3 (January–June 1964) is a good example of the miner's approach to the region. In the Yellowstone archives are occasional gems, such as James Gourley, "Narration of a Mining Trip Into the Yellowstone Country, 1870." A good summary of mining activity at Cooke City is T. S. Lowering, "The New World or Cooke City Mining District, Park County, Montana," U.S. Geological Survey Bulletin 811-A (Washington, D.C.: G.P.O., 1930).

Two Yankee Quakers and a Dane

The best and most readily available source for the story of the Cook–Folsom–Peterson expedition is Charles W. Cook, David E. Folsom, and William Peterson, *The Valley of the Upper Yellowstone,* ed. Aubrey L. Haines (Norman: University of Oklahoma Press, 1965). Readily available material on the visit of certain Montanans with Father Kuppens is in Thomas Francis Meagher, "A Journey to Benton," ed. Robert Athearn, *Montana, the Magazine of Western History* 1, no. 4 (October 1951).

The Washburn Expedition

Here there is no shortage of material. Orrin and Lorraine Bonney, *Battle Drums and Geysers* (Chicago: Sage Books, 1970) tells all that need be said about Lieutenant Doane. Nathaniel Pitt Langford, *The Discovery of Yellowstone Park,* Foreword by Aubrey L. Haines (Lincoln: University of Nebraska Press, 1972) is a recent reprint of a good narration of the expedition, as is Cornelius Hedges, whose "Journal of Cornelius Hedges," *Contributions to the Historical Society of Montana,* vol. 5 (Helena: 1904; reprinted Boston: J. S. Canner & Co., 1966) gives his version of the trip.

The Creation of the Park

The work of W. Turrentine Jackson some thirty years ago is a good place to start. His "The Creation of Yellowstone National Park," *Mississippi Valley Historical Review* 29, no. 2 (September 1942) gives the basic story, but without essential information which has since come to light. See also his "Government Exploration of the Upper Yellowstone," *Pacific Historical Review* 11, no. 2 (June 1942). Louis C. Cramton, *Early History of Yellowstone National Park and Its Relation to National Park Policies* (Washington, D.C.: G.P.O., 1932) is an excellent survey. For the adventures of the Hayden expedition, see Thurman Wilkins, *Thomas Moran: Artist of the Mountains* (Norman: University of Oklahoma Press, 1966), and William Henry Jackson, *Time Exposure* (New York: G. P. Putnam's Sons, 1940). A fine work containing information on the creation of the park and continuing its history into the twentieth century is H. Duane Hampton, *How the U.S. Cavalry Saved Our National Parks* (Bloomington: Indiana University Press, 1971).

Index

Absaroka Range, 8–10
acid tracts, 41
Adams, John Quincy, 195
Adventures of Captain Bonneville, The (Irving), 99
alkaline areas, 42
Allen, E. T., 37, 40, 47
Allen, William, 129
alpine meadows, 53
Altowon: or Incidents of Life and Adventure in the Rocky Mountains (Stewart), 113
Álvarez, Manuel, 103
American Fur Company, 103
American Journal of Science and Arts, 201
amphibians, 71
Anderson, Lou, 131
animal life, 4, 55–72
antelope, 65–67
aquatic plant community, 53
Arapaho Indians, 135–36
Ashley-Henry expedition, 101
aspen forest, 53
Astor, John Jacob, 101

badgers, 58
Bannock Indians, 80, 86, 87–92, 112
Barlow, John W., 140, 189–93
Baronett, Jack, 28, 140, 183, 184–86, 187, 191, 204
Barth, Thomas F. W., 48
Bartram, William, 194
bats, 57–58
Beale, Merrill D., 100
bears, 61–64
Beartooth Mountains, 22; geology of, 5–8
beaver, 60
Biddle, Nicholas, 95
Biography of a Grizzly, The (Seton), 29
birds, 4, 71–72
bison, 70
Blackfoot Indians, 80, 81, 84, 86–87, 92, 98, 102, 104, 112, 119, 130, 144, 146, 203
Blackmore, William, 20
Blaine, James G., 188, 189
Bloss, Donald, 48

Bonneville, B. L. E. de, 112
Bottler, Frederick, 168
Bottler brothers, 153
Boulder Ditch Company, 148
Bowles, Samuel, 196
Bridger, Jim, 103, 106, 112, 113–15, 144
Broad Gauge Company, 127
Bryant, William Cullen, 194
Budd, Robert, 207
buffalo. *See* bison
Bull, John, 130
Bunsen, Robert Wilhelm Eberhard von, 44–45, 46
Byrd, William, 194

California Yosemite Commission, 196
Cameron, Bill, 136
Carnegie Institution, 36, 37
Catlin, George, 194
cattlemen, 119
chipmunks, 58
Chittenden, Hiram Martin, 99
Clagett, W. H., 198, 201, 206, 208
Clark, William, 94–95, 97, 98–99, 100. *See also* Lewis and Clark expedition
Cleveland, Grover, 167
Colfax, Schuyler, 196, 208
Colter, John, 10, 26, 87, 97–101, 144
Columbia Fishing and Trading Company, 104
Comanche Indians, 81
Cone, Jack, 139
Conness, John, 195
Connor, Patrick, 92
Cook, Charles W., 125, 148–63, 165, 168
Cook-Folsom-Peterson expedition, 150–63, 164
Cooke, Jay, 141, 188, 189, 206, 207–8
Cooper, James Fenimore, 194
coyotes, 64, 69
Cramton, Louis C., 209
Crèvecoeur, Hector St. John, 194
Crow Indians, 80, 84, 85–86, 87, 89, 92, 98, 100, 112, 119, 141, 168, 170

Davis, John C., 125, 127–28
Dawes, Chester M., 189
Dawes, Henry L., 189, 199, 206
Day, Arthur L., 37, 39, 40, 41, 47
De Lacy, Walter W., 121–26, 127, 128, 143, 164–65, 192
de Smet. *See* Smet, Pierre Jean de
deer, 67–69
D'Église, Jacques, 93
Delano, Columbus, 201
Descloizeaux, Alfred, 44–45
Diary of the Washburn Expedition (Langford), 204
Diggers, 82
Dixon, Joseph, 97
Doane, Gustavus C., 32, 166–83, 186, 189, 192, 202, 205
Dobie, J. Frank, 64
Dorf, Erling, 30
Douglas fir forest, 53, 54
Drouillard, George, 98
Ducharne, Baptiste, 102
Dunlevy, James, 147

Early Man, 75–80
earthquakes, 12–20
Edward Warren (Stewart), 113
elk, 68–69
Elliott, Henry, 189
Emerson, Ralph Waldo, 194
Enabling Act (Yellowstone Park Act), 208–9
Evans, John, 93–94
Everts, Truman C., 147, 181, 183–87, 201; in Washburn-Langford-Doane expedition, 166–80
expeditions
　Ashley-Henry, 101
　Cook-Folsom-Peterson, 150–63, 164
　Hayden, 188–93
　Lewis and Clark, 12, 20, 26, 87, 94–95, 96, 98, 99
　Princeton University, 27, 30
　Raynolds, 113, 115–16
　Washburn-Langford-Doane, 126, 164, 166–83, 200, 202, 203

fauna. *See* animal life
Ferris, Warren Angus, 103–4, 144
Fischer, William A., 19
fish, 70–72
Flathead Indians, 80, 86, 87, 89, 92, 96, 98, 119, 201–2, 208
flora. *See* plant life
Folsom, David, 84, 125, 148–63, 165, 168
forest fires, 54
forests, 53–55

fossil forests, 30–31
Frémont, John Charles, 195
Freneau, Philip, 194
fumaroles (steam vents), 37, 39, 41. *See also* geysers; hot ground areas
fur trappers. *See* trappers

Gardner, Johnson, 102
Garfield, James A., 199, 208
geology: of surrounding area, 5–22; of Yellowstone, 23–50
Geophysical Laboratory of the Carnegie Institution, 37–39
geyser basins, 42
geysers, 19, 33–34, 35, 42–49
Gilded Age, The (Twain and Warner), 199
Gillette, Warren C., 166–82
glaciation, 8, 24–26, 27–28
Gourley, James, 132–36, 138, 139
Grant, Ulysses S., 193, 196, 197, 206

Hague, Arnold, 10, 24, 36, 40
Haines, Aubrey, 77
Hamilton, William T., 113, 137, 138
Hancock, Forest, 97
Hancock, Winfield S., 168, 202, 207
hares, 58–60
Hauser, Samuel T., 147, 163, 183, 188, 201, 202, 206; in Washburn-Langford-Doane expedition, 166–82
Hayden, Ferdinand Vandiveer, 20, 21, 32, 54, 115, 125, 126, 140, 144, 164, 188–93, 199, 200–201, 206–9
Hayden expedition, 188–93
Heap, David P., 189–93
Hector, 194
Hedges, Cornelius, 143, 145–47, 183, 184, 188, 201, 203–5; in Washburn-Langford-Doane expedition, 166–81
Helena Daily Herald, 169, 183, 203–4, 205
Henderson, A. Bart, 129–36, 137–41
Henry, Andrew, 87, 101
Hibbard, Ed., 132–36
Hidatsa Indians, 85
Hine, Thomas J., 191
Holmes, William Henry, 24–25, 26, 27, 30
hot ground areas, 38, 41–42
hot springs, 19, 35, 36–37, 39 40–41, 42. *See also* geysers.
Hudson's Bay Company, 101
Humphreys, A. A., 32, 193
Hunt, Wilson Price, 87, 101, 112
Huston, George, 129, 141

Ice Age. *See* glaciation
Iddings, J. P., 50

Indians, 80–92, 117, 135–36, 149, 171; Arapaho, 135–36; Bannock, 80, 86, 87–92, 112; Blackfoot, 80, 81, 84, 86–87, 92, 98, 102, 104, 112, 119, 130, 144, 146, 203; Comanche, 81; Crow, 80, 84, 85–86, 87, 89, 92, 98, 100, 112, 119, 141, 168, 170; Flathead, 80, 86, 87, 89, 92, 96, 98, 119, 201–2, 208; Hidatsa, 85; Nez Perce, 80, 86, 87, 89, 92, 96, 129, 141; Paiute, 80, 87; Piegan, 86, 87, 112, 145, 203; Shoshone, 80–85, 86, 87, 88, 92, 96, 112; Sioux, 84, 89, 119; Tukarika, 81, 82–85, 95, 107, 154; Ute, 89
Irving, Washington, 99, 194
Ives, George, 150

Jackson, Andrew, 195
Jackson, William Henry, 189, 191, 193, 201, 206
James, Thomas, 98
Jay Cooke and Company, 206. *See also* Cooke, Jay
Jefferson, Thomas, 94, 95
Jones, Jack, 130
Jones, William, 84
Journey to the Land of Eden, A (Byrd), 194

Kansas City Journal, 114
Kelley, William Darrah, 199, 206–7, 208
Kennerly, William Clark, 113
King, Clarence, 141
Klukus, Richard W., 77
Kuppens, Francis Xavier, 87, 144–45, 146–47, 203

Lahoutan, Baron de, 93
Langford, Nathaniel Pitt, 32, 127, 150, 163, 166–83, 188, 200, 201, 202, 204–5, 206, 208
Laroque, François Antoine, 96
Lewis, Meriwether, 81, 87, 97
Lewis, Samuel, 100
Lewis and Clark expedition, 12, 20, 26, 87, 94–95, 96, 98, 99
lichen, 51–52
Lisa, Manuel, 97
lodgepole pine forest, 53–54
Logan, William B., 189

Mackay, James, 93–94
Mackenzie, Sir George, 43
Madison Canyon, 13–17
Madison Slide, 17–18
marmots, 58
Maynadier, H. E., 115
Meagher, Thomas Francis, 145–47, 203, 204
Meek, Joseph L., 102, 103

Menard, Pierre, 87
Merriam, C. H., 59
mice, 56
Miller, Adam, 132–36
Miller, Horn, 138, 139
Miller, Joaquin, 143
miners. *See* prospectors
mink, 58
Montana Post, 147
moose, 69
Moran, Thomas, 183, 189, 191, 193, 201, 207, 208
Mullan, John, 121, 144
muskrats, 58, 61

Nashville Clarion, 96
national parks: concept of, 194; precedents for, 194–97
Nettleton, A. R., 206, 207, 208
New World mining district, 141
New York Tribune, 196
Nez Perce Indians, 80, 86, 87, 89, 92, 96, 129, 141
Nidda, Krug von, 43
Norris, Philetus W., 31, 84, 168
North West Company, 101
Northern Pacific Railroad, 21, 126, 188, 206–8

obsidian, 49–50
Old Faithful, 19, 43, 180
Old Gabe. *See* Bridger, Jim
Olmsted, Frederick Law, 195, 196–97
Omaha Herald, 129
Overland Monthly, 182, 183, 200, 205

Pacific Railroad surveys, 144
Paiute Indians, 80, 87
Peale, Albert C., 40, 190
Personal Memoirs of Philip H. Sheridan (Sheridan), 168
Peterson, William, 148, 150–63, 165
petrified forests, 30
Pick and the Plow, The, 137
Piegans (Blackfoot tribe), 86, 87, 112, 145, 203
plant life, 4, 51–55
Pomeroy, Samuel C., 199, 201, 206
porcupines, 59–60
Potts, Daniel T., 101–2
Potts, John, 87
Powell, John W., 129–30
Princeton University expedition, 27, 30
Pritchett, George A., 183
prospectors, 117–42, 143–44

rabbits, 58–60
railroads, proposals for, 126, 142, 188. *See also* Northern Pacific Railroad; Union Pacific Railroad
Raymond, Israel Ward, 195
Raynolds, W. F., 115, 144
Raynolds expedition, 113, 115–16
Red Eagle (Tukarika chief), 84
Red Streak Mountain Coal Company, 127
Republic Mine, 141–42
Richardson, Albert, 196
Rickard, Reuben, 141–42
Roberts, W. Milner, 207, 208
Rocky Mountains, The (Irving), 99
rodents, 56–61
Russell, Osborne, 83, 87, 104–11, 144
Ruxton, George Frederick, 113

sagebrush-grass community, 53
Scribner's Monthly, 183, 200
Seton, Ernest Thompson, 29
sheep, bighorn, 64–65
Sheep Eaters. *See* Tukarikas
Sheridan, Philip H., 168, 189, 193, 202, 206, 207
Shoshone Indians, 80–85, 86, 87, 88, 92, 96, 112
shrews, 57
Sioux Indians, 84, 89, 119
Smet, Pierre Jean de, 112, 114, 121, 144
Smith, Jacob, 166–81
snakes, 71
Specimen Ridge, fossil forests at, 30–31
Springfield Republican, 196
spruce fir forest, 53, 54–55
squirrels, 58
Standifer, Jeff, 129, 137–38
steam vents (fumaroles), 37, 39, 41. *See also* geysers; hot ground areas
Stewart, Sir William Drummond, 113
Stickney, Benjamin, 166–82
Stuart, James, 127–28, 168
subalpine meadows, 53
Sublette, William, 102

Targhee (Bannock chief), 92
thermal activity. *See* fumaroles; geysers; hot ground areas; hot springs

"Thirty-seven Days of Peril" (Everts), 183–84
Thompson, David, 93
Thorkellson, Thorkell, 46, 47, 48
Thoreau, Henry David, 194
Three Years Among the Indians and the Mexicans (James), 98
trappers, 101–15
travertine areas, 41–42
Trumbull, Walter, 200, 201, 205, 206; in Washburn-Langford-Doane expedition, 166–83
Tukarikas (Shoshone tribe), 81, 82–85, 95, 107, 154
Twain, Mark, 199

Union Pacific Railroad, 126
University of Montana, 78
Ute Indians, 89

Van Horn, R. T., 114
Vest, George Graham, 199
volcanism, 7, 23–24, 26

wapiti, 68–69
Warner, Charles Dudley, 199
Warren, K., 115
Washakie (Shoshone chief), 85
Washburn, Henry D., 163, 164, 165, 166–83, 187, 188, 201, 202
Washburn Range, 28–29
Wilkinson, James, 96
Williams, Bill, 113
Witkind, Irving, 14
wood rats, 57
woodchucks, 58
Wyeth, Nathaniel, 104

Yancey, "Uncle John," 29
Yellowstone caldera, 23–24
Yellowstone National Park, *passim;* creation of, 147, 187, 194–210; legislative history of, 197–209
Yellowstone National Park (Chittenden), 99
Yellowstone Park Act, 208–9
Yellowstone Park Bill, 193
Yosemite, as precedent for Yellowstone National Park, 195–97
Yosemite Act of 1864, 195–97, 209